Studying Hinduism in Practice

"*Studying Hinduism in Practice* is an innovative approach to presenting a religion such as Hinduism. Too often textbooks and readers are concerned only with texts. This work greatly embellishes the study of religion with first-hand, first-person accounts of not only the living traditions, but the research activity itself as it has transpired in real time. The book would be a wonderful companion in a course on Hindu traditions, or a course in Anthropology where field-work is addressed."
Guy Beck, *Tulane University, USA*

Drawing on personal experiences of Hinduism on the ground, this book provides a reflective context within which religious practices can be understood and appreciated. It conveys the rich realities of the Hindu tradition and the academic approaches through which they are studied. The chapters cover a wide range of topics, including dance, music, performance, festival traditions, temples, myth, philosophy, women's practices, and divine possession. The engaging narratives are accompanied by contextual discussions and advice on such topics as conducting fieldwork, colonialism, Hindu seasonal celebrations, understanding deities, and aesthetics in Hinduism. All the entries are accompanied by photographs and suggestions for further reading.

Hillary P. Rodrigues is Professor of Religious Studies at the University of Lethbridge, Canada, where he has been honoured with a Distinguished Teaching Award. His books include *Introducing Hinduism* (2006) and *Ritual Worship of the Great Goddess* (2003).

Studying Hinduism in Practice

Edited by Hillary P. Rodrigues

Routledge
Taylor & Francis Group
LONDON AND NEW YORK

First published 2011
by Routledge
2 Park Square, Milton Park, Abingdon, Oxon OX14 4RN

Simultaneously published in the USA and Canada
by Routledge
711 Third Avenue, New York, NY 10017

Routledge is an imprint of the Taylor & Francis Group, an informa business

British Library Cataloguing in Publication Data
A catalogue record for this book is available from the British Library

Library of Congress Cataloging in Publication Data
Studying Hinduism in practice / edited by Hillary Rodrigues.
p. cm. – (Religions in practice)
Includes index.
Hinduism. I. Rodrigues, Hillary, 1953–
BL1108.2.S77 2011
294.5–dc22 2010053477

ISBN: 978-0-415-46847-3 (hbk)
ISBN: 978-0-415-46848-0 (pbk)
ISBN: 978-0-203-81028-6 (ebk)

Typeset in Bembo
by HWA Text and Data Management, London

MIX
Paper from responsible sources
FSC® C004839
FSC www.fsc.org

Printed and bound in Great Britain by
CPI Antony Rowe, Chippenham, Wiltshire

Contents

List of Figures

Series Preface: Studying Religions in Practice

General Editor: Hillary P. Rodrigues

The intent of this new series is to assemble an assortment of texts that primarily instruct by addressing two aspects of human activity. One aspect is the practice of religion, and the other is how such practice is studied. Although these books may be profitably consulted on their own, they are ideal supplements to a comprehensive introductory textbook on each of the traditions in question. This is because introductory texts are rarely able to attend adequately to the range of activities that are integral features of most religious traditions. However, religious practice is a vast field of study, and each anthology in this series makes no claim to providing a complete picture of either the religion it addresses or its rich assortment of practices. Instead, the objective in this series is to provide the reader with vignettes of religious practices within particular traditions, as viewed through the experiences of scholars engaged in the study of these religions. As such, the series offers readers a window onto both the "doings of religion," and the scholarly study of those doings.

As scholars who study religion in its varied dimensions, and as instructors who teach about religion, we routinely scout for resources to enhance our students' learning experience. We wish to teach them about various religions, but also to teach them about the scholarly endeavor of studying religion. Introductory textbooks, however comprehensive they might be in providing necessary factual and foundational information, are typically unable to convey the richness of religious life as experienced by practitioners. By necessity, introductory textbooks tend to favor history, intellectual developments, and teachings from written sources of and about the tradition. Even when they address religious practice, the tone in these textbooks is generally distant and explanatory, rather than descriptively engaging and evocative. Additionally, since the author's persona and presence are often excised from the accounts, these books do little to get across to students what scholars who engage in research actually do and experience. This series is designed to address some of these lacunae.

Each book in this series contains an assortment of pieces written specifically for the anthology in question by established scholars in their field. Other series that focus on practice tend to be collections of translations of religious texts about religious practices, or are anthologies of classic articles previously published in scholarly journals. Texts of the former type are actually still slanted to the textual tradition, while those of the latter type do not have novice students as their intended audience. The essays in the volumes of this series are purposely crafted differently from typical articles published in scholarly journals, chapters in edited academic volumes, or papers presented at scholarly conferences. They are even different in style from what one might find in textbooks and ethnographic anthropological literature, although recent writings from the latter category are probably closest in stylistic character. The writings in these collections derive from the memories, notes, photos, videos, and such, of scholars who were in the process of studying, and who still continue to study, some aspect of religious practice.

The sensibilities within, and tone of, these writings are partly derived from postmodern orientations that indicate that, regardless of whether one is an insider or an outsider, one's understanding of reality is always partial. A pervasive and generally erroneous belief is that insiders to a tradition (i.e., adherents) know the *real* meaning of what is transpiring when they engage in religious activities. However, even for religious insiders, that is, believers and participants in a religious practice—such as a pilgrimage or rite of passage—the understanding of the phenomenon they are experiencing is always mediated by their own backgrounds, cultural familiarity, age, experience, degree of interest in their religion, and so on. They do not necessarily know "the" meaning of what is going on, simply because they are insiders. Each insider's understanding is partial. Nevertheless, one effective way to learn about religious practice would be to read about these activities from the perspective of insiders. But the volumes in this series are not collected writings by religious insiders about their practices, however valuable and interesting such accounts might be. Rather, these are writings by persons engaged in the academic study of religion.

Those who embark on the scholarly study of religious phenomena are often outsiders (although not exclusively so), and place themselves in an unusual position. They often seek to understand as much as they can by engaging as deeply with the phenomenon studied (striving to become akin to insiders), but then also attempt to convey what they have understood to others (typically fellow outsiders). They may read the literature of the religion, study the ancient languages of its scriptural texts, learn local contemporary languages, travel to distant places, and live among the cultures where the religion is found and practiced. In certain respects, this often makes them more informed than the unschooled insider. Anthropologists refer to the process of immersing oneself within a culture, while maintaining a scholarly stance, as participant observation. Although not all of the contributors to these anthologies utilize a robust anthropological field methodology, they all utilize the approach of participation, observation, and reporting back on what they have experienced, observed, and reflected upon.

The final category of reflection is particularly significant when distinguishing the insider's experience from that of the scholar. Religious practitioners need not report on their experiences to anyone. Their religious activities typically emerge within the framework of their cultures. Their lives are affected in particular ways during the course of their activities, and these effects influence and orchestrate the practitioners' subsequent thoughts and actions. These processes work to sustain and transform the cultural matrix of the practitioners. In contrast to this, scholars immerse themselves into the practitioners' religious culture and patterns of activity, seek to inform themselves about the traditions that they are studying, and strive to extricate themselves from those contexts to report back to their own milieu on what they have learned. Unlike the conventional scholarly formats in which they report their findings, which may include reading papers at academic conferences, publishing articles in peer-reviewed journals, writing book-length monographs, or contributing chapters to edited scholarly volumes, the contributions in these collections are perhaps unique in character. The authors are expected to reveal something about their process of engagement with the activities they study.

The discipline of Religious Studies is often misunderstood. Some people think it is religious education, others that it is akin to theology. Neither of those is true, for the study of religion is not conducted to inculcate others into a particular religious tradition, and it does not have the objective of developing the religious content of a particular religion. The study of religion takes religion in all of its manifestations, including religious education and theology, as its object of study. Scholars of religion attempt to understand, with a vigorous blend of objectivity and empathetic curiosity, all facets of the human religious response. The methodological tools for such study may be drawn from other disciplines such as anthropology, sociology, literary criticism, history, psychology, and so on, often selected because they are well suited to the religious phenomenon under consideration. As previously mentioned, since the focus of the contributions in these anthologies is on contemporary practices, the methods of participant observation central to the discipline of anthropology are highlighted here. This does not mean that all the scholars featured in these volumes are anthropologists, or even that their primary methodology is anthropological. However, the basis of their narratives is an anthropologically grounded experience of being scholars who are active participants in some phenomenon related to the practice of religion, which they are attempting to learn about, understand, and eventually convey to others.

Studying religious practice can be a messy and challenging process. One does not always know what to expect, where to go to best observe it, where to situate oneself during a rite, the degree to which one should participate in the practice, the amount of primary preparation needed, or the amount of descriptive content to provide when sharing the experience with others. One does not always understand aspects of what one has observed, what certain actions and activities might mean, and how other participants, particularly insiders, are experiencing the processes. One does not always have the best attitude, the most open-mindedness, optimal physical health, and other such attributes when actually engaged in the process of research. It may take many hours, days, weeks, years, and even decades of experiential immersion in a culture, and painstaking study of texts and other material, for scholars to deepen their understanding sufficiently to report on it. And even that is always regarded as a work in progress, a contribution that may be refined by the subsequent work of the same or other scholars. The contributions in these anthologies are written from the disposition that the scholarly study of religion is an ongoing process. And it is a process in which we invite the reader to participate by revealing aspects of the research process often concealed from view in most scholarly literature. Moreover, these contributions are not exclusively written by outsiders for outsiders. They are written by scholars, who, whether or not they belong to the religious tradition under study, assume a scholarly stance of engaged objectivity and empathetic distance with that religion as they engage in their research. Through their descriptive narrative vignettes, they invite the reader to share in their experiences, however briefly and partially, while they were engaged in some features of their research.

Almost anyone who has some experience with teaching about religion and culture knows the efficacy of story-telling. Not only is it an ancient and well-tested technique through which religious beliefs are conveyed and culture transmitted, but the narrative is equally effective in eliciting and maintaining the attention of a student audience. The first-person story is one of the most engaging forms of the narrative. Tell a person what you did, saw, thought, and felt, and you are much more likely to garner their interest. Within that encounter there is the possibility for learning to occur.

The objective in these chapters is primarily pedagogic. These are true stories of the experiences of real persons engaged in some of the activities of their discipline. It is hoped that they convey to the reader not only some details of what the study of religion entails, but as significantly, the rich textures of humanity's religious life. One might find within these narratives revelations that the author did not always use good judgment in certain instances, that they initially misunderstood what was transpiring, and so on. The honesty within the narrative portion of each contribution would likely be suspect if these stories did not contain features of surprise, puzzlement, or missteps. However, these narratives are not relatively superficial journalistic or travelers' accounts of adventures written to satisfy the reader's need for entertainment or to satiate some passing curiosity. Embedded within the narrative descriptions and in the discussions that follow the reader will also find remarkable details and useful information that derives from corollary facets of solid and rigorous scholarly work. It is hoped that the reader comes away with an enhanced appreciation and understanding of the religious tradition they are studying, as well as of the disciplines and methodologies through which it is studied.

Acknowledgments

I wish to thank many people whose labors and support were intrinsic to the successful realization of this collection. The first among these is Lesley Riddle, the senior publisher in religion and anthropology at Routledge, for taking a chance on an experimental series such as this. My colleague, John Harding, who is editing *Studying Buddhism in Practice*, has been an invaluable consultant as the vision for the series and its volumes moves from conceptualization to manifestation. The contributing authors were unanimously enthusiastic about the project, and nobly complied with the instructions to craft essays in the prescribed non-traditional style and format. For some, the processes of remembering and self-revelation were especially challenging and even poignant. Their willingness to write for the benefit of initiates reveals much about their commitment to mentoring, as well as to the religious tradition and the scholarly discipline. My initial respect and admiration for them has continued to grow over the course of the project. I also wish to thank the many scholars who were excited about the project's approach and anxious to contribute, but because of health or heavy workloads could not.

Scores of my students in my Spring 2010 introductory course on Hinduism voluntarily read and provided feedback on early drafts of the articles (a process to which the authors had courageously consented—after all, how often do second-year students get to comment on one's writing with uncompromising honesty?). The enthusiasm with which the students greeted the assignment was somewhat surprising (for one, they actually had to do a fair bit of extra reading), and their delight in the contributions (some even passed copies to family members or friends) confirmed the pedagogic effectiveness of the approach. Bev Garnett laboriously deciphered and typed up the hundreds of pages of handwritten reviews. All the authors benefitted from the feedback they received, even if for some the consensus opinion simply acknowledged that their pieces were well written, interesting to read, and informative. My editorial assistant, Lisa Kozleski, painstakingly read my edited versions of various drafts, and frequently communicated with the contributors on my behalf. As a non-specialist in Hinduism, her perspective on the essays was especially welcome. We collectively hope that instructors and students, through being entertained, informed, instructed, and inspired, find as much satisfaction in using this book as we did in constructing it.

ACKNOWLEDGMENTS

Introduction

Studying Hinduism in practice

This book is a collection of contributions written by specialists especially for readers relatively new to the academic study of the Hindu religious tradition. In accord with the intent of the *Studying Religions in Practice* series, to which this compilation belongs, the chapters are designed to serve two purposes. These are: 1) to highlight features of Hinduism as it is actually practiced, and 2) to illustrate some of the authentic experiences of researchers engaged in the study of those practices.

These contributions have other features that make this collection distinct. Although many of the authors may have strong affinities for the Hindu tradition, and some may even be deeply immersed in aspects of its practices, these are not chapters by Hindus telling the reader how they practice and experience their faith, and then explaining how or why these practices might make sense to non-Hindus. This book is grounded in the secular, scholarly study of Hinduism. It is also focused on the doings of Hindus, that is, their practices. This is because even well-written comprehensive introductory textbooks—and there are several in use in university undergraduate courses—cannot adequately convey the life of the Hindu religious tradition as it is experienced by Hindus. A textbook may talk about the Hindu caste system, and even describe how distinctions are made between the casteless Untouchables and high-caste Brahmins, but it rarely transports us into the midst of a scenario in which this distinction is played out. A textbook may tell us that the majority of Hindus live in small villages, that they enjoy varieties of folk entertainment with religious themes, and that modernization is bringing with it irreversible changes to rural life, but it does not carry us into the experiences of the people who are living those realities. And such books almost never reveal to the reader anything about the experiences of the researchers as they are making those discoveries. Effective textbooks are typically designed to convey information and serve as useful and comprehensive references on Hinduism.

This collection is intended to serve as a complement to a good textbook and a knowledgeable instructor. It makes no pretensions to providing a comprehensive coverage of the practices of Hinduism. Frankly, one should be highly suspicious of any book that makes such a claim. Hinduism is an inordinately complex and rich tradition, with an astounding array of practices. Its expressive forms vary considerably across regions of India, where it is widespread, in neighboring lands, such as Nepal,

Sri Lanka, and Bali, where there are large Hindu populations, and across the globe, wherever Hindu communities of any reasonable size are found. Any attempt at an all-encompassing treatment of Hindu practices would require a small library of volumes. Nevertheless, this concise collection of chapters is felicitously broad in its temporal and topical coverage. When viewed as a whole, a knowledgeable reader will note that the chapters touch upon contemporary practices from half a century ago up to the present day, as they were actually observed. Within its corpus there are discussions of devotional worship, pilgrimage, folk dramas, music, dance, village life, temple traditions, exorcisms, possession, healings, the epics, rituals, oral traditions, women's practices, puranic myths, tantric, yogic, and other philosophies, as well as festival traditions. It illustrates the more marginalized realities of Hindu women, Dalits, the lowest members in the social hierarchy, and villagers, along with the views of the more dominant groups, such as urban, upper-caste Brahmin men. Its perspectives emanate from north and south India, as well as from the Hindu world beyond India.

Unlike other collections that concern practice, but which focus primarily on the translation of ancient texts that discuss religious practices, these chapters address current expressions of Hinduism. Thus the anthology is an excellent source for the study of contemporary Hinduism. Although some of the chapters address the changes that certain researchers have observed over decades of study, their contributions to this volume do not focus on how classical texts prescribe Hindu practice, but with how select groups of Hindus actually engage in their religion today. And, unlike the content of other collections that deal with the life of Hinduism, these chapters are not culled from larger works written by academics for the benefit of their scholarly peers. These are pieces written by highly trained, professional researchers and instructors specifically for readers with little or no background knowledge of the Hindu tradition. The contributors span a range from scholars at the early stages of their professional careers to those with emeritus professorial status or its equivalent. Many enjoy the reputation of eminence among their peers for their lifetime of contributions to the study of Hinduism. Some are scholars who do not or no longer work primarily within a university environment. Some tell stories about their journey through academia. All tell stories about their discoveries and processes of learning about Hinduism. Moreover, there is research material not published elsewhere, contained within some of these chapters. Apart from volumes in this series, there is currently no other published collection of contributions of this sort.

Another distinctive feature of this collection is the form in which the chapters are written. Authors were encouraged to comply with an innovative, experimental, prescribed structure, allowing moderate flexibility for the subject matter and the dispositions of the contributors. Having trained in both textual and anthropological methodologies, and being deeply committed to pedagogy, I was continually struck by how effective story telling can be in the process of teaching. Even a superficial probe into most religious traditions will reveal the enormously influential role that stories have in conveying religious teachings. Hinduism is especially instructive in that respect. In fact, I quickly recognized that when I taught my classes, my students most often remembered the myths that I recounted from epics, such as the *Rāmāyaṇa,* or from the Purāṇas, far better than the philosophical arguments and other material presented to them in a non-narrative manner. Moreover, when explaining where I took particular photographic slides (long before the advent of PowerPoint), I found that the stories I told about the circumstances surrounding those experiences, or the anecdotes that I used to illustrate particular points, such as interactions with religious specialists, my emotional responses to music or other performances, to sculpture or architecture, and so on, held my students' attention best. In evaluations at semester's end, there were frequent remarks on how much they enjoyed and learned from those aspects of the Hinduism course. Years, even decades later, former students I encountered would sometimes comment on how those stories inspired them to read or study further into Hinduism, long after they had graduated and gone on to other occupations. A few were even inspired to take up the academic study of religion. These observations and experiences are not unique, and are likely shared by most teachers. The narrative, particularly a personal one, is an undeniably compelling form of communication and can be a powerful teaching instrument. It is for this and numerous other reasons that the contributors begin their accounts with a self-implicated narrative, telling a story about their raw experiences while they were engaged in studying some feature of Hindu practice.

An early draft of my chapter included in this volume served as a guide to the authors. In it I begin with a description of some of my research experiences in Varanasi during two consecutive occurrences of the autumn Navarātra, an annual goddess-centered celebration. The chapter provides a sense of the diversity of practices that take place in the city, both prior to and during the festival, as well as the challenges facing any researcher. It touches upon domestic and temple devotional rites (*pūjā*), urban pilgrimage, sacrifice, and various other aspects of the living practice of Hinduism. It then uses this descriptive narrative as a springboard for discussing the Hindu calendrical system, and introducing readers to some of the major festivals that are celebrated through the year.

Authors were instructed to tell their stories in a form that is not typical in scholarly papers, where narrative is often wholly absent. But even in such papers that include narratives, the story is kept brief, mostly stripped of its colorful descriptors and with little or nothing revealed of the researcher's personal response to the experience. Embedded within or immediately after the narrative, the scholar typically provides extensive interpretations and explanations often derived from their years of subsequent painstaking analytic work. There are obvious merits in that design, among which is its effectiveness in conveying information to one's academic peers. Among its demerits are the distance it constructs between the specialist and the novice, and the illusion it can perpetuate that the researcher possesses a mature understanding in the midst of raw experience. It is more akin to a polished performance. In contrast to that format, the intention in these chapters is pedagogic. Here the authors tell about their experiences in as honest a manner as they remember, including indications of their thoughts, and their sensory and emotional states. What were they seeing and hearing, what did the experience cause them to feel, and what did it make them wonder about? In so doing, and by minimizing specialized terminology, the aim is to first draw the reader into the experience alongside the researcher. The narrative is intended to be more of a description of raw experience than a well-processed explanation of the observed practices. This is because experience, whether it is that of the researcher or the observed practitioners, has a potency that derives from its immediacy. It is compelling because it carries qualities of sensory, emotional, and intellectual stimulation. Explanation, by contrast, is second-hand, a reflection upon experience.

By being drawn into companionship with the author through the narrative, the reader may be better able to share vicariously in the experience of observing and participating in the religious practices that are being described. They may find themselves having emotional responses, such as of excitement and awe, or even fear and revulsion, which resonate or contrast with those experienced by the researcher. They may find themselves asking questions about features of the experience described in the narrative that the researcher does not appear to ask. This is intended as a heuristic strategy. Moreover, the discussion that ensues in the chapter may not address any of the questions that may interest the reader. Authors were instructed to use the narrative as a launching point dicussing for any of a number of related topics. They might contextualize some features of the narrative with information. Alternately, they may go into a discussion about certain aspects of the experience, providing a much broader context and explanation about the phenomena described in the narrative. Some choose to touch on theoretical issues, while others offer advice to novice, would-be researchers.

In my own chapter, for instance, I do not provide theoretical explanations about *pūjā* or pilgrimage, or temple worship, or sacrifice, or renunciation and devotion. Nor do I go into extensive specific explanations about the nature of Durgā, her mythology, and the modes of her worship. Instead, I choose to inform about Hindu festivals and their place in the annual cycle. The readers are thus not provided with a neatly packaged story with its authoritative explanations and interpretations seemingly providing answers to all anticipated questions and an end to all further discussion. Instead, they are encouraged, if not induced, to turn to their instructors, read their textbooks more pointedly, and consult the suggested readings where many of their unanswered questions might be addressed in much greater detail. This process will have already transformed them into inquiring agents rather than passive recipients of knowledge. Readers may also find some answers to their inquiries, but certainly more questions, in other contributions in the anthology, because a discussion provided in one chapter may have instructional value and explanatory relevance for other narratives in the collection. Similarly, various narratives may touch upon overlapping subject matter, similar themes, and describe related forms of practice. Let me now turn to a brief account of the contents of the collection. My brevity is deliberate, because I do not wish to precede the authors' stories with lengthy summaries and analyses, which can diffuse their impact. Our intent is to let the phenomena of religious practices and their study take the lead, and to let reflections by the reader follow in their wake.

Brenda E. F. Beck's contribution centers on her early experiences in an Indian village in the 1960s. It tells how she, almost by happenstance, came upon aspects of Hinduism that served as the basis for some of her most significant scholarly contributions and current activities. In particular she discusses her discovery of the system of right and left castes, and the *Elder Brothers Legend*, a folk narrative, which she is now transforming into a series of animated films. She illustrates the value of fieldwork, and offers advice and guidance on how to benefit from it.

Jeffrey Brackett's chapter describes his visits to rural and urban temples to the monkey god Hanumān in the state of Maharashtra. These took place on different years on the occasion of the festival celebrating the deity's birth. His narrative illustrates the dazzling variety of temples dedicated to Hanumān, and leads to a discussion on why Hindu temples develop their distinctive popularity and eminence.

Paul B. Courtright tells about his investigation into the outlawed practice of *satī* (widow burning). These lead him to myths of the goddess Satī, which in turn are linked to places such as Kankhal in north India. He demonstrates how such myths can be fertile sources for interpretation, yielding layers of meanings for whosoever contemplates them.

Patricia A. Dold describes her encounters at the renowned temple of Kāmākhyā in Assam, with women who carry the tradition of singing devotional songs known as Nām to the goddess(es) abiding there. She tells of the ritual contexts in which these songs are performed, particularly the Debaddhanī festival, which entails phenomena such as supernormal empowerments, possession, and blood sacrifice. Her discussion focuses on the Mahāvidyās, the cluster of goddesses that figure most significantly as forms of Kāmākhyā as she is actually worshipped today.

Jason D. Fuller recounts his first encounter with Hindu sacred space in an unexpected place, the temple complex at New Vrindaban in West Virginia. He also discovers experiential parallels during his visit to the Hare Krishna temple in Mayapur, Bengal. This leads to a discussion of *Tīrthas*, Hindu conceptions of sacred crossing points that ford mundane and transcendental realms.

Anne-Marie Gaston gives an account of her absorption into Indian classical dance at a time when it was infrequently taken up by persons outside of the temple traditions within which it had formed, much less by foreigners. She tells of particularly memorable performances, choreography, and her progressive understanding of Hinduism through the medium of dance. This leads to a discussion of issues of purity and pollution, caste distinctions, as well as the aesthetic theories of Hinduism as they relate to dance.

Alf Hiltebeitel's piece deviates somewhat from the pervasive structure in the contributions because his topic does not submit particularly well to it. His concluding discussion is short because he embeds commentaries on context and theorizes within his lengthier narrative. He discusses his attempts to track a hypothesis within village enactments during a festival dedicated to Duryodhana, the villain of the *Mahābhārata* epic, who is worshipped as a god. His search for the widows of the Kauravas, the family defeated by the heroic Pāṇḍavas, is based on various clues and hunches, most of which prove to be misguided. He thus offers valuable insights into the process of learning through fieldwork, while providing us with colorful descriptions of festival rituals.

Knut A. Jacobsen begins his chapter with a description of his observations at the Kāpil Maṭh, perhaps the only monastery in India dedicated to the Sāṃkhya philosophical tradition. He witnesses the practices and participates in rituals that align with values promoted by Sāṃkhya, such as detachment, tranquility, and self-realization. We learn about the master-student relationship involved in the transmission of teachings, and he provides a more extensive discussion of Sāṃkhya teachings.

Jeffrey Lidke's story centers on his early experiences studying the *tablā* in Nepal, and performing as he gained greater proficiency. This forms the basis of a discussion on the intimate relationship between the performing arts and Hindu spirituality, which are particularly well articulated in aesthetic philosophies of Tantra.

William Sax's chapter recounts his experiences among the Harijans (Untouchables) of the Himalayas, where spirit possession and exorcism play significant roles in the diagnosis and treatment of maladies. He offers detailed descriptions of the ritual processes entailing music, chanting, and blood sacrifice, through which healing is enacted. His discussion probes the notion of possession in the social and religious lives of communities.

Bruce M. Sullivan describes his experiences studying the ancient dance dramatic form known as Kūṭiyāṭṭam, which originated within temples. This leads to a discussion of the classical Hindu theory of *rasa* (aesthetic enjoyment), which is the purpose of such dance dramas. He also tells of transformations that have been affecting the tradition as India modernizes.

Paul Younger tells of his experiences studying Indian religions in the early period after Indian independence, when hierarchical and colonial attitudes strongly prevailed, even among academics. He describes his progressive movement into the examination of Hindu temple traditions, particularly at Śrīraṅkam and Citamparam, and his study of festivals, including those not centered primarily on temples.

The contributors did not read each others' works and did not purposefully craft their contributions to resonate with them. And yet, as was suspected, thematic relationships and connections are everywhere evident. Lidke, for instance, makes passing reference to notions in Sāṃkhya and Yoga philosophy (which is discussed in greater detail by Jacobsen), to the *devadāsī* tradition (also discussed by Gaston), and to *rasa* theory (discussed by Gaston and Sullivan). The overall form of the anthology is intended to be synergistic in its effects. While the prescribed structure for each chapter was encouraged, the contributors followed it with varying degrees of rigor based on their capacities, professional habits, and the subject matter with which they were dealing.

These chapters may be used to get glimpses and insights into an assortment of Hindu practices. For instance, one might read Younger, Fuller, Brackett, Rodrigues, and Dold to get perspectives on pilgrimage, while aspects of temple traditions are found in Fuller, Brackett, Younger, Rodrigues, Dold, Courtright, and Jacobsen. Dimensions of Hindu philosophy are addressed in Jacobsen, Younger, Lidke, and

Fuller. One can read about sacrifice, including blood sacrifice, in Rodrigues, Sax, Hiltebeitel, and Dold. Jacobsen and Dold offer translations and information on living, oral hymn and song traditions. Younger, Gaston, Sullivan, Beck and Hiltebeitel represent south Indian Hinduism in their pieces. Fuller and Lidke touch upon Hinduism outside of India. Women's religious practices are evidenced in Dold, Hiltebeitel, and Gaston, for instance, and the experiences of women scholars in Beck, Dold, and Gaston. Issues related to caste and untouchability are found in Beck, Sax, Gaston, Hiltebeitel, and Younger. Mythic tellings and enactments about gods and goddesses are touched upon in Beck, Hiltebeitel, Dold, Sullivan, Courtright, Rodrigues, and Younger. Possession and exorcism are treated in Hiltebeitel, Dold, and Sax. The crucially significant relationship between the teacher (*guru*) and the student is evident in Gaston, Lidke, and Younger. Dold, too, reveals processes of transmission within women's oral traditions. The oft-ignored, but intimate relationship between the performance arts and the Hindu religion is explored in Gaston, Lidke, and Sullivan. Such Hindu aesthetic and philosophical notions as *rasa*, often rendered as taste, flavor, mood, emotional state or response, appear in the chapters by Lidke, Gaston, Sullivan, and Fuller. Priestly traditions and ritual performances are discussed in Sullivan, Rodrigues, Brackett, Hiltebeitel, and Younger. Aspects of village Hinduism are described in Beck, Hiltebeitel, Younger, and Sax. There are numerous other overlapping treatments of topics, which will be apparent even upon cursory reading. Since all the chapters deal with contemporary realities, they are a valuable resource for the study of modern Hinduism.

As the thematic overlaps mentioned above indicate, there were many options available in which to order the contents of this volume. However, no particular grouping seemed adequate. For instance, one could have placed Sullivan, Lidke, and Gaston's chapters under a category such as "Performance in the Hindu Tradition." But this would have excluded performative acts by mediums and healers in the chapters by Dold and Sax, for instance. And, by labeling those chapters as dealing with performance, it might have done disservice to the discussions of philosophy, social structure, and other such themes embedded in them. In other words, any viable grouping seemed to diminish the richness of the constituent chapters, undercutting potential benefits derived from such categorizations. My decision, therefore, has been arbitrarily to simply place the chapters in alphabetic order following the author's surnames.

On transliteration and pronunciation

Transliteration is the method in which words that are typically written in foreign scripts are depicted in the English or Latin-based alphabet. Since the languages of India, such as Sanskrit, Tamil, and Hindi, have their own alphabets that do not always correspond with the English alphabet, the scholarly convention is to use diacritic marks. Diacritics are dots and dashes that are placed above or below certain letters in an alphabet giving it a sound variant. For instance, the Sanskrit alphabet has three sibilant letters, or "s" sounds. One sibilant sounds like the common "s" in "sassy," but there are two others, which sound more like the "s" in "sugar," or "Sean." These are rendered "ś" (as for the god, Śiva), and "ṣ" (as for the god Kṛṣṇa). You will sometimes see these gods' names written as Shiva or Krishna, to clarify the pronunciation without using diacritics.

We have decided to use diacritics, both because they are widely used by most scholars, and because they actually give you a much better indication of how to pronounce a word. When you see a diacritic dot under a letter, place your tongue near the roof of your mouth, and then say it as you would in English. If you see a dash over a vowel, as in the word Hanumān, for instance, just extend the sound of that vowel, so it sounds like "Hanumaan." And the letter "c" in Sanskrit is always pronounced like the "ch" in "chair," and not with the "k" sound as in "cat." So "Cōla dynasty" is pronounced like "Chōla dynasty," and not "Kōla dynasty." There is much more that one can say about proper pronunciation, but this should suffice to enable you to read the essays in this volume effectively. You should consult a good textbook on Hinduism if you are interested in learning more about Sanskrit transliteration and pronunciation.

In this book, we opted to use diacritic marks for most terms, but not for place names, or names and terms that are normally rendered without diacritics even in India. So you might see "Varanasi" instead of "Vārāṇasī" and "Ramakrishna" instead of "Rāmakṛṣṇa." Since India has changed the names of many cities in the last few decades, you might often see references to cities by their older and more commonly used names. Sometimes the alternate name is placed in parenthesis beside the first occurrence. So you might see Bombay (Mumbai) or Kolkata (Calcutta) or Varanasi (Banāras). On occasion, you might also encounter "Gaṅgā" instead of "the Ganges," because it struck the author as more appropriate to call the river by the name of the living goddess that it is believed to be by Hindus, rather than by the mundane English equivalent.

In some cases, authors chose to transliterate terms according to regional conventions. So, although the terms will be spelled consistently in a particular chapter, you might find variations in the spellings of the same word in different chapters throughout this volume. For instance, you will see the name of the great south Indian temple to Śiva rendered as "Citamparam," a spelling derived from the Tamil script, while the derivation from Sanskrit would be "Cidambaram." Since it is a place name, it might also be written "Chidambaram." We have included a list of such spelling variants here.

List of common variant spellings

Brahmin	Brāhmaṇa	
Brahminic	Brahmanic	
Cidambaram	Chidambaram	Citamparam
Gaṇeśa	Ganesha	Ganesh
Gaṅgā	Ganges	
Kṛṣṇa	Krishna	
Kolkata	Calcutta	
Madras	Chennai	
Mumbai	Bombay	
Nataraja	Naṭarāja	
Sāṃkhya	Sāṅkhya	
Śiva	Shiva	
Tamil Nadu	Tamilnadu	Tamilnātu
Varanasi	Banāras	
Vrindaban	Brindavan	

Chapter 1

Discovering a Story

Brenda E. F. Beck

Preamble

In the spring of 1964 I was a doctoral student at the Institute of Social Anthropology, (technically Somerville College), a part of Oxford University in England. Having just completed a B.Litt., I was now ready to set off for two years in the field. I had been told to "immerse myself" in the culture of a strange land, in my case a Tamil-speaking village in south India. That was the route to a membership badge that would later gain me acceptance into the world-wide club of academic professionals. It was whispered quietly in the Institute's dark halls that completing one's research alone, abroad ... for two years ... was *the* initiation ritual required of all serious anthropologists. The rumor mongers were right!

My chapter tells of some of my early fieldwork experiences and then moves onto discussing how those experiences led to discoveries that shaped my academic career and ongoing interests. From my current vantage point, I offer some counsel to those embarking on studies involving fieldwork.

Narrative

It took me took several months to decide exactly where to settle in south India. Finally around mid-February of 1965 I decided on a village named Olappalayam. Roughly translated this means "place of the palmyra palm trees." The leaves of this palm, called *olai*, are greatly appreciated and have many uses. Traditionally they were especially valued as a kind of writing paper. All the old manuscripts in this part of India were once written in books made of this particular leaf type. It seemed a suitable place for a scholar to establish herself. Using modern paper I wrote several letters to my parents around that time. Here is a taste of what I had to say:

> I have a very nice little house with a little open central courtyard, a separate storage room which securely locks, and a semi-outside cooking and bathing space. The house is built in the old, very tasteful style with a quadruple-thickness tile roof to keep it cool, and with a whitewashed interior and dark brown supporting posts. The roof/ceiling is slanted so that drainage is into a

small central court. The whole area together is perhaps 18 by 30 feet. I've had a workable latrine built in a vacant lot just to the south. My floor is earthen, but is washed every few days with a cow dung mixture which smells quite sweet and is definitely antiseptic. There is no electricity in my house but I have an excellent kerosene table lamp which gives adequate light for work. I have a cheap wooden table and a chair which I managed to bring by ox-cart from the city. I have one lovely rope cot, made here, for sleeping.

I recently bought a cheap kerosene stove for cooking but my cook/companion prefers the mud stove we sourced here for seven cents. It uses wood fuel. We have just bought a two-month supply for $2.20. The house rent, by the way, is $1.20 a month! And the washerman charges 50 cents a month to do all my laundry. All this gives you some picture of the village economy. Best of all is that people here have been very friendly. My house companion is a real gem of a woman, about 45 years of age and a cook by caste. She comes with me everywhere and seems to give very favorable explanations and reports of my activities. Her son, also very nice, is a priest for the lower and smaller village-level temples. I expect to learn a great deal from him. My companion's salary is food and lodging plus $5.50 a month. Neither mother nor son speaks a word of English.

Some people come back after having seen the cities of India and say there is no air of the exotic (after having read Kipling or the like) but here in the village it is an entirely different world! I'm wearing an eight yard sari—village style—for the first time today (the "modern" sari is only six yards of cloth). People have reacted *very* enthusiastically. I have also been wearing my hair in a long braid for about a week.

The most exciting event on my birthday was that Papamma (my companion) told me that she had been frightened the night before by an evil spirit. She always moans and makes loud sounds at night, so I didn't pay particular attention that night, but I do remember her noises being extra loud and more word-like. She afterwards explained that the spirit came towards her and pushed her backwards, so that she fell, apparently, onto some rice and other goods, knocking their pots over. She shouted some words to frighten it and then quickly lit a little kerosene light, which we usually keep burning at night but which had somehow gone out. She then took the household broom and lay down, putting it under her head. The spirit didn't return. She explained that a broom, or a pair of old sandals placed near one's head, will frighten an evil spirit away. Some spittle applied to the forehead three times has the same effect, but the best remedy of all is to bring some sacred ash from a particular temple, not too far from here, and place it over the lintels of the doors. She thinks that the spirit was that of the old landlord of the house. He went mad and died about ten years ago, after losing his second wife. I guess my house doesn't have a very happy history. Papamma says that male spirits will only trouble women, and female spirits, only men. Olappalayam (the village where I stay) is just bursting with interesting ideas and

> customs—I just wish I could speak this **** language better. Boy, it is *really* foreign! The grammar, the pronunciation, the vocabulary, everything is tough!
>
> As I write, at least ten people lean over my table watching my hand move. (They don't see a person writing very often, and never have seen someone write in a foreign language such as English). I feel a bit self-conscious but they are all very pleased to know that I am writing to my parents. Your portrait, which hangs on the wall in my one large room (along with grandmother's), has acquired a flower garland recently. Nowadays a small light, which my clerk has constructed out of bits of wire and old battery cells, is reverently switched on for an hour each evening. I hope all three of you duly appreciate the attention!
>
> Yesterday my assistant, Sundaram, had his head shaved, in completion of a vow to a god on the top of a small mountain (Sivanmalai) about 18 kilometers from here. (He has been growing his hair and beard for this purpose for more than three months now.) Papamma, Sundaram's brother, and I all accompanied him to the temple. We cycled the 12 kilometers by bike, in the hot sun, and then climbed the mountain, barefoot. As a result, I feel like a true pilgrim. But he looks like a young Buddhist monk now, and he has plastered his bald head with sandalwood paste. I tried to explain to him what a Buddhist monk was, but I don't think he really understood, never having heard of the Buddha.
>
> I scheduled my first interview with an untouchable informant yesterday and, unfortunately, it caused somewhat of a stir. The man with whom I share my front outer courtyard complained (even though other Harijans have walked there before without his objection). I had not intended to invite this guest of mine inside the house—nor even suggest that he sit on the porch outside. I was going to merely squat in the shade with him in this outer open space. It would have been impossible to interview a man by us squatting together outside the furthest door, along the main thoroughfare, where we would have been in full view and also in the hot sun. (So finally) Papamma offered the courtyard of her own house and we went there to sit. The man was an excellent informant and very willing. But even so, he had to sit on an old gunny sack, on the ground, while I and Sundaram (my clerk) sat on a mat, on the raised porch of his house. Our guest had to drink the water we offered him from a coconut shell, so as not to touch our cups, and he had to eat the breakfast we gave him off of a dried old leaf. All this was accepted by the Harijan, but I can't say that I felt very much at ease treating him thus.

So much for my letters home. At the time that I discovered storytelling was a popular form of local entertainment I was still struggling to understand the language. So it occurred to me that if I collected a few stories and then studied them I might learn quite a bit. My cook's assistant, Sundaram, didn't know a word of English. But he could very effectively break down complex sentences for me and explain them with simple gestures and vocabulary he knew I had mastered. I had brought a tape recorder I had planned to use for interviews, and so I thought "why not use up a few of the many tapes I had with me and collect language-listening material?" I went about this new project methodically. I first asked people who was the best storyteller in the village, and then I asked them to tell me their favorite story. To my surprise, there was pretty well a consensus. Ramasamy and his nephew (both barbers) made up the best storytelling team around, and the best story of the lot was what they called the "Annanmar Kathai" or the "Story of the Elder Brothers." So I found Ramasamy and asked if he would mind my recording this story as he and his nephew sang it. He agreed and expressed pride that I would actually want to record his words using a machine. We set up a time and a small payment. He always sang at night, and each evening as he started up many others in Olappalayam would instantly hear his drum and come running.

I started to tape record the performance of the two bards, Ramasamy and his assistant Palanisamy, without thinking ahead. But I soon became worried about my battery supply. The singing of this one story had lasted all evening and it still was not finished! Soon the word got around that I didn't have enough batteries to finish the job. But then I had a happy surprise. The official lineman came to visit. He was responsible for bringing electricity to Olappalayam and he already had a single feed wire strung as far as the little Ganesh temple clearing nearby. He told me he could supply an (illegal) hot wire to the performance area and that I could run my tape recorder off of that. With his help we got this set up working … and I was very glad of it! I had forgotten to ask how long this Annanmar story was! My notes say that we started recording on June 23,1965, and finished 19 (night) sessions later on the September 1! I had collected a story of epic proportions without ever realizing what I was doing!

I remember these taping sessions as being a mixed experience. I really enjoyed the singing and the rhythms the two men used. I enjoyed the interaction and the dramatic back-and-forth I could observe. The audience was always attentive and keen. And I could tell from their faces when a particularly moving part was being sung. But frankly I couldn't understand a whole lot as the men sang. It took patience to sit through 19 long night sessions. I frequently amused myself by watching the great black shadows that moved behind the two singers on the white wall behind them as they sang and narrated.

I imagined the characters of the story riding horseback, crying, begging, fighting, and more. All these emotions seemed writ large through their portrayal via moving silhouettes. To this day I believe these shadows served as a spring board for my radical idea—to attempt a computer-based "animation" of this story. It required some 40 years of computer development and modern software design before such a concept finally became feasible, both technically and in terms of my limited financial resources.

At the end of their 19 nights of singing the two bards requested a special *pūjā* (worship ritual) be done for my almighty tape recorder. This "magical machine," people vaguely understood, now held the entire performance within itself. This was demonstrated when, to everyone's amazement, I was able to play back a short segment on the last night, while they listened intently!

Figure 1.1 Shrine set up for the story's performance

The final ceremony for the recorder included painting stripes on the machine with sandalwood paste, and then sprinkling it with coconut water. I objected to the latter, but was promptly put in my place. I was assured that it was the god's sanctified water and that it could not possibly harm this sacred project. Fortunately, my hardy Uher machine survived the loving attention and remained undamaged. It continued to work like a charm.

Let me now flesh out a few more details pertaining to the context that was so important to the collection of this legend. At the time I arrived and settled in the village of Olappalayam no homes had been electrified. So in the first few weeks I worried a lot. How would I pass all those hours between sunset and sunrise? I thought I would be very bored, having only a kerosene lantern and a few books for company. How wrong I was! It was not more than a few days into my stay when I began to discover that the nights were full of interesting events, generally activities far more exotic than what I could see during the day. First of all, the drums would start

Figure 1.2 Bard-singers receiving gifts

soon after dark. There would be people telling stories, people getting possessed by spirits (both benign and threatening), people playing games and those just gathering to gossip. I quickly learned that these were the hours for recreation, that wick lamps provided a dim flickering light very conducive to imaginative thinking, and that this was also the time for festival events of all kinds. I soon discovered that full moon evening was the most exciting of all. I quickly took the decision that I could never afford to be away from Olappalayam, ever, for this key night each month!

Even before I had finished recording the story in full, I realized that I must have collected something special. Nonetheless, I had little more than a dim idea of what the tapes contained. I was afraid to scrub my five inch reels to actually listen to it in pieces. I didn't want to damage those valuable tapes and furthermore, my offer of free electricity vanished at the completion of these formal recording sessions. It was about two weeks after that, therefore, that I came up with what seemed like a bright idea. Why not invite the same bard back and have him recite the whole story over again over many days? This time I would ask my assistant Sundaram to serve as my scribe. The two men agreed to my plan (after all it would make them some money). So I soon held daily narration sessions in my house. Although I repeatedly reminded Ramasamy to tell the story exactly as he had sung it—I didn't want him to change a single word—at the end I made a key discovery, a new perspective on my field research and something that I had never anticipated. When I started looking at them in depth, those two versions of the story were *so* different!

I never started my stint of fieldwork in India thinking that I would collect folktales. But now I have virtually built my career around this unexpected stockpile of data. After first stumbling on the "mother of all stories" I went on to collect many more smaller ones. I developed an almost insatiable appetite for this. Perhaps it was like a second childhood, a time when I used to beg the elders around me, night after night, for just one more story ... how much has been lost to the world of storytelling with the disappearance of the unlettered, but richly educated, village storyteller!

Discussion

I now had collected two versions of the Elder Brothers' Legend from the same bard, one performed and documented electronically on tape, the other dictated and hand-written on paper. Both were in Tamil. These two records were completed just weeks apart. How different would they be? At first I assumed that they were (nearly) identical. How wrong I was! Years later the marked differences in these two documents has become a gold mine that has taken on a life of its own. Where else had a folklorist conducted this type of controlled experiment? A study of the detailed contrast between these two versions now reveals so much. The differences demonstrate what (must have also) happened elsewhere ... as so many other great epics first got written down by scribes. As I look at these two versions today I find many, many exciting patterns of divergence. I will list just a few: 1) a shift from a first person to a third person narrative voice; 2) a great foreshortening of the mythological embroidery included; 3) an extreme reduction in sexual innuendo and other colorful types of colloquial phraseology; 4) and a loss of deliberate thematic emphasis through a marked decline in repetition. Of course, the absence of drum rhythms and also of a great variety in expressive intonation (via use of the human voice) are also vital to understanding this transformation process.

Following close on the heels of the bright new bare-bulb house lights in Olappalayam after its rapid electrification came the explosion of the Indian commercial cinema. The nearest theater was just an eight-mile bicycle ride away. Then came the mass availability of affordable television, and (still more recently) computer games and DVD playback machines. The old traveling drama troupes soon began to lose revenue and audience interest. Even when I revisited Olappalayam a few years later these popular folk performances were already being replaced with loud speakers that could blare out cinema songs. The folk stages too, began to fill with more modern fare, especially (male) Bollywood wannabees who could entertain their friends with dance steps and gestures inspired by what they had seen at the theater. Industrial-scale storytellers and writers all come out of the big cities now. What legends are left to tell have largely lost their connection to local bards and their live entertainment. The result has been the lightning-fast demise of a rich oral story-telling culture in India's rural areas. It is very difficult to find a skilled, professional, practicing bard, anywhere nowadays. People who still do know these legends are rapidly aging. There are very, very few new enthusiasts training to replace them. India's culture of storytelling has undergone a change of earthquake proportions.

By the late 1960s, this electrification had reached nearly every village in India. Before this introduction, the night was the main time people had to relax and let their minds wander. No one realized that this special oral culture belonged to a world of semi darkness. Even I did not realize until much later ... how effectively the personal imagination becomes freed by watching the natural shadows that move behind a storyteller's body ... when it is lit only by the light of a small, flickering oil lamp.

I believe that what I find myself doing now is similar to what that church mural painter recently did for St. Paul's Cathedral in London. He painstakingly uncovered (and touched up) the original, magnificent artwork that told Saint Paul's story in vivid images that are live with action and color. I am doing the same by animating the Elder Brothers' Legend ... unveiling a magnificent (nearly lost) tradition through animation, and bringing it back to life bit by bit. Hopefully, as a result, this great legend will once again be available to be seen, heard and enjoyed by all. It has been wonderfully rewarding to assist with a project that gives a great (temple of) story energy and spirit once more!

But why bother with a long and exotic village legend? Surely India has bigger, greater and much better epic stories to share with the world? There are many answers to this question I am asked so frequently. First, this story is important precisely because it was been handed down in the villages of one specific area. Second, it is nearly unique in that it was collected directly from oral singers. Third, it is a kind of crystallized gem that simplifies and judiciously balances many great themes and concepts that swirl around in South Asian Hindu culture. Thus it serves as a window on something much vaster. And fourth, it provides a very self-confident, regionalized, non-Brahmin view of this wider cultural world. It puts forth a rare warrior-farmers' perspective that plays with (and even inverts) some of the wider

Figure 1.3 Family ceremony at folk temple in the animated Elder Brothers Legend

thematic threads of Hinduism. I believe the story takes this form in order to paint a proud picture of the Kongu region of Tamilnadu and its unique social identity. Other regions of India have similar stories that have a similar function. How these regional assertions of identity take form and assert local pride, in relation to a set of well-established wider cultural norms, is well worth study. Indeed, this is a truly modern issue that we are very familiar with in Canada as well. Of course it is not the story tradition in an active sense that does the asserting, but rather the bards who have handed their story down over the generations. Their local school has devised and perpetuated this contrastive form. They know what appeals to their local audience(s) and systematically mine this, both for maximum impact and for maximum popularity.

Although there are many Indian folk epics cited in the literature, this type of story is little known, rarely well translated, and almost never mined for its insights. In many ways the Elder Brothers Story provides a road map of Hindu religious beliefs that is balanced and comprehensible. Śiva and Viṣṇu are matched as a pair of brothers-in-law, each having their own special strengths (and weaknesses). The epic provides a geography that links its key social communities to landmarks on earth and it also describes the pilgrimage path one must take to find Lord Śiva's famous abode in the sky (Kailāsa) while passing over rivers of snakes and of stone, winding over Himalayan peaks and so forth. Even the underworld is described at a few points. But the story also lays out three generations of human characters and their many struggles with moral and ethical issues. As individuals these characters must face disease, famine, exile, succession problems, death, and much more. The story also outlines much about common life in medieval south India, depicting the relations between kings and subjects that virtually no other sources describe. This legend also has great emotional depth. Its songs melt the heart and bring tears to the eyes of those who can appreciate the fine poetry.

The Legend of Ponnivala has grown on me gradually, increasing in importance year after year for more than four decades. It has become a kind of Rosetta Stone in my mind, being a key to understanding almost everything I found surprising and challenging during my Olappalayam stay. Every one of these surprises I now understand better by considering it in relationship to the wider canvas of the brothers' story. The evil spirits my cook encountered are akin to those the warriors of Ponnivala had to propitiate before they raised their great war-drum in preparation for battle. My assistant's shaved head was a form of ascetic practice. His casting off of a handsome head of hair was a mild form of the many personal hardships the heroine-mother of the Ponnivala heroes underwent in order to speak to Lord Śiva at the gates of heaven. The tape recorder ritual undertaken at the end of the ballad singing project was an acknowledgment of imbedded power and hidden story knowledge that lay within it. That act was motivated by feelings similar to those the heroes of the larger story experience when they honor the stone image that is their family goddess.

I have studied this epic and thought about it for 45 years now, and yet hardly a day passes without some new insight jumping into my conscious thoughts and demanding its due. Furthermore, with every book I read, new questions quickly spring to mind about how The Elder Brothers' story also stick-handles that particular topic, be it fate, causality, moral codes, the afterlife, and more.

I was trained as a social anthropologist and I left Oxford to study Indian village social structure. Little did I expect to be looking at stories. Significantly, when I actually started collecting data I became more and more confused. Then I became worried. Nothing was fitting into a pattern. Instead I seemed to have notes on some kind of jumbled network. I couldn't find the neat hierarchy I was looking for anywhere - indeed, I felt I was far from it. This is where the interview with the untouchable temple drummer, mentioned in one of my letters home, became meaningful. My conversation with him was about a key festival for the goddess Mariyamman. He was a drummer at that festival and I was asking him what he did. I wanted him to describe his responsibilities. As a kind of throwaway comment near the beginning of the conversation, however, he happened to mention that his first duty used to be to construct a kind of gateway across the road leading to the temple ahead of the festival itself.

Then, to my surprise, the drummer told me that only the right-hand castes were allowed to pass through this special ritual gate. He also said that they had stopped building this archway some years back and that I could no longer see the gate he was referring to. I was curious and of course intrigued by the term "right-hand caste" he had used. And so I asked who these people were. He thought for a moment and then gave me a list. Of course I wrote it down. Then I asked if there was any opposing category, say a "left-hand" group of castes? To my surprise he said "yes." Then I pushed him to name those communities. That was harder for him but he came up with quite a few. I'd never heard of this kind of social system and so when I got back to my house I spent the rest of the day laying all of my field notes out in big heaps on two sides of my porch. All the data I had on people the drummer had named as "right-hand castes" went on one side and all the data associated with those he named as "left-hand castes" went on the other. Then I looked through the piles and thought about it for a while.

Bingo! I had suddenly discovered something very interesting. As soon as I had made this separation of caste types a neat and understandable pattern jumped out at me. The "left-hand castes" could pretty well be ranked, amongst themselves. They also had no common identity. But the right-hand castes were like a club. If one excluded the lowest groups (the Harijans) they had a lot in common. Their wedding ceremonies seemed to be identical and they were pretty much willing to share food. Their women all wore the same symbol on their wedding necklaces, and so on. This was a huge "ah ha" for me and it was also a great relief. Here was the gem of an idea. Well, of course I then began to pursue this new pattern and to ask many more questions about it.

During one trip to the city of Madras (now Chennai), I also discovered that some of the old British records about the area actually mentioned a right–left caste rivalry. I later learned that historical inscriptions from the area mentioned it as well. Although it wasn't something that many people I talked to knew much about, a few elderly people did remember the terms. This key idea later became the core theme of both my doctoral thesis and, after reorganization, the topic of my first book. The point I wish to make, and the advice I have for other researchers, is always watch for the unexpected. When you stub your toe against something you don't expect and don't understand ... pursue it with vigor. The best discoveries are serendipitous. It is worthy of note that this second great find of my Olappalayam stay was linked to temple ceremonies. I would not have discovered this pattern had it not been for that one key interview with an elderly Harijan temple drummer. He was like a guru who opened up a whole new world of thinking before my eyes. Carrying the generalization further, I would say that looking behind temple rituals at their social symbolism can provide a very rich goldmine of information. And I particularly recommend befriending and talking to the lowest ranks of temple servants. These desperately poor and marginalized groups tend to retain their stories and customs longer than the more modern upper-caste communities. They also sometimes do not have electricity in their homes, even today. For this reason they know the oral culture of the area more deeply and fully than do others. If one is looking to understand the past and its imprint on the present this is an excellent place to look for fresh ideas.

I can also link my right–left discovery back to the great Ponnivala legend. Although the terms "right and left" are not found in the story, the pattern of opposition between certain types of castes is very clearly present. Indeed one can say that the opposition between the farmers (right-hand) and the artisans (left-hand) is one of the main social rivalries that fuels this epic account. I discovered that story echo fairly early on, but its significance has continued to grow on me over the years. Other types of serendipity have been equally important to my research.

A little folk story I learned from my research assistant early on during my stay goes like this: There was once an old man who was very poor. So he set off to wander carrying only a small bag on his shoulder. Soon that bag became heavy and he sat down to rest. Opening it up he found a stone inside. Thinking this was the reason the bag had felt heavy he threw the stone away. Then, a little later, he got up and started to walk again. But the bag got heavy a second time. So he set it down, opened it and lo and behold he found a second stone. He threw that one away too. This sequence of events then repeated itself a third time (as with many a good story). Finally the man found a place to settle down for a while. He built a small hut and set his bag in the corner. When he opened it for the fourth time—there was that stone again! This time he knew its significance. It was indeed a positive divine force that had been with him all along. So now he made a little shrine and set the stone on it. Every day he paid it his respects. Metaphorically that poor man was me. The moral: never throw a bothersome stone away. It may indeed become the center of your lifelong career! Perhaps there was more than one stone. But together their initial weight has now become the inspiration for 45 years of work.

My chapter began with a description of just a few of the many early experiences I had in Olappalayam as I adjusted to a very new life and to a totally new language. Memories of each of these adventures (and many more, of course) have come back to me again and again in the years since. Many of them can be linked to the Ponnivala story, but there is no space for all those details here. Each fresh discovery, in hindsight, was a ground mover. Each took me one step further into a new world—a world where I had to become a child again—and had to be helped. I was forced to relearn how to walk "while wearing a sari" and, of course, I had to relearn how to talk. Ritual initiation, that is, being (symbolically) forced through a second childhood, is not uncommon in religious rituals. In India I discovered first hand why this can be an extremely powerful experience. One must stand on the shaky ground (as if an earthquake has hit), one must live through the humiliation of being laughed at, one must experience a second childhood, in order to finally exit onto new ground and find a new sky. It is this process, this passage, which is the real knowledge one gains from fieldwork. It is also something that is best done alone. There should be no spouse there to lean on, no best friend, and no one in the vicinity to whom you can speak in your native tongue. Psychological loneliness is a powerful emotional driver. Sometimes one must be forced into liminality in order to come out the other side of a tunnel with a new vision. It is like being blown at high speed, in total darkness, through a dark wind tube, or sliding down a water slide in darkness. There are parallels with the traditional vision quest of young native braves so central to many North American native cultures. Because of vulnerability, through confusion, and stemming from frustration and self doubt, the mind is somehow loosened—allowing one to learn so much—and so much faster.

* * *

As soon as I returned to Oxford, my Indian field data in hand, I was instantly recognized and accepted as a serious degree candidate. There was a palpable change in my status at the Institute the day I walked back through its doors upon returning from Tamilnadu. That was in September of 1966. I now felt a new welcome, something I had never experienced while being just a student there two years earlier. Now I had passed the "hazing" test, the formal initiation ritual. About a year and a half later I completed my written doctoral thesis. That final trial by verbal fire occurred in the spring of 1968 when an external examiner came up from London to grill me on my research findings.

Having succeeded in crossing these multiple barriers, I quickly left Oxford to begin what I thought I wanted—an academic teaching career. At first I served as a sessional lecturer at the University of Chicago. Then, with one year of practice under my belt, I welcomed the offer of an assistant professorship at the University of British Columbia. Fifteen years later I decided to resign what had by that time been upgraded to a tenured full professorship. I liked university but I decided to leave to explore a much wider world focused on modern communication technologies. The inspiration came from an opportunity the CBC had extended to me to serve as a cultural consultant for a series David Suzuki was then creating on India. Leaving the University of British Columbia was tough. The stint with

Figure 1.4 Beck with pottery horse

the CBC soon came to an end. I now faced a second extended period of initiation, this time in another milieu that felt very foreign—the corporate business world. The transition was challenging in every respect. But there too, I learned a lot!

The third phase of my lifelong commitment to professional teaching has only just started. Finally I have found the time and the opportunity to blend the two former periods of my life together. As I write this chapter I find myself totally immersed in the animated production of a two-part television series (26 shows). These shows tell an important and almost unknown story. It is the very legend I once collected with a tape recorder from a singing bard … in that small Indian village where I did my anthropological fieldwork some 45 years ago!

It is often by a painful initiation that one learns to become two (or three) persons in one. Like the modern immigrant to North America, a true and intimate personal encounter with a foreign culture can make a person strong. If that experience is ultimately positive, the new strength acquired will remain with that pilgrim for a lifetime.

Readings

Key books that particularly influenced my own early thinking include Louis Dumont's *Une sous-caste de l'Inde du sud: organisation sociale et religion des Pramalai Kallar* (*A South Indian Sub-Caste Community: The Social and Religious Organisation of the Pramalai Kallar*) (La Haye: Mouton & Co., 1957), an important work that has not yet been translated. A classic in ethnographic fieldwork is E. E. Evans-Pritchard,

Nuer Religion (Oxford: The Clarendon Press, 1956). And two works by Claude Lévi-Strauss, *La Pensée sauvage* (Paris: Plon, 1962) (later translated into English as *The Savage Mind*) and *La Voie des masques* (Paris: Plon, 1967) (later translated into English as *The Way of the Masks*) were also important. Each of those three authors was a personal friend, teacher, and mentor.

On village life and the right and left castes, you may consult, Brenda Beck, "Colour and Heat in South Indian Ritual," *Man*, Vol. 4, 1969, pp. 553–72 and *Peasant Society in Konku: A Study of Right and Left Subcastes in South India* (Vancouver: University of British Columbia, 1972). On the *Elder Brothers' Legend*, see *Annanmar Katai*: Vols I & II (A folk epic of Tamilnadu in Tamil and in English, on facing pages), (Madras: Institute of Asian Studies, 1992) (approximately 780 pages), collected, translated and edited by Brenda Beck.

Author

Brenda E. F. Beck is a senior South Asian scholar who now lives east of Toronto in a farmhouse that doubles as an animation studio. She taught at the University of British Columbia for 15 years and then worked as a business consultant and an active documentary video producer for more than two decades. In recent years Dr. Beck has lectured around the world, including having been a visiting professor at The University of Madras, as a guest of the government of India. She is the author of five books and roughly 60 articles. These include: "The Goddess and the Demon: A South Indian Festival in its Wider Context," *Purusartha: Récherches de sciences socials sur l'Asie du Sud*. Pt. 5, Paris: École des Hautes Études, 1981, pp. 82-136; *The Three Twins: The Telling of a South Indian Folk Epic*, Bloomington, IN: Indiana University Press, 1982, and *Folktales of India* (Beck is first of joint editors and also a contributor) Chicago, University of Chicago Press, 1987. You can visit her website: www.legendofponnivala.com for more information about *The Legend of Ponnivala*, including the 26 animated episodes telling this story.

Chapter 2

Hanumān Jayantī in Maharashtra

Jeffrey Brackett

Preamble

Lord Rāma's story is well-known from Vālmīki's epic *Rāmāyaṇa*. There are countless regional variations of Rāma stories, but the basic outline is as follows: Rāma is banished from his would-be kingdom of Ayodhya; he travels to the forest with his brother Lakṣmaṇa and wife Sītā, who is abducted by the demon-king Rāvaṇa; Rāma and Lakṣmaṇa are assisted by Hanumān and his monkey-troops in a great battle of good and evil; ultimately Rāma's side wins, and he returns to Ayodhya with Sītā and Lakṣmaṇa. Rāma and Kṛṣṇa are today the two most popular "earthly embodiments" (*avatārs*) of the great god Viṣṇu, and Hanumān is considered to be Rāma's faithful servant (*dāsa*) and model devotee (*bhākta*). Hanumān also is one of the most widely-recognized Hindu deities in contemporary India. In the present-day state of Maharashtra, located in central-western India, Hanumān is called Mārutī in Marathi (Sanskrit: Māruti), and he enjoys unparalleled popularity. Maharashtrian Hindus (and even some non-Hindus) engage in wide-ranging devotional practices for his annual festival, Hanumān Jayantī ("birthday"), which occurs precisely at sunrise each year on the first full-moon of Caitra (March–April), the first lunar month of the Hindu calendar. In the following section I describe my observations of Hanumān Jayantī celebrations at two locations: atop a hill in a rural area (1999), and at a few of the numerous temples in the modern city of Pune (1998). These two sites illustrate in part the immense fluidity one sees during the course of a single festival day. I use my field notes, photos, and video footage (from Pune) to describe this annual festival.

Narrative

Hanumān Jayantī: celebrating the birth of god

Rural temples

A surprisingly warm breeze blows across the start of the trail up to the famous hilltop Mārutī temple at Jaraṇḍeśvar ("J" here is pronounced as "Z"), which will take at least an hour to ascend. It's only 4:30 a.m. and there are cars and buses at the foot of the hill. The day of the first full-moon of the lunar month of Caitra (March–April) is believed by Hindus to be auspicious ... but I'm mostly thinking about the heat. "It's surely not going to be as hot at the top, which is nearly 4,000 feet above sea level and has plenty of trees for shade," I mumble to myself as I make the arduous climb. I was right.

Atop the plateau is the largest Mārutī temple I'd seen in Maharashtra. Śrī Jaraṇḍeśvar Devasthān ("temple") is certainly regionally famous, and, according to some accounts it is the most important Mārutī temple in all of Maharashtra. Today the hilltop is swarming with people. The crowd causes me to wonder, "Is this spot 'famous' only on festival days? What is this whole notion of 'fame' anyway? I rarely see more than a few devotees here on non-festival days. Ah, but who really has time to climb this hill regularly? On the other hand, a normal Saturday draws a continuous stream of devotees to more accessible temples in cities like Pune."

People say Jaraṇḍeśvar's Mārutī is courageous and brave; hence, this Mārutī's right hand is raised and ready to strike enemies, his left hand is placed across his chest, and he is crushing a demon under his left foot. Mārutī's raw physical power is other times symbolized by his holding a mace, his special weapon for vanquishing evil beings. I think, "Well, maybe it is this extreme power that makes this place 'famous.' But there's got to be more to this notion of fame than yet another 'powerful' Mārutī image."

My thoughts shift moment-to-moment, sometimes doubting my research goals, other times thoroughly enjoying the festival atmosphere: "Maybe I'm just tired of going to so many Mārutī temples." I sometimes think there's nothing new to find. "What *really* sets this place apart from other Mārutī temples? Yes, it's 'powerful.' And, yes, devotees have 'testimonials' about its healing powers. But every Mārutī temple makes claims about 'power' and 'fame.' I can't see any raised hand or crushed demon in the Mārutī. All I see is a large roundish image that covers any of those details." Not seeing Mārutī's hand or other details is common after priests apply layer upon layer of *sindūra*, a mix of powders and oil that gives the image a bright orange color.

What is striking is that this Mārutī image is also regarded as a self-manifested embodiment of the divine. That is to say, it is not a hand-crafted image. It's naturally appearing at this spot makes the image extremely powerful, alive, and awake. Certain details—like Mārutī's painted mustache and eyes—remind me of seeing Gaṇeśa, the elephant-headed deity, naturally appearing in tree trunks. I wonder, "Do painted mustaches and eyes highlight or diminish the miraculous? Other Mārutīs in this region sometimes have a mustache, but those are hand-crafted images. Either way, these elements help me to recognize the images more readily."

Priests, devotees, and written sources all suggest to me that the miraculous abounds at Jaraṇḍeśvar. "I came here on the advice of my guru. You see, I used to be a wrestler in my youth," the head priest tells me. "Look for yourself," he says as he extends his hand. "The leprosy stopped because of the healing powers of Jaraṇḍeśvar. You surely know the *Rāmāyaṇa* story of Mārutī carrying a mountain filled with healing herbs to revive Lakṣmaṇa, Rāma's brother. This *very hill* is a piece of that mountain. It fell on this spot! If you look closely, you'll also find healing herbs right next to the footpaths," he declares. "The amazing panoramic view itself surely has some 'healing' effect, too," I think to myself.

Our early arrival today allows my research partner and me to see this famous Mārutī before the doors to the inner sanctum close for final ritual preparations. We sit on the temple floor between the inner sanctum and a raised platform, above which hangs a small, lavishly decorated cradle for Mārutī's birth moment. At the precise auspicious moment, a group of priests emerge from the inner sanctum, descend the steps and transfer two platters filled with flowers and magenta powder—and several items too small to recognize—to the cradle. One of these items is the tiny festival image of Mārutī, not visible from my spot; I only glimpse it later when I have an opportunity to peer into the cradle. Soon after, one priest pulls a coconut from the cradle; members of the crowd cheer and chant as the priest tosses flowers their way. A priest then carries both platters through the crowd. Another priest continues tossing flowers from the cradle and its plinth. People reach toward the platters as the priest weaves through the temple.

Everyone hopes for *darśan* of the divinely charged materials. To take *darśan* entails seeing and being seen by the divine, but it can include touching this platter or cradle, too. Eventually, a priest and several helpers sit on the plinth handing out food blessed by this powerful Mārutī. I realize that getting *darśan* of the permanent Mārutī abiding within the temple will take patience today, as the long line snakes its way well outside the temple, and does not diminish in size all day long.

I'd been to very crowded village festivals before, but none that took such physical exertion to attend. It was tempting to conceptualize "village" and "urban" Hindu practice as somehow separate, as if to suggest that the very fluidity of festivals and rituals could be contained geographically … or any other way, for that matter. I suppose I was still seeking that special feature that made this place so famous.

"Where are you from?" I casually ask two men. "We are from Rajasthan." "And you travel *here* for Hanumān Jayantī," I inquire. "Actually, that is our native home. We live in Maharashtra now. We enjoy this festival, the surrounding beauty, and so we come here every year now. There are other Rajasthan devotees here too, mainly Vaiṣṇavas. But we are Jains." Speaking with Jains from Rajasthan (who now live in the urban sprawl of Pune) further challenges my understanding of "Hindu" practice. The conversation with these Jains, who happen to be relatives, destroys (yet again) imagined boundaries of religious practice. "This is my seventeenth consecutive Hanumān Jayantī at Jaraṇḍeśvar. It's number 14 for my brother. Other Jains also come here," they tell me. Once again, I am reminded how nothing "Hindu" is ever neatly categorized. I still am left thinking, nonetheless, of stylistic differences between rural and urban festivals. The attendees may come from various places, but the ethos of the festival experience remains different.

In fact, each time I ventured outside Pune—over time, to countless Mārutī shrines—there was no denying that rural and urban practice have significant differences. This rural festival scene couldn't have been more different from the previous year's (1998) Hanumān Jayantī that I witnessed in the urban centre of Pune.

Figure 2.1 Hanumān in Nashik, Maharashtra

Urban Temples

I stayed in Pune for a long stretch (1996–1999) conducting research on Mārutī traditions in Maharashtra. My research partner and I, recognizing the challenges we faced, had mapped the quickest route to visit as many Hanumān temples in the city as possible on the one festival day of Hanumān Jayantī (1998). Out of sheer exhaustion, we finally stopped at 22.

In Indian astrology, each day of the week is ruled over by the influence of a particular planet. Tuesday is Hanumān's day in much of India. But Saturday is ruled by the malevolent Śani/Saturn and happens to be Mārutī's special day of the week in Maharashtra. Mythically, only Mārutī proved powerful enough to defeat Śani, so he is believed to have the power to protect devotees from Śani's evil. Since this Hanumān Jayantī fell on a Saturday in 1998, we anticipated big crowds.

The day begins early with excitement and anticipation. Ah, our cameraman is here! We greet one another and quickly squeeze into the rickshaw we hired in advance for the day. The first stop: Balabhīm Mandir. Seeing "Balabhīm" on the signboard, my mind drifts to the first stanza of Samārtha Rāmdās Swāmi's (1608–81) *Bhīmarūpī Stotra*: *bhīma-rūpī mahā-rudrā, vajra-hanumān mārutī, vanārī añjanī-sūtā, rāma-dūta prabhañjanā.* The words speak of Hanumān's physical prowess, his being the son of Añjani, and a messenger of Lord Rāma. Mārutī's raw power is complemented by his other main trait: devotion (*bhakti*)—often in the form of unquestioning service (*dāsa*)—to Lord Rāma.

Two things stand out in my memory of that visit. First, just inside the temple entrance, a woman is giving a religious discourse that one might call a sermon. She faces the white stone *dāsa* Mārutī while she speaks; turning one's back to a deity would be inappropriate and highly disrespectful. Typically a *dāsa* image stands facing Lord Rāma in a Rāma temple … but Rāma is rarely present in Mārutī temples. I had never seen a woman teaching in a Mārutī temple. In spite of my initial confusion of witnessing a woman leading the festivities here, I am more impressed by the fact that we are welcome to walk right into the middle of a talk, film it and leave at our leisure. This openness and unending hospitality accorded foreigners like myself is not lost on me; nor is this the first or last time I would reflect on such matters.

A second memory is my early morning questions and thoughts: "Is this *all there is* for an annual festival? What about crowds? Where are the flashing lights, or at least something a bit more glitzy? The temple seems too quiet … not many more visitors or pilgrims than one would expect to see on a typical Saturday … and I can hear birds outside! Shouldn't there be more noise inside the temple?" I am confident that this serene environment will change throughout the day.

With a growing list of unanswered questions, we quietly leave for Hanumān Ṭekaḍī, a hill where we encounter many devotees chanting the *Bhīmarūpī Stotra* (Marathi) or the *Hanumān Cālīsā* (Hindi) on the way up the trail, as they typically do especially at sunrise. After a ten-minute hike up the trail we reach the top of Hanumān Ṭekaḍī. There, we immediately see the first (and much larger) of the two hilltop Mārutī shrines. It is at this moment that I feel Hanumān Jayantī really kicking into gear.

It's barely past sunrise, and we are pleasantly surprised by the large crowd. On most days, hill walkers give a quick "hello" (*namaskār*) greeting in the direction of Mārutī and continue on their way. Others pause for a moment, but not for any ritual formalities involving a priest. Today, however, there is a priest accepting devotees' offerings of coconuts and garlands to Mārutī. He also hands back the blessed food. Meanwhile a second priest chants Sanskrit verses.

There are some 50 people crowded in front of the Mārutī image today. Group chanting and (semi-rhythmic) clapping begins when a priest waves a camphor flame before Mārutī. At the appropriate moments, devotees respond with a joint "*jay*," each time the priest throws in a quick Hindi "*mahā rudrā hanumān kī*" … All the while, the chanting priest hands out blessed food items. I would like to linger, to watch and participate in the celebrations here. I think to myself, "You can watch it all again later. There's much more to see today."

We certainly don't want to miss the special sunrise *kīrtan* that we have learned is going on at another temple. *Kīrtan* is a mix of religious storytelling and song, and the styles vary widely. The *kīrtan* performer stands facing Mārutī, but the temple is Śrī Daśabhujā Gaṇapati Mandir on the ever-crowded Karve Road. Men sit with backs to walls, forming two lines. This area runs parallel to the elevated Gaṇapati temple. Women are seated up there near the railing. It is frustratingly difficult for me to make out much of the performer's Marathi words, as his singing competes with the constant traffic noise.

A drummer and harmonium player accompany him. I feel better when I can finally hear some words, such as "Tuka says" (a.k.a., "Saint" Tukārām), "messenger of Rāma," and "son of Añjani"—the last two refer to Mārutī's character. Since I was audiotaping the performance, I figured I would be able to listen to it later. As the *kīrtan* ends, a number of people approach the performer for *darśan*. Others gather near Mārutī for group chanting, much as we saw at Hanumān Ṭekaḍī. As the chanting is finishing, participants chant the familiar "Hāre Kṛṣṇa" mantra: "*hāre kṛṣṇa, hāre kṛṣṇa, kṛṣṇa kṛṣṇa, hāre hāre, hāre rāma, hāre rāma, rāma rāma, hāre hāre.*"

Our next stop is Parvatī Mārutī Mandir. "Parvatī" is a popular spelling and pronunciation of *parvatīya* ("mountainous" in Marathi). This word is not to be confused with Pārvatī, the name of a Hindu Goddess. The temple is located across the street from the bottom of Parvatī, another well-known hill in Pune that has several large temples on its plateau. This Mārutī temple is not lavish; its plain rectangular exterior is normally hardly noticeable. However, it would be hard to miss the temple today.

A colorful cloth canopy extending from the temple entrance marks the special day. Loudspeakers broadcast Sanskrit chants. Extra vendors setup devotional materials (oil, coconuts, and *ruī*-leaf garlands) in anticipation of supplying devotees' ritual offerings until late in the evening. A five or six feet long, two-dimensional painted image of young Hanumān hangs on an exterior wall. He flies upward, reminding one of his mythic leap to eat the sun, which he had mistaken for a piece of fruit.

This temporary, painted festival Hanumān image contrasts severely with the aesthetic one encounters inside the temple: framed photos of people and deities placed here and there, many in desperate need of cleaning—or at least a fresh garland—and in my experience of Mārutī temples, no planned order to the décor. At the same time, I'm struck by how this seemingly haphazard mix of imagery adds a sense of uniqueness to each temple.

Today two men hand devotees' offerings to a priest, who was seated inside the small inner sanctum. The festival offerings add variety to the usual coconuts and leaf-garlands, including split cantaloupes and whole watermelons. Mārutī's small, garland-covered cradle sits atop a railing in front of the inner sanctum. Directly below the cradle—yet behind the metal railing—about a foot above the floor, rests a small traditional Mārutī image that couldn't be more than six inches tall.

Back outside, I now see on the chalkboard a Marathi quote by the much beloved Sāne Gurujī (1899–1950), a Gandhian freedom fighter, socialist, follower of Vinobā

Bhāve's teachings, and prolific author, especially of children's stories. One could surely imagine links between Mārutī and politics, which tend to be associated with militant Hindu ideologies. I'm pleased, however, to see a less controversial figure quoted for this festive occasion. Some may attribute "controversy" to Sāne Gurujī: after all, he is a Maharashtrian Brahmin who underwent a "death-fast" for temple entry rights of (now former) Untouchables.

Meanwhile, young women are completing a beautiful *rāṅgoḷī*, an intricate design of colored powders created on the ground near the temple steps. Its diameter is roughly six-feet across, with a white ॐ (*oṁ*) surrounded by a bright red circle right in the center of their *rāṅgoḷī*. I can't help smiling each time I see a *rāṅgoḷī*. It adds color—literally and symbolically—to any occasion, and surely would be missed if absent on a festival day.

Another *rāṅgoḷī* is just beginning to take shape at our next stop, Bhikārdās Mārutī Mandir. Bhikārdās ("servant of the poor") is named for the "holy man" who donated money to begin building the temple. His memorial marker is near the Mārutī image within the temple, which is located in the largely Brahmin neighborhood of Sadāśiv Peṭh in Pune's "old city." The Mārutī once lay against a tree, which toppled more than 100 years ago. Today Bhikārdās Mandir is one of Pune's two most famous Mārutī temples. It also completely blends into its surroundings. But, like Parvatī Mārutī Mandir, the vendors' flowers, leaf-garlands, and stacks of coconuts, set the temple entrance apart from its drab background. We approach the temple entry under another ornate cloth canopy.

I notice for the first time a *svāstika*—a sign of auspiciousness in Hindu lore—of tiny orange light bulbs above the doorway leading to the hallway that has a rack for footwear. I'm a bit surprised by this discovery, since this is the temple I visit more than any other ... and it only took me three years to see it! Well, this is the first time the lights are on.

Today there is a police officer at the end of the hall, where we make a 90-degree clockwise turn to enter the temple. We can barely see the image of Mārutī through the crowd. Devotees often do a quick *namaskār* in Mārutī's direction and continue on this path to the adjoining street and vice versa. I don't see anyone doing that today. Normally, devotees easily approach Mārutī with offerings. Today, there are two assistants: a priest is seated facing Mārutī, and a young boy is actually standing inside the inner sanctum. The boy is placing leaf-garlands atop Mārutī—not around his neck—while the priest quickly waves coconuts in a small circle before Mārutī, and then smashes them to the ground to crack them open. The priest and his assistant barely keep up with the deluge of offerings.

Meanwhile, people circumambulate Mārutī's sanctum clockwise. Though the crowds in temples on festival days may seem chaotic, there's a sense of flow that I've grown used to seeing. Everyone seems to know where to go, and in which direction, despite the absence of any single way of engaging in devotion. I used to be baffled by the lack of "order." Now, I sometimes forget to look for nuances that differentiate temples. It's easy to get lazy, thinking, "Oh, it's just another temple," when each place provides me the opportunity to learn more not only about the variety of forms of Mārutī devotion, but about the unique stories about Mārutī that are related to a specific temple.

I do notice several of the "regulars" doing their usual, focused walking around the inner sanctum. And the priests are especially interested to know how I'm enjoying the festival. Once again, the hospitality makes me feel at home. I tell them how glad I am to see the crowds and they are pleased to hear of our plans to visit so many Mārutī temples in one day. I happily accept the specially prepared paper-wrapped, blessed-food packet before bidding them farewell for the day. As I step down to the lower section of the temple, I finally notice Mārutī's garland-covered cradle hanging slightly higher than the temple bell. Some devotees touch the ground in front of two elderly gentlemen who appear to be holy men (*sādhus*). Others place a few coins in their metal cups.

In this lower section of the temple one finds various framed posters and pictures, some at eye level, and many more along the edges of the ornate ceiling. Off to one side, there is a shrine to Samārtha Rāmdās Swāmi, a Brahmin *sant* ("saint") and embodiment (*avatār*) of Mārutī. Normally the doors to this wooden "cabinet-like" shrine are closed, but not on such an important day. In the Marathi-speaking region of Maharashtra, Rāmdās adds a significant regional flavor to Mārutī devotion. In fact, most Mārutī shrines in Pune have a framed image of Rāmdās adorning their walls.

Facing Mārutī, there is also a Rāma temple, which was constructed recently. Typically, if there is an image of Rāma, he is the center of attention. One would then expect to find a *dāsa* ("servant" and "devotee") Mārutī facing Rāma or kneeling near his side. Since a "brave" (i.e. one ready to strike an enemy) Mārutī is the original image, its facing Rāma is highly unusual. In any case, Mārutī is the center of attention here, and I rarely even see devotees approach Rāma's image here.

Right after leaving Bhikārdās Mārutī, we enjoyed a brief lunch break before heading to our next stop, a privately owned temple, "Akrā Mārutī Mandir." *Akrā* translates as "eleven," referring to special set of eleven Mārutī temples established by Rāmdās. These eleven temples form a pilgrimage circuit for some devotees.

Pune's "Akrā Mārutī Mandir" is right in the middle of the courtyard of a private residence. The temple is a six or so foot high white "stūpa" that has eleven niches housing Mārutī images around its circumference. Unlike the images in the eleven temples established by Rāmdās, these images look exactly alike. The temple is enclosed by a wood lattice fence, with two entryways. Each image has a single, multi-colored flower garland in addition to the usual leaf-garland. A toddler stands before an image and waves incense sticks.

Just a few footsteps from this scene is a rather large Rāma temple. Inside it are two Mārutīs. One of these is a black stone *dāsa* Mārutī that is draped with orange robes today. A *dāsa* pose is natural in a Rāma temple, but the smaller white Mārutī in front of it catches our eyes. A gentleman here tells us that this is the only Mārutī image in all of India in which Mārutī has a carved bow over his shoulder. Once again I'm reminded of a special trait associated with each temple I visit.

From here we head back to the other of the two most famous Mārutī temples in Pune: Śanipār Mārutī Mandir, which sits right in the middle of a road, atop a *pār* (elevated "bench" around a tree); hence, "Śani-pār." Śanipār, as it is locally known, couldn't be more different from Bhikārdās in spite of their being separated by such a short distance. Here, devotees queue up directly facing the images of both Mārutī and Śani. The orderly line may be due in part to the destitute people who sit on either side of the queue, awaiting blessed food offerings or pocket change from devotees. Śani, the malevolent one who rules the planet Saturn, is especially powerful on Saturday (*Śanivāra*). Mārutī defeated evil Śani, who now protects those who appease him or worship Mārutī; otherwise, Śani interferes in one's astrological chart to afflict a person with troubles (especially illnesses) for a period of seven and a half years. At Śanipār devotees regularly pour oil on both Śani and Mārutī.

Śani is also present in Nava Graha ("nine planets") temples and at Ḍulyā Mārutī Mandir, which has a black stone image of each *graha*. Ḍulyā is in the middle of a traffic intersection. This wouldn't be the last temple we would see in a road, but it is a good reminder of how Pune's development has engulfed—yet accommodated—religious structures in the midst of ever-increasing vehicular traffic.

Lesser known among Pune's innumerable Mārutī temples are three others situated amidst intersections or roads: Lakeryā Mārutī, Uṇṭāḍe Mārutī, Pañcamukhī Mārutī, and Sūryamukhī Mārutī. Uṇṭāḍe's fantastic flashing lights fill the temple with just the sort of fun I hoped for when the day started at Balabhīm Mārutī Mandir. It also has a permanent signboard in Marathi and English listing prices for special rituals.

Sūryamukhī, however, reminds me of the meeting of antiquity and modernity in Pune. Like Śanipār it sits atop an elevated bench. An enormous tree is right behind Mārutī's enclosed sanctum, but it is a covered open-air shrine with a modern tile floor and metal railing around its perimeter. This modern temple incorporates a Peepal tree that has five very old looking black stone upright Nāgas (snakes, especially cobras).

Nāgas have diverse roles in Hindu lore. Each Nāga is raised up as if to strike, yet has five heads that are extended forward slightly to offer protection to barely decipherable smaller images under their extended hoods. Other stones with two intertwining snakes also lean against the base of the tree. Each stone has at least a flower, if not an entire garland placed on its head(s), as well as various colored sprinkled powders. During one's circumambulation of Mārutī, devotees would touch the top of each Nāga, and then hang a leaf-garland on the same spot on the tree. Lots of strings were hanging from limbs; others wrapped around the trunk.

The Nāgas and strings remind me of hero stones and "wish-granting" trees I would see during research trips. Such images are much more common in or near village temples, and are a pleasant reminder of the immensely diverse forms of temples, images, and devotional styles at Mārutī temples in Maharashtra.

Across town in Pune, on a road adjoining a well-known shopping district, at least 100 devotees await their turn to enter the large Mārutī temple situated there. Strings cross the street above the temple: small orange cloth squares fluttering in the breeze. And Mārutī's offerings are a good reminder of why generalizations regarding devotional practices are futile. It also challenges romanticized visions of "religion" that glorify antiquity or impose dichotomies of "tradition" and "modernity" as if it were so simple. For, at this temple, the large, roundish *sindūra*-smeared image—much like ones we had seen earlier—is adorned with garlands of rupee notes ... 10-rupee notes, 100-rupee notes, and another of 500-rupee notes. Are these garlands really so different from the single flower or garland placed on Mārutī, in the hopes of having one's wish fulfilled?

Discussion

Hanumān Mūrtis and temples: power, fame, and miracles

Following from my preceding observations of Hanumān Jayantī, I could address various topics related to Hanumān-Mārutī. For example, I could describe Mārutī's rise in popularity among urban-dwelling Hindus (especially the middle class); Mārutī rituals that only women engage in during Śrāvaṇa (August–September); highly technical *upāsanā* ("worship") techniques aimed at correcting specific troubles, including illnesses; Samārtha Rāmdās Swāmi's importance to modern understandings of Mārutī's significance; tantric ritual practices; or, a whole host of other devotional patterns that enable devotees quick, direct access to Mārutī's multiple forms of power.

Important though these themes may be for a more complete understanding of Hanumān-Mārutī, I will limit my discussion to a few themes associated with how a given temple becomes "famous" (*prasiddha*). One should keep in mind that, although "famous" is a common translation of *prasiddha*, a temple's "fame" is also its sense of importance; it is what sets *this* temple apart from others, and what makes *this* temple special (or even unique). My sources are Marathi "worship" guide-booklets and pamphlets, as well as stories that devotees told me. In combination, these two sources—textual and oral—contribute to a more nuanced perspective on Hindu practice.

One could surely find similar themes of "fame" related to other deities and their temples, so these notions should prove useful beyond the limited descriptions of Mārutī temples in Pune and Maharashtra. Two important ways that Mārutī temples become famous is through their temple origin stories and through miraculous events. Other Hindu temples may have special texts such as Māhātmyas or Sthalapurāṇas narrating elaborate—often lengthy—temple origin stories that praise their fame and extraordinary characteristics.

Mārutī temple descriptions, on the other hand, are short descriptive prose pieces that appear in Marathi worship booklets and in one lengthy, dictionary-style book that is a compendium of such stories from around the subcontinent. Regardless of the descriptive style, these Mārutī images are deemed to be especially powerful and therefore famous. Temple origin stories regularly narrate miraculous events associated either with the temple's origin or devotees' subsequent experiences of miraculous powers. These personal experiences confirm and increase the famous and powerful character of the temple.

Before one hastily claims that such reasoning is circular, recall the example of Jaraṇḍeśvar: if it is a piece of the medicinal mountain (Droṇagirī), it is natural to hear devotees speak in terms of healing. Hence, the head priest showed us the leprosy that no longer afflicts his hand and told us we could find healing herbs around the mountain. This particular example links a sub-regionally important temple with a well-known event of pan-Indian fame, namely, Mārutī's carrying of Droṇagirī in Vālmīki's epic *Rāmāyaṇa*.

Frequently, miraculous temple origins are attributed to the person who either installed or found a temple image (*mūrti*). When the origin is uncertain, Samārtha Rāmdās Swāmi regularly is cited as establishing the image. Or, the image is simply very old—hundreds of years—or it dates to time when the Brahmin Peśvās ruled from Pune, before being ousted by the British in 1818. Another response to questions of origins is simply, "Who knows?"

Whether the origins are certain or not, miraculous powers (past and present) take several forms. Often an otherwise hidden image is located/discovered, leading it to have special powers. Bāhe Mārutī, among the eleven (*akrā*) Mārutīs established by Rāmdās, was discovered at the bottom of the Kṛṣṇa river. The Mārutī had been at the bottom of the river since the deity diverted the flow of the rising river to keep it from disrupting Rāma, who was engrossed in devotion to the Śiva-*liṅga* he just established. Rāmdās dove into the Kṛṣṇa, stayed there for several hours, brought the Mārutī to the riverbank for a short time, and then created a temple image resembling that ancient Mārutī. At Pārgāv, Rāmdās pulled the Mārutī image from his cloth bag. These are just two of several miraculous events linking Rāmdās with Mārutī's regional fame. Often the image itself shakes or moves in a manner that increases its power.

Another common event attesting to this type of miraculous power is when the accumulated layers of bright red/orange (vermilion) oil-powder mix (*sindūra*) suddenly fall off the image. At Lakeryā Mārutī (Pune), a priest spoke of filling several sacks of the fallen *sindūra* and gave me a small piece as a "souvenir." The same miracle occurred at Gañjī Mārutī (Pune), which now has a beautiful black Mārutī. This sudden event relates to other images that are known for movement—at regular intervals, or at some point in the distant past.

Ḍolṇārā Mārutī ("involuntary movement" or "swaying") in Amaravati District, for example, was discovered at a riverbank. It was so heavy that it could not be moved from the riverbank to the platform constructed for it; the villagers finally gave up hope, only to be surprised the next morning to find the Mārutī had miraculously moved to the platform! Moreover, since 1968, this same *mūrti* is said to move every two or three minutes, but never from the waist down.

Written documents claim that the Ḍulyā Mārutī (Pune) image shook out of sadness and frustration as the Maratha army was being defeated in the Battle of Panipat (1761), north of Delhi. Ḍulyā ties together other themes that contribute to its fame. For instance, the priest and printed stories both report the image to be

Figure 2.2 Gaṇeśa naturally appearing in a tree at Bāhe, Maharashtra

hundreds of years old, increasing its renown. Other sources suggest that Rāmdās installed the temple image, linking it to a famous "saint" (*sant*). Finally, it seems that the Brahmin Peśvā rulers in Pune sought Mārutī's advice, or verdict (*kaul*), at this very temple.

At Śakunī Mārutī (Pune), one ascertains Mārutī's advice by simply placing a flower on the small roadside image. As a shop owner explained to me, "You then wait to see where the flower lands. The direction of its fall determines how one should proceed, or whether one's wish will be granted."

While fame accrues to Mārutī temples via associations with various miraculous events, Pune's Mārutīs are also famous for their interesting names. Each name has a story behind it, but I will leave those stories untold, important though they are to neighborhood histories. Some names refer to people or events, while others are geographic markers of sorts. Here is a sample of entertaining names, each of which is followed by "Mārutī Mandir": Potato (*Baṭāṭyā*), Bhāṅg (*Bhāṅgyā*:

variously known as hashish or cannabis), Well (*Khāṅyā*), Glass Bangle (*Lakeryā*), Grass (*Gavat*), Grain (*Dāṅe*), Our (*Āpla*), Tied-Up (*Bhandhācī*), Hay Stack (*Gañjī*), Whoring (*Chināl*), Gold (*Sonyā*), Village Border (*Gaokos*), Jilabī (*Jilbyā*: a deep-fried, pretzel-shaped orange sweet), Camel (*Uṇṭāḍe*), Pumpkin Intersection (*Bhopaḷā Cauk*), Truthful (*Satyavān*), Head (*Ḍoke*), Bhavani ([Goddess] *Bhavānī Mātā*), and National (*Rāṣṭrīyā*) ... and there are many, many more.

Odd names, locally important stories, miraculous events, saints, powerful and famous images: all serve as reminders of Mārutī's immense and diverse regional popularity throughout Maharashtra. And, Mārutī's fame far exceeds the boundaries of Maharashtra state, extending around the globe and creating exciting opportunities to add new stories of Mārutī's importance.

Readings

For the most comprehensive treatment of Hanumān, see Philip Lutgendorf, *Hanumān's Tale: The Messages of a Divine Monkey* (New York: Oxford University Press, 2007). Lutgendorf critically examines the historiography of Hanumān studies before turning to other important issues such as historical developments and regional variants in Sanskrit and popular literature (mainly Hindi), iconography, ritual performance, politics, and the contemporary significance of Hanumān in India and beyond. For shorter pieces of this puzzle, begin with two of his numerous essays: "My Hanumān is Bigger Than Yours" (*History of Religions* 33.3: 211-45, 1994) and "Monkey in the Middle: The Status of Hanumān in Popular Hinduism" (*Religion* 27: 311-32, 1997). For more details on Hanumān-Mārutī in Maharashtra, see Jeffrey M. Brackett, *Practically Hindu: Contemporary Conceptions of Hanumān-Mārutī in Maharashtra* (PhD dissertation, University of Pittsburgh, 2004). For a nice overview of Hanumān in the *Rāmāyaṇa*, see Catherine Ludvik, *Hanumān in the Rāmāyaṇa of Vālmīki and the Rāmcaritamānasa of Tulsī Dāsa* (Delhi: Motilal Banarsidass, 1994).

Author

Jeffrey Brackett (PhD) teaches Religious Studies at Ball State University. Recent essays include "The Upwardly Mobile Monkey-God: Village and Urban Mārutīs in Maharashtra," in Manu Bhagavan and Anne Feldhaus (eds), *Speaking Truth to Power: Religion Caste, and the Subaltern Question in India*, (New Delhi: Oxford University Press, 2008, pp. 78-91), and (with Vijayā Dev) "Hanumān at the Center of Maharashtrian Village Life: A Translation of Vyankatesh Madgulkar's Marathi Story, 'Temple,'" *Journal of Vaishnava Studies* 12 (2) 2004: 105-116.

Chapter 3

Searching for Satī

Paul B. Courtright

Preamble

Research in India has a way of taking its practitioners in unexpected directions. Several years ago I began what I expected would be a straightforward historical look into the early stages of British colonial rule in India, focusing on what British civil servants and amateur scholars learned about Hinduism and how they learned about it. As I read around in books, East India Company reports, memoirs, and correspondence from the latter part of the eighteenth and early nineteenth centuries, the period during British interests in India expanded from trade and profit to administration and revenue collection, I kept running across eye-witness accounts and discussions of the Hindu practice of the burning of widows on the funeral pyres of their deceased husbands. The sources I came across from the earlier part of this period generally agreed that the practice, however despicable to Europeans, was a part of the Hindu religion where such women were venerated for their devotion to their husbands.

In keeping with its long-standing policy of not interfering with Indians' religious traditions, the British refrained from intervening. However, after a lengthy debate among British administrators and Protestant missionaries, and among Hindu traditionalists and reformers, from about 1805–1829, the Governor-General finally ordered that the practice of widow-burning, or *suttee* as it came to be called, was indeed not a religious obligation and therefore its abolition did not abrogate the policy of non-interference in Indians' religious traditions. This part of research took me to libraries and archives. Somewhere along the way I became aware that there was a connection between the practice of *suttee* and the wife of the Hindu god Śiva, the goddess Satī, who also entered a fire, albeit under different circumstances. Indeed, the story of Satī appeared in many ancient Sanskrit texts from the *Mahābhārata* to the numerous compendia of myths and ritual lore called Purāṇas. My research took me another step into discovering the connection between the story of Satī and a series of shrines in her honor that extend across the South Asian lower Himalayas. What I had assumed was a historical and textual project evolved into something that I needed to look into on the ground in India. How did Hindus understand the connection between Satī the goddess and the wives who joined their dead husbands on the pyre? How could I better understand the ways texts and historical materials fit with what I could learn by being there and talking with people in some of these shrines?

Narrative

"Just over there"

My search for Satī's story took me from Delhi to the pilgrimage city of Hardwar, a city of temples and religious establishments located along the banks of the Ganges River at the point where the river slows its descent from the Himalayas to the plains below. From there it was only a few miles taxi ride to the small town of Kankhal, which is also adjacent to the Ganges. My destination was a large temple called the Daksheshwar Mandir, the temple to Dakṣa's Lord, that is, Śiva. I arrived one hot afternoon in May, along with a good friend who is a native speaker of Hindi. The taxi dropped us off near an open lot where several vendors had set up their carts selling soft drinks, snacks, pamphlets, and tape cassettes of devotional songs. From there we wandered into the temple, past two large cement statues of lions and visited the main temple to Śiva, joining the queue of devotees entering the white marble enclosure. Around the outer walls of the temple were a series of bas-relief sculptures depicting the various episodes in Satī's story. In the center of the temple, slightly beneath ground level was the pillar-shaped *śivaliṅga*. The *liṅga* is the marker of Śiva's presence. A priest, dressed in a red monastic tunic, sat next to the deity and received garlands of flowers from the devotees and marked each worshipper's forehead with red *kuṃkum* powder as she or he passed by the *liṅga* and moved on back outside into the temple courtyard.

After we had paid our respects to the shrine of Śiva we wandered over to the nearby shrine of Satī to view her in her white marble image dressed in elegant silk. She was facing a three-layered square fire pit where priests periodically offer *homas* or Vedic fire offerings. From there we walked down a series of steps to the bank of the Ganges where a number of devotees were worshipping the river and another priest smeared red powder on our foreheads. We walked back up the stairs from the river, past a large and very old banyan tree with its many tendrils hanging down. At the base of the tree was a square marble platform on top of which a couple of dozen small stone *liṅgas* had been placed. Several young men were pouring offerings of milk over the *liṅgas* and placing flowers on their tops while softly chanting "*oṃ śivāya nāmaḥ*" (om, homage to Śiva) as they circumambulated the sacred tree.

Across the courtyard from the tree we saw that the *mahant*, the senior monk in charge of the temple, had come out of his office and was sitting in a chair surrounded by one other priest and some of the pilgrims. We walked over and introduced ourselves. I explained in my stilted Hindi that I had come to the temple to learn more about the story of Satī and asked if he would have a few minutes to tell it to me. The *mahant*, known there simply as Lāl Bābā (the honored one dressed in red, the color of his monastic order), was a man of medium height and a sturdy build. He had deep-set eyes, a graying beard, and wore a red turban to match his red shirt. It only took one look into his eyes to see that he was a man comfortable with his own authority even as he was gracious in his hospitality. The temple is managed by an order of ascetics called the Mahanirvani Akhara, the order of the great enlightenment. The order has many affiliated communities across India.

"Yes," he answered, "it was just over there." He gestured with his chin to the shrine where Satī's image was located and the Vedic fire altar. "It all happened there." He then went on to tell us the story of Satī, a story he said was "in the Purāṇas." I felt astonishingly lucky that he happened to be there and was willing to take time to retrace Satī's story for this passing foreigner. It was also a great relief to sit on the cool ground in the shade. This moment was a lot of why I had come to India in the first place: to hear the story told by one whose authority to tell it was unquestioned by his tradition, and to hear it at the very place where its tradition says it happened. In that moment, story, place, and voice converged. As I recall his telling, and from the scribbled notes I made as he was telling it, the story of Satī goes briefly like this.

Once, long ago, the gods Viṣṇu and Brahmā were worried that Śiva was not married. He lived on his mountain all alone. Viṣṇu and Brahmā persuaded Śiva to go with them to visit the Great Goddess, Ūmā, and ask her to take birth and marry Śiva. She said that she would meet their request and take birth as Satī, the daughter of the great King Dakṣa. But, she warned them, if anyone failed to respect her she would abandon that body and return to her divine form. After some time the arrangements for the wedding ceremony were complete and the two were married and went to live in Śiva's home on Mt. Kailāsa.

Sometime later Dakṣa decided to host a great sacrifice at his home in Kankhal. He invited all the gods, all the kings, all the humans, all forms of life, and all units of time. All were invited except Śiva and Satī. When he announced his intention to host the great sacrifice his priest, Dadhici, protested that no sacrifice would be effective without Śiva. Dakṣa answered that once before, when he had sponsored another sacrifice, Śiva had failed to pay him proper respect when he entered the sacrificial enclosure. Besides, Dakṣa continued, Śiva was a man without kin, he lived in a cremation ground, and he drank intoxicants out of a human skull. He was not fit to be included in such an important event as a great sacrifice.

The preparations for the sacrifice continued, and the guests began to make their ways across the sky in their chariots. Satī saw them as they went past and asked Śiva where everyone was going. He replied that they were going to Kankhal for the great sacrifice. She told him she wanted to go also. He said that they had not been invited and it was not proper to go where one is not invited. She answered that since it was her father who was hosting the event and they were members of the family no invitation was needed. Śiva refused to attend, but he did agree that Satī could go if she wanted to and sent his companion Nandi and a number of servants to accompany her.

When Satī arrived at Kankhal and saw that seats for each of the gods and members of her family had been set out around the sacred fire, she asked her father why she and Śiva had been excluded. Dakṣa spoke to her abruptly, "Your husband is a filthy beggar! He has no kin. He is a *kalpālin*, a radical ascetic who lives in a cremation ground and drinks intoxicants from a skull. He insulted me once before by not paying respect to me at another sacrifice." He went on to say that he had only agreed to Satī's marriage to Śiva because Brahmā had insisted on it.

Satī was filled with rage at hearing her father insulting her husband. She spoke back angrily to him, "I will no longer live in this body I have received from you!" With that her body began to flame up with the fire of her yoga (*yogāgni*).

The news of Satī's death by fire quickly reached Śiva. He was overwhelmed with grief and flew into a rage. He pulled a lock of his hair out of his head and threw it on the ground. Immediately an enormous figure named Vīrabhadra sprang up. Śiva instructed Vīrabhadra to go to Kankhal and destroy Dakṣa's sacrifice. Quickly Vīrabhadra assembled a band of Śiva's retinue and went to the sacrificial arena. When they arrived there they immediately destroyed the sacrifice, scattering the offerings and utensils, and chasing off the guests. Dakṣa tried to escape, but

Figure 3.1 Śiva and Satī image at Kankhal, Uttarkhand

Vīrabhadra grabbed him. Vīrabhadra tore off Daksa's head and threw it into the sacrificial fire. Then Śiva arrived and saw Satī's body smoldering in the fire. He picked up her body and wandered off into the mountains consumed with grief. Soon the whole world began to collapse. Viṣṇu and the other gods went after Śiva. Viṣṇu took out his discus-weapon (*cakra*) and threw it at Śiva and Satī. As the discus struck Satī's body it cut off pieces that fell to the ground. At each place the piece of her body was transformed into her whole form, and Śiva took the form of the *liṅga* to remain at each place. These are the *śāktapīṭha*s, the places of her divine presence.

I do not recall how long it took for him to tell the story. By the time he had finished I noticed that a small crowd of devotees to the temple had gathered, perhaps amused at the scene of a foreigner sitting at Lāl Bābā's feet or appreciating hearing a story they probably already knew being told by such a distinguished figure. He invited me to come back and stay in the temple's guesthouse. It was another example of legendary Indian hospitality.

Later on I had the opportunity to visit several of the shrines that mark the spots where pieces of Satī's body had fallen. At one of them I again had the opportunity to ask an elderly priest to tell me Satī's story. I was struck by how remarkably similar it was how Lāl Bābā's version. The experience of hearing a second version reminded me of how orally transmitted narratives and shrines dispersed across a vast countryside hold traditions intact. It is said there are 51 places where pieces of Satī's body had fallen. Some of the shrines are famous pilgrimage destinations in their own right; together they form an implicit structural framework for devotees to venerate the many distinct yet connected forms of the Goddess.

Discussion

Placing the story

What struck me most directly in listening to Lāl Bābā's narration was how much the story was about *where* it happened, in Kankhal, "just over there" as he had said earlier. Many of the versions of the story in the Purāṇas mention Kaṇkhāla, or Gaṅgādvāra—the doorway of the Ganges, as where Dakṣa's sacrifice and Satī's self-immolation took place. Why Kankhal? Kankhal is located next to the sacred Ganges at the place where the river slows its plunge down the Himalayas and meets the plains below. At Kankhal, and Hardwar a few miles up the road, the sacred river slows its pace and it is possible for pilgrims to bathe in it.

In addition to the geographical convergence of the mountains and the plains, the story reflects a violent but ultimately benign resolution between two very different configurations of Hindu tradition: the Vedic practitioners of sacrifice and their social order, represented by Dakṣa, and the ascetic antinomian practitioners represented by Śiva. Satī stands in the middle, the daughter of one and the wife of the other. Historically, perhaps Kankhal was already a sacred site about which there was some dispute as to who controlled it. The story of Dakṣa's sacrifice, Satī's self-immolation, and Śiva's victory may be a way the Hindu tradition as a whole has remembered what had been a conflict between the Vedic-Brahmanic religion of the plains and the yogic-tantric religion of the mountains. Between the mountains and the plains flows the river, the embodiment of the goddess. The religion of the plains undergoes a disruption by the religion of the mountains, a rupture that is first resolved by including the religion of the mountains, and later expanded to include the religion of the river. In other words, the story of Dakṣa's sacrifice is a tale of convergence and transformation that is embodied in the very landscape of plains, mountains, and river. At this level of understanding the story is fully inscribed on the land itself.

Returning to Satī. According to the story, when her father insulted her husband she abandoned her mortal body and burst into flame. Satī became the sacrifice. Through her self-immolation she brings about the confrontation between Dakṣa and Śiva that leads to Dakṣa's dismemberment and his recognition of Śiva, whom he had excluded, as the true lord of the universe. But, Dakṣa only comes to this recognition when he gets a new head, the head of the sacrificial goat. When Śiva comes to the sacrifice and carries Satī's body away, the gods follow them and cut her body into many pieces and distribute her body across the landscape. Here the story draws on the ancient Vedic hymn (*ṚV* 10.90) about Puruṣa, the original one, whose body parts made up the universe. Now it is Satī's body, the female body, that extends its animating power (*śakti*) across the world.

Eventually, long after I had left Kankhal, I looked at the story in relation to its place of narration. It made sense to me that Kankhal, as a sacred destination for millennia, linked together Vedic-Vaiṣṇava, Śaiva-yogic, and Devī-tantric traditions at the place where the mountains and the plains are joined together by the river. In other words, place, story, and the internal history of the Hindu tradition in this locale all fit together into a kind of *yantra* or framework of connections.

After Kankhal

But, there is another dimension to the story that I keep noticing now after many readings of the many versions in the Purāṇas and elsewhere. This dimension takes the story beyond its particular Hindu framework and moves it into a meditation on the relations among the main characters: Dakṣa, the father and father-in-law; Śiva, the son-in-law and husband; and Satī, the daughter and wife. These three characters form a triangle that links them together and separates them from one another. Many Hindus I have talked with about this story have told me that Satī was the perfect wife in the way she immolated herself rather than submit to her father's abusive tirade against her husband. Dakṣa is the villain. He violates the dharma of family relations by speaking ill of his son-in-law. A piece of advice often given to the father of the bride at Hindu weddings is "Don't be like Dakṣa!"

As I think about the story, I wonder if there is more to the matter of Dakṣa's hatred of Śiva than he is telling us, or more than he himself may be aware of. Is the story exploring an unconscious dimension in family relations? Dakṣa says his animosity toward Śiva links back to Śiva's failure to pay him appropriate respect at a previous sacrifice, and that Śiva's lifestyle offends him. This all makes sense. But he agreed to the marriage at the requests of the gods, and the Goddess had specifically warned them that she would abandon her Satī body if she were mistreated. Dakṣa's rage at Śiva seems to me too excessive, as though something else is going on, something hidden. What is it that Śiva has that Dakṣa may not have? Satī. Here I think the story is exploring the forbidden world of incestuous desire. There are two things Dakṣa wants that he cannot have. He wants to own the whole world, symbolized by the sacrifice without Śiva in it; and he wants the woman he cannot have, his daughter. Śiva, the ash-smeared outsider, has her. Moreover he is obliged to pay respects to his son-in-law, something he accuses Śiva of failing to do toward him. When Satī refuses to submit to Dakṣa's insult, it is her body, the body that came from him—the rest being the incarnation of the Goddess—which she surrenders into the fire, or that becomes the fire. There is a powerful irony in Dakṣa having to witness powerlessly as his most beloved one ignites as his sacrificial offering. Only after Dakṣa loses his head and Śiva gives him the goat's head, the head he deserves, does he understand his own limits. Only when his goat eyes enable him to see Śiva as the lord of the universe does he experience the inner peace of the devotee.

For me, as a foreign reader who inevitably brings my own cultural categories and forms of knowledge, this story is—whatever else it is, which is a lot—about primal family relations, relations across sex and generations. I am, of course, drawing from a particular constellation of analytic tools derived broadly from both Western and Indian psychoanalytic traditions to offer certain insights into the Dakṣa–Satī myth (the works of Kakar and Obeyesekere listed in the Readings section provide a thoughtful and detailed discussion of this). This approach stresses the importance of myths as narrative vehicles for exploring profound and often hidden meanings about human drives, fears and desires. Myths, like dreams, may have many interpretations. To me, the Dakṣa–Satī myth is also a story about what must not be spoken about directly. Dakṣa's "original sin" is that he wants everything. He has no internal constraints; he must be taught a painful but ultimately redeeming lesson. In giving his daughter in marriage, even though he agreed to it out of deference to the gods, he had to let go of that which was from him—his seed—but not of him, a different sex and generation—his daughter.

Here I think the story explores the complexities of human desire that resist constraints and the requirements of society and culture that require them. The story turns to the father–daughter bond as a place to narratively explore this paradox. In Hindu marriage traditions the father must "give" his daughter to the groom. She is the "gift of the daughter," the *kanyādāna*. The husband is "given" the very thing the daughter's father is denied. I do not think the story is so much about incest as a sexual transgression; rather it is about the father coming to terms with the limits of his power in general. Just as Dakṣa, goat-headed at last, had to acknowledge Śiva as lord of the universe, the daughter's father has to acknowledge the lordship of the husband in relationship to his daughter. Even as he welcomes his son-in-law into his home, the father-in-law carries his own sense of loss, pushing it below the level of awareness.

It is said in the Hindu tradition that a daughter is a visitor in her own family. From the moment she is born her parents know she will one day leave. This fragility of the daughter's place in her natal home may bring with it a bond that is bottomless. As the daughter leaves her natal home to live with her husband, her family of origin may be relieved that she has been successfully married. But there is also a loss, an inevitable and irreplaceable loss and separation the women sing about as the young bride leaves home.

In the story Satī is carried away and distributed across the land, joined by her husband in her shrine. Just as Dakṣa, through his ordeal of arrogant attempts at controlling a universe that excluded Śiva and led to his own beheading, finally attains a greater and more inclusive wisdom, so the reader or hearer of the story may have a glimpse of what Dakṣa finally sees.

Now, a number of years after my first visit to Kankhal, after having read through the many versions of the story from the classical Purāṇa texts, to Hindi pamphlets I purchased at the shrine, to comic book renditions of the story of Śiva and Satī and Dakṣa's sacrifice, I get a glimpse of my own journey. It started off as a rather straightforward inquiry into the historical circumstances of a practice in India, and then moved along a trajectory that took me to the story behind the story—the Satī behind *satī*—to the one place where it is said to have taken place. Living with the story, with my photographs of Kankhal in front of me, I feel like I have travelled through some of the distinctively Hindu dimensions of the narrative that have to do with sacrifice, marriage, gods, and goddesses. For me, and perhaps only for me, the story reaches down into a hardly noticed and much resisted terrain, a place some call the unconscious. Here, in this shadowy landscape, the tale of Śiva and Satī explores forbidden desires and the inevitable violence their pursuit brings upon those who act on them. Here the story enters a primal triangularity: father/father-in-law, daughter/wife, husband/son-in-law. These are some of the most fundamental relations human beings inhabit. For me, the Dakṣa story, like that of Oedipus—also a story about a primal triangle—is one of the truly great myths of the world. In remembering this story the Hindu tradition has preserved an elaborately layered inquiry into the deepest recesses of the human heart.

As a place, Kankhal remains for me a revealing and haunting location. I have had the good fortune to visit many places in India, but it is in Kankhal, down the road from Hardwar, alongside the sacred Ganges, where it all began. "Just there," Lāl Bābā said, "just over there."

Readings

The titles of the following books point to their contents. See, John Stratton Hawley, ed., *Sati: The Blessing and the Curse* (New York: Oxford University Press, 1994); Andrea Major, *Pious Flames: European Encounters with Sati 1500–1830* (New Delhi: Oxford University Press, 2006); Lata Mani, *Contentious Traditions: The Debate on Sati in Colonial India, 1708–1833* (Berkeley, University of California Press, 1998); H. C. Upreti, and N. Upreti, *The Myth of Sati: Some Dimensions of Widow*

Figure 3.2 Courtright engaged in fieldwork

Burning (Bombay: Himalaya Publishing House, 1991); and Catherine Weinberger-Thomas, *Ashes of Immortality: Widow Burning in India* (Chicago: University of Chicago Press, 1999). For more reading on Western and Indian psychoanalytic traditions see Sudhir Kakar, *The Inner World: A Psycho-analytic Study of Childhood and Society in India* (New Delhi: Oxford University Press, 1981) and Gananath Obeyesekere, *Medusa's Hair* (Chicago: University of Chicago Press, 1984).

Author

Paul B. Courtright (PhD) is a professor in the Department of Religion and Graduate Division of Religion, Emory University, Atlanta, Georgia, USA. He is the author of *Gaṇeśa: Lord of Obstacles, Lord of Beginnings,* and co-editor of *From the Margins of Hindu Marriage.* He is currently writing a book on Satī the goddess and *satī* the practice in its Hindu and Western interpretations.

Chapter 4

Pilgrimage to Kāmākhyā through text and lived religion

Some forms of the Goddess at an Assamese temple site

Patricia A. Dold

Preamble

Hindu traditions use a variety of strategies to convey the nature of divinity, to convey worshippers' beliefs about the nature of divinity, or to express both local presence and transcendent essence of a god or goddess. In Śākta (goddess-centered) traditions, one strategy for describing divinity is to invoke groups of divine females such as the seven Mothers, the nine Durgās, the 64 Yoginīs, or the ten Mahāvidyās. Sometimes, groups of goddesses are presented as different manifestations or forms of one all-encompassing goddess. So the goddess Kāmākhyā, the presiding deity of an important goddess-centered temple site in Assam, dwells there with her ten major manifestations, the Mahāvidyās. In the following section, I describe some of my experiences in field research at the Kāmākhyā Temple site. My description draws upon interviews, audio and video recordings, and field notes from three periods of field research at this site: a brief visit in 1992, a two-month stay in 2008, and a three-week stay in August 2009. Much of this fieldwork was collaborative. To record, transcribe, and translate religious songs (Nām) sung by women residents of Kāmākhyā, I worked with Ms. Jayashree Athparia, a local authority on the folk traditions of the site. Our work on these Nām is wholly dependent on the generosity of many of the women of Kāmākhyā who allowed us to record their singing. Several of the song performance leaders have given me permission to use their real names.

Narrative

The Goddess Kāmākhyā at Kāmākhyā

When I first visited the temple site of the goddess Kāmākhyā in 1992, I was anxious to find connections between contemporary religious life at the Kāmākhyā site and a Sanskrit text I had been translating for my PhD research. This intriguing text, the *Mahābhāgavata Purāṇa*, contains an elaborate account of the origin of Kāmākhyā, a Māhātmya (glorification) of the site and its goddess, and some general instructions for ritual practices to be performed there. My quest was urgent for I had been unable to find any evidence of knowledge of the text at the Kāmākhyā site, neither in other Sanskrit texts nor in scholarship on the site. The text knew the site but the site, so to speak, did not seem to know the text. As a textual scholar, I found this utterly bewildering. Clutching text and dictionary tightly in my arms, I questioned the value of textual scholarship. How could a Sanskrit text be so irrelevant to the lived religion?

To my relief, I soon found connections between the *Mahābhāgavata's* depiction of the ten Mahāvidyās and the lived religion of the Kāmākhyā site during my first visit in 1992. Oral narratives, modern lithographs, and even several of the smaller temples at the Kāmākhyā site featured the Mahāvidyās, a group of ten goddesses who are locally described and enshrined as forms of the Goddess Kāmākhyā herself. In both the local tradition and in the *Mahābhāgavata Purāṇa*, these ten forms were linked to the site through the story of the goddess Satī, a story that explains the origin of the Kāmākhyā site. Clearly, parts of the *Mahābhāgavata* were known at Kāmākhyā, even though none of those parts were traced by the local tradition to any text called *Mahābhāgavata Purāṇa*.

"Why are the Mahāvidyās here?" I asked the president of the Kāmākhyā Temple Board, Jñanada Prasād Sharma, in 1992, as we looked at his handwritten list of the many temples of the site. There were temples to Gaṇeśa, and to the goddesses Bana Durgā, and Lalitā Kaṇthā, to five forms of Śiva, and temples of seven Mahāvidyās (with the remaining three housed in the main temple). Although Mr. Sharma did not know of the *Mahābhāgavata Purāṇa* by name, his answer to my question described a distinctive element in that text's story about the goddess Satī. He explained: "Satī's father Dakṣa, an *aśura* king, calls a *yajña* [a Vedic ritual]. He wants to insult Śiva; he does not invite him. Śiva refuses permission for Satī to go to the *yajña*. She is furious, becomes the Mahāvidyās, and scares Śiva, who must yield. At the *yajña* she kills herself by yoga." Similarly in the *Mahābhāgavata's* account, Satī, who is portrayed as the supreme Goddess (and supreme deity), has agreed to be born as Satī and marry Śiva. Their marital bliss collapses when their discussion about attending Dakṣa's sacrifice without an invitation deteriorates into argument and insult. In the end, Satī decides to show Śiva her power. She reveals herself as the dark, fear-inspiring, but radiant goddess Kālī, and then as the ten Mahāvidyās who surround a terrified and confused Śiva. During that 1992 visit, I found a lithograph at Kāmākhyā that depicts this climactic scene. An angry Satī and a fleeing Śiva are shown in the central panel, which is surrounded with images of the ten Mahāvidyās, each looking perfectly calm, returning the viewer's gaze (see Figure 4.1).

The power of this scene has become increasingly clear. Already in Western academic contexts, whenever I present my work on the *Mahābhāgavata*, it is this scene that inspires comment. And it was my description of this scene that provoked a crucial question from my colleague Stephen Inglis a few days before my return to Kāmākhyā in 2008. "Are there performance traditions at the temple?" he asked. Feeling every inch a textual scholar, I realized I had no idea.

"Oh yes, there are many performance traditions at Kāmākhyā. Women have one of their own. They sing to Kālī and the Mahāvidyās too." It was Emilie Arrago,

Figure 4.1 Śiva and Satī surrounded by the Mahāvidyās

a PhD candidate from L'École des Hautes Études en Sciences Sociales conducting research at Kāmākhyā, who first told me about Nām, the women's religious songs, shortly after I arrived in Assam in 2008. She introduced me to Jayashree Athparia and to Gita Das, a leader of Nām performance. We women sat together in the Athparia family home on the evening of January 27 as Gita Das sang a Mahāvidyā Nām and following it, a Nām to the goddess Kālī, the leader of the Mahāvidyās and an alter ego of the goddess Kāmākhyā herself.

As Gita Das sang, the emotional power of the moment hit me and I felt the sting of tears in my eyes. As a female academic in the discipline of religious studies, I have often felt overwhelmed by males, maleness, male imagery, and male authorities in the religious institutions and texts I study. Not in my wildest dreams did I envision such a scene and suddenly here I was in the middle of it: four women each focused in their own way on other females whether scholars, worshippers, or the goddesses of Kāmākhyā. Here we were: Emilie Arrago and I, learning from the women of a living religious community such as Jayashree Athparia, who was helping to preserve Kāmākhyā women's Nām, and Gita Das, a wife and mother with a powerful physical presence despite her petite stature, singing about Kālī and her extraordinary appearance and behavior.

Mother Kālī, what game are you playing now?
With ten arms, holding weapons, you kill demons.

Put on clothes, Mother of the universe, put on some clothes.
Put on sandal paste, put a hibiscus blossom in your hair.

Put on clothes, Mahāmāyā, put on some clothes.
The gods, seeing you, are embarrassed.

Eternal, infinite Kālī, you sustain the universe.
Nārāyanī, you are the protector of the world.

Honor to you Great Kālī, your face smeared with blood,
You see [Śiva,] the bearer of the trident under your feet.

...

Now, enough with other work!
Just be enslaved at the feet of mother Kāmākhyā [and] say "Rām, Rām."

As I listened to Gita Das, I remembered my teacher David Kinsley's poignant questions about women's vernacular hymns to goddesses. Bhakti lineages have preserved male and female poets' songs to gods and males' songs to goddesses but "where are the women's songs to goddesses?" he would ask. "I think I know," he would then say, mysteriously. And—music to my ears!—here they were, in women's oral traditions. As an oral tradition, these women's hymns would have remained invisible to historical records. Here in the Kāmākhyā oral tradition of Nām performance, there is no official lineage for the hymns as one typically finds in textualized Hindu *bhakti* song poems. There is no formal institution controlling performances of the songs, nor any signature line in which composers of songs offer their names and their closing commentary. Here, there simply is a repertoire of hymns performed only by women, preserving through generations the local tradition about the many gods and goddesses of the Kāmākhyā site.

Noticing the tears in my eyes during Gita Das's performance, Emilie Arrago remarked on the power of this event for us as female scholars. "Can you imagine," I recall her asking, "what it is like to sit with a group of a dozen or more women as they sing?" I would not have to imagine it for I would return the following Thursday evening as a group of women gathered in a small shrine to the goddess Śītalā, a few hundred meters south and down the hill from the main Kāmākhyā temple.

Darkness is falling as 20 women from the neighborhood sit on blue plastic tarps spread on the floor of the shrine to the goddess Śītalā and begin the ritual they do every Thursday. Led by Gita Das, the women conduct a *pūjā* (ritual of worship) to Śītalā with food offerings contributed by several households in the neighborhood. Then these women, mostly married women and some widows, sing Nām for perhaps an hour, marking the rhythm by clapping. Nothing interrupts the women's singing, not even the racket of hammering from construction work underway on the shrine itself. At the close of the ritual performance, the women share the *pūjā's* food offerings as *prasād* (a blessing from the deity) and return to their homes.

That evening, the women performed for me the Mahāvidyā and Kālī Nām I'd heard from Gita Das a few days before. The refrain (*pada*) of the Mahāvidyā Nām lists these goddesses and affirms their connection with the goddess Kāmākhyā. In this, the Nām echoes a key principle of local theology: the Mahāvidyās are the goddess Kāmākhyā's ten forms and the site is a powerful sacred site (*pīṭha*) because all 10 of Kāmākhyā's forms are here. The women sang:

> Jay Kālī, Jay Tārā, Chinnamastā, Bagalā,
> Bhuvaneśvarī, Bhairavī, Mātaṅgī, Kamalā,
> Lakṣmī, Sarasvatī, in the middle, Bhāgirathī;
> Goddess Kāmākhyā, beloved of Śiva who is Hara.

This refrain is sung frequently whether to begin a Nām performance, to introduce a particular Nām, or as the refrain in an entirely different Nām (such as the one discussed at the end of this section). The verses of Gita Das's Mahāvidyā Nām focus on Kālī, suggesting, as some lithographs do, that Kālī represents all of them (see Figure 4.2). The focus on Kālī surprises me. Though Kālī is frequently declared to be Kāmākhyā herself, she is not typically worshipped by women. Yet, here at the Kāmākhyā, site, the women sing:

> Victorious, Joyous Kālī, Gentle Kālī.
> Remembering these [goddesses], there is dharma, wealth (*artha*), and pleasure (*kāma*).
>
> Kālī, Kāli, Great Kālī, whose name is "Terrible Kālī,"
> Śiva meditates under her feet.
>
> Victorious, Joyous Kālī, whose face is smeared with blood,
> Flicking her tongue, she is the killer of demons.
>
> ...
>
> Body black like a cloud, naked,
> Her hair is loose and messy, flying wildly.
>
> ...
>
> I submit to your feet, protect [me], Mahāmāyā.

My research priorities change: I cut short my planned stay in Varanasi for Sanskrit translation work to take up an invitation from Jayashree Athparia and her family to stay in their home for the month of April and record and translate Nām in collaboration with Jayashree. We accomplish a great deal through deliberate effort, but sometimes by happy coincidence. For example, we often sat with a group of women outside the northern doors of the main temple where Nani

Figure 4.2 Lithograph depicting Kālī at the centre of the Mahāvidyās

Devi, a woman my own age, leads Nām performance every evening after final *āratī* (the offering of light) and *prasād* (blessing). Yet, it was not until the end of my stay at Kāmākhyā that we stumbled upon a particularly important Nām in Nani Devi's repertoire.

On May 1, 2008, in the heat of mid-afternoon, Jayashree and I sit with Nani Devi in her home not far from the main temple of Kāmākhyā. With diligence and pride, Nani Devi consults her library for parallels to the Nām she is performing for us. She keeps several notebooks, which contain handwritten texts of Nām she knows. She worries about the future of the Nām tradition and so finds great meaning in the help she has been able to give us. No one owns these songs, she says. Although Jayashree and I must not use our texts or recordings to teach others to perform the songs, we can work together to help preserve them and make them known beyond Kāmākhyā. I watch Nani Devi's face as she watches Jayashree work and I see a mentor's pride in her smile. I wonder if she sees herself as something like a *guru* to Jayashree. Does she contemplate teaching Jayashree to a point where Jayashree herself could lead, sing, and pass on?

When I hear Nani Devi sing the opening lines of the following Satī-Mahāvidyā Nām, one that Jayashree has stumbled upon in Nani Devi's handwritten collection of Nām, I excitedly nudge Jayashree and mouth the question: "This is the story?" She nods, smiling.

> Lord Śiva heard the request:
> "I will go to see the ritual at my father's home."
> Śaṅkar says [to Satī], "[If] you go to your father's house without an invitation, you will get disrespect."
>
> ...
>
> She says to her husband, "don't speak like that.
> A daughter [just] goes to her father's house, where is there need for an invitation?"
> At this moment, Śiva does not give permission to Satī.
> Angry, Satī becomes Kālī, with a fear-inspiring appearance
> Hair loose, [dark] like a great cloud, her teeth like fangs.
>
> With corpse like form, her howls ear-splitting,
> Wearing a garland of bloody heads,
> In [one] left hand, a bloody, severed head,
> In her other left hand, a knife.
>
> Her two right hands make the gestures "fear not" and "ask a boon."
> Her tongue lolling, blood streaming from both corners of her mouth,
> Her third eye, a half moon, is shining on her forehead.
> Seeing her, he is afraid and turns his face away.
>
> Becoming Tārā, Satī stands before Śiva
> Blue in color, her tongue lolling, her mouth smeared with blood,
> Her hair matted into a single lock forms a cobra's hood over her head.
> On the back of her hair is a half moon, its light on her forehead.
> Three-eyed, with a big belly, wearing a tiger's hide,
> Her four hands adorned with a blue lotus and a snake from the ocean,
> On the other side [in her left hands], a bow and arrow.
> Seeing her, Paśupati, the ten-faced one, is afraid; he wants to run away.

The Nām continues in this vein, describing each of the Mahāvidyās as the forms through which Satī (as Kālī) manifests herself to her husband. Each one is fearfully encountered by Śiva, who trembles, and is rendered speechless and confused. He squeezes his eyes shut and flees from each of the remaining eight Mahāvidyās. "Is this the story?" I ask Nani Devi, handing her the Mahāvidyā lithograph (Figure 4.1). Yes, it is.

Bearing in mind the importance of context, I ask, "Is there any specific festival occasion when this Nām is performed?" Nani Devi's answer is immediate and enthusiastic: Yes, on the first day and as the opening observance of the Debaddhanī festival, the Deodhas gather at the Tukreśvar temple, one of several temples of Śiva at the Kāmākhyā site. Accompanied by the singing of this Nām, led by Nani Devi, and following the rhythm set by the women's clapping, the Deodhas (echoes or voices of the gods) dance as they receive the god or goddess whom each man will embody through the three days of the festival. This opening ceremony is the only occasion during Debaddhanī when the Deodhas dance to anything other than the festival drums. And this Satī Mahāvidyā Nām, as Jayashree would emphasize to me later, this—the account of Satī's revelation as the Mahāvidyās—is the myth of origin of the Kāmākhyā site itself. So, the performance at Tukreśvar is well attended; the tiny temple and its courtyard are packed with people. Unless the women singers make a mistake in the song in which case a Deodha (or rather his deity) will snarl at them—everyone is happy, Jayashree tells me. I can well imagine that all would be happy. The gods and goddesses are "here" as living, breathing presences in human bodies! They are re-performing the creation of Kāmākhyā as a sacred site with the help of a song of the women's oral tradition. In this context, the only text important to the lived religion is the text that the women sing. That the crucial scene of Śiva's fearful encounter with Satī as Kālī and the Mahāvidyās is described in a Sanskrit text, in the *Mahābhāgavata Purāṇa*, is irrelevant. The current leader of the Deodhas, for example, knows the story of Satī revealing herself as the Mahāvidyās. Yet, neither he nor Nani Devi knows the *Mahābhāgavata Purāṇa* as the Sanskrit source of the scene.

Caring less and less about local knowledge of any Sanskrit texts, I return just over a year later for the Debaddhanī festival. I am, of course, especially eager to see the opening ceremony at the Tukreśvar temple. But even as this much anticipated occasion arrives, it slips away for the ceremony is delayed again and again. Word circulates through the neighborhood that the Deodha leader is feeling ill and cannot take on the physical demands of his ceremonial role in the heat and humidity of midday. It is late in the afternoon when we finally see the Deodhas gather. Their bodies are rubbed with red *sindur* powder and each man wears garlands of flowers around his arms, legs, and neck. Slowly the Deodhas climb the steep stone stairway, pause briefly beside the main temple, and then turn west to Tukreśvar. I have been told to watch the behavior of the Deodhas as they make their way up the steep stone stairway and along the path to Tukreśvar. The men will behave normally, casually, I have been told. They will be chatting and smoking cigarettes. But all will change when the women sing: the Deodhas will transform their manner as they manifest the persona of their god or goddess.

When we arrive at Tukreśvar, women are singing inside and the Deodhas enter the temple. But we can barely hear the women because the festival drummers are enthusiastically beating their drums in the temple courtyard. Inside, some of the Deodhas gesture to the women, cupping their ears with a hand to indicate that they cannot hear the singing, but mostly they simply dance as they move from inside the temple out to the courtyard and back inside. As an impressive crowd watches, the drummers play without interruption, and the Deodhas dance. Finally, the drummers accompany the Deodhas back to the main temple where they will dance and receive worship from a massive crowd of devotees.

I am devastated. What happened? Nani Devi was not even there to lead the singing of the Satī Mahāvidyā Nām! The drums were deafeningly loud and were not *supposed* to play at Tukreśvar at all! There was no dramatic transformation of the Deodhas energized by women's performance of Nām. Later, over tea at Nani Devi's house we learn some of the answers. Beginning a few years ago, women began to disagree about which Nām should be sung at Tukreśvar on the first day of Debaddhanī. Feeling disrespected by the group, Nani Devi decided she would no longer lead or attend.

But, the festival must go on. I join the thick crowd of residents and pilgrims sitting on the tiers of stone seats that create a kind of amphitheater on the north

Figure 4.3 Kāmākhyā Temple in Assam

side of the main temple. Thirty festival drummers as well as several horn and cymbal players stand in a long line along the bottom tier. Their constant and vigorous playing provides the rhythm for the "dancing" of the Deodhas. The Deodhas, each wielding the weapon(s) and wearing the color favored by their god or goddess, move along the line of musicians, now bobbing in time with the music, now gazing intensely up at the crowd, now running into the Naṭa Mandir, the large "performance room" at the west end of the temple. With the heat and crowd of the festival, the Naṭa Mandir is an oven. The deep throbbing from the row of kettle drums being played inside feels like a massive heartbeat, the heartbeat of mother Kāmākhyā, as my colleague and fellow pilgrim James Mullens observes. Some Deodhas are more theatrical than others: Kālī's Deodha sticks out his (her?) tongue and triumphantly lifts Kālī's curved sword to the sky. All are received as deities by the assembled crowd. One by one, people approach different Deodhas with cautious reverence, giving them money, wrapping them in clothes and piling garlands so high around their necks that soon only their eyes are visible. They look like moving, living *mūrtis* (icons of deities). Within this intense atmosphere, I marvel at the sweetness of some of the exchanges between devotee and Deodha. I see great reverence and tenderness as I watch a woman and her son attempt to gain the attention of the goddess Calantā's Deodha. She holds up a garland, following the Calantā's dance back and forth. Finally, the Calantā bows his head slightly to accept her garland, listens to her plea, and gently places his hands on the son's head and caresses the boy's cheek. Then he gives both mother and son a *tilak* (forehead marking) using red *sindur* powder he rubs from his own forehead onto theirs. They bend to touch his feet. Such interactions, easily seen as a *pūjā* (worship) to the Deodha's deity, are constant.

Late in the afternoon, the leader of the Deodhas, the Mahārāj (a deified devotee of Bhairavī) emerges from the sacrificial hall carrying a large sword, a *khadga*, normally used to decapitate buffalo in sacrifice and the kind of sword Kālī carries. Two Deodhas hold each end of this sword, cutting edge up, as one after another of the goddess Deodhas, the Śaktis, climb upon and then "dance" on the sharp edge of the blade. I am too far away to see exactly what the Deodhas' feet do on the sword, but my attention is soon focused elsewhere. The crowd surges forward and its mood intensifies as a priest appears carrying a live pigeon. As the bird flaps its wings, the priest lifts its head to the mouth of the Deodha now standing on the edge of the sword. With a dramatic chomp of his teeth and shake of his head, each Deodha bites the head off two or three birds. As the women's piercing, high-pitched, and triumphant cry, "ooolulululu" fills the air, the Deodha chews, swallows, and then spits out clumps of flesh and feather. Like the goddesses these Deodhas embody, the Deodhas are receiving animal offerings, *bali*. Is this bloodlust? Animal sacrifice is done regularly at Kāmākhyā and people watch it with serious solemnity and the moment of the animal's death is sacred and so priests do not allow it to be photographed. *Bali* is not a celebration of death or of the power to kill. Perhaps then, the crowd at Debaddhanī celebrates the living presence of goddesses as the Deodhas accept the animal offerings.

At a ceremony to open the festival activities for the following day, I again experience the presence of goddesses of Kāmākhyā in a different but no less dramatic way. It is August 18, 2009, and with the mid-afternoon sun breaking through a thick haze of monsoon humidity, I sit with 25 women in a ground floor room of a family home. We sit facing an open doorway to an adjoining room, which, for the duration of Debaddhanī is the *āsan*, the temporary sacred home of two Deodhas. Taru Devi, a vigorous young woman, leads the women in the singing of Nām. As the women sing, the two Deodhas casually walk around their *āsan*, now pausing before the altar in one corner of the room, now looking at the women, now wandering outside. They seem to be waiting.

As the women sing of the goddess Kāmākhyā with a lengthy Nām, the Calantā's Deodha kneels down at the altar and touches his forehead to the floor. Taru Devi watches him carefully. The Nām speaks of young women singing to the goddess at the main temple, which houses the Calantā, the "moveable image" of Kāmākhyā, as well as the famous *yoni mūrti* (the natural stone image of the goddess in the shape of a vulva):

All the young women are at the Kāmākhyā temple performing songs.
Now, protect us, Goddess Kāmākhyā, we remain touching your feet. (refrain)

You grant the desires of Hara; you are the wife of Hara,
Mother of Kārttik and Gaṇeśa
Say "Queen Durgā," all beings remember her two lotus feet.

This Nām is extremely complex and evocative; it not only names all ten Mahāvidyās and gives brief descriptions of each, it alludes to mythic accounts about Satī, Pārvatī, and others, and it has five different refrains. As the women repeat the refrain quoted above, the Deodha, still kneeling before his altar, suddenly cries out as if in pain and then throws his arms behind his back. The women, still singing, need very little prompting. Taru Devi immediately leads them in singing of the familiar refrain of the main Mahāvidyā Nām of Kāmākhyā (which Gita Das and her group sang for me in January):

Jaykālī, Jaytārā, Chinnamastā, Bagalā

...

Goddess Kāmākhyā, beloved of Śiva, who is Hara. (repeat)

As the women continue to sing, the Deodha becomes increasingly agitated; he throws his arms up over his head, swings them down to his sides and then, as he arches his back, he cries out as if in pain and fear, stretching his arms behind his back. The women are singing and clapping for rhythm. They sing loudly, the pace quickening and they adopt the voice of the goddess:

"Do not be afraid! Do not be afraid," again and again [the goddess says],

"In the form of a shadow I dwell in your heart." (repeat 4 times)

Now the Deodha rises to his feet, and begins to dance as he takes his deity's weapons, a gesture that confirms his identity as the Calantā. The Calantā Deodha turns to face the women, lifts his hands to his forehead, bowing to the women before turning to leave the *āsan* and begin his day's appearance at the main temple. All the while, the women sing:

> She, Tārā, is a boat and the guru is the helmsman.
> Protective Kālī, protect us in the beginning as Bhairavī.
>
> Oh Kālī Kālī Kālī, wearing a garland of heads,
> Forever we remain your slaves.

Moments later, the women begin a Nām of the goddess Mānasā, whose Deodha now approaches the altar and kneels before it. Soon he too cries out, and as his persona transforms; the women resume their singing of the Mahāvidyā Nām refrain and verses once again. When the Mānasā Deodha leaves, the women share *prasād*, the deity's blessing but very literally, their satisfaction or pleasure with the worship just received. That *prasād* is shared implies that all emerge from the ritual pleased and satisfied. In this instance, the blessing is a meal of fruits and vegetables presented on a split bamboo shoot. Clearly though, it is not just this shared food that conveys the deity's involvement in the ritual. The Deodhas become embodiments of deities and the women, whose voices help transform ordinary men into "voices of the gods" (*deodhas*), have this ability because they are natural embodiments of *śakti*, the feminine divine principle of power.

Discussion

The ten Mahāvidyās

As the ten forms of the goddess Kāmākhyā, the Mahāvidyās are an important group of deities in the lived religion of the Kāmākhyā temple and pilgrimage site. As I learned through my fieldwork, they are featured in lithographs, housed in temples large and small, embodied by Deodhas, and invoked in the Nām of women residents. But the Mahāvidyās, both as individual goddesses and as a standardized group of ten, are also known quite apart from the Kāmākhyā site. They are described in several Sanskrit texts of fairly late date, especially in texts of the genre known as Tantras. By the modern period, interpretations of the collective character of the ten Mahāvidyās have become bewilderingly diverse. The Mahāvidyās are sometimes partnered with the Nine Planets and will help the worshipper overcome malevolent astrological influences. Or, the Mahāvidyās correspond with the ten avatars of Viṣṇu and so protect from chaos. They will attack one's enemies through ritually provoked aggressive powers (the "six acts" or *ṣaṭ karma*). Occasionally, they are described as ten sisters. They represent the stages of a female's life (from Ṣoḍaśī, the youthful "16 year old," to the elderly widow Dhūmāvatī), or the fearsome and benevolent aspects of the Great Goddess. In yet other interpretations, they are the phases of the moon, the stages of consciousness, the great (*mahā*) goddess mantras (*vidyās*), all forms of knowledge, all powers or perfections (*siddhis*), and all meditative states or moods (from Kālī as an ego-transcending awareness of Self to Kamalā as a materialistic "mood"). Probably the most common interpretation says that the ten Mahāvidyās are manifestations of one supreme Goddess. In the following discussion, I will focus on a general interpretation of the group that is emphasized in the texts and living religion of the Kāmākhyā site: the Mahāvidyās express the full divine nature of the Goddess as a protective divine *presence*.

The account of Satī and the creation of the Śākta Pīṭhas ("seats" of sacred sites of the Goddess) is now a well-known account of the origin of the Mahāvidyās. It presents the Mahāvidyās as direct embodiments of the one Goddess and as protectors who reside at the "seats of the goddess" (Śākta Pīṭhas). Śiva's wife, Satī, reveals herself to him as Kālī, an awesome, black, fearsome goddess, and then as the Mahāvidyās when he insults her during their argument over attending Dakṣa's sacrifice without an invitation. The oldest Sanskrit puranic telling describes the scene in a way very similar to the oral narratives, lithographic depictions, and Nām lyrics described in the previous section:

> Seeing her, the Goddess, her lower lip trembling with rage, the pupils of her eyes resembling the doomsday fire, Śiva shut his eyes. But she laughed loudly, her mouth full of terrible fangs. Hearing her, the great god was bewildered and become very afraid. Forcing his eyes open, he looked at her, the terrible one. … She whose roar was dreadful, was adorned with a garland of human heads.
>
> (Mahābhāgavata 8.47-49, 51b paraphrased)

Terrified, Śiva flees and so the goddess tries to stop him: "Do not be afraid," she says "loudly, laughing uproariously and most terrifyingly" (8.54-55). This does not help. On the contrary, Śiva runs away again. Then, out of compassion, Kālī manifests as the ten Mahāvidyās whose presence eventually brings Śiva's flight to an end.

This account suggests that Kālī's character defines the group as a whole. Śiva responds fearfully after seeing each Mahāvidyā, as if all had the frightening appearance of Kālī, even though some of the Mahāvidyās, Kamalā (also known as Lakṣmī, the goddess of good fortune and prosperity), for example, are not typically described as fearsome. Iconographically too, Kālī's image seems to spill over to that of some of the other Mahāvidyās: nudity, a garland of heads, male deities sitting or lying beneath the goddess's feet, allusions to death and cremation grounds, and transgression of mainstream values—all of these are recurring elements in the iconography of several Mahāvidyās. Tārā and Kālī are often depicted naked. Both wear a garland of severed heads, wield knives or swords, and stand on a prone Śiva whose eyes are closed. Chinnamastā is also often depicted naked, and stands upon one or two prone figures. Her image also has strong representations of bloodshed and death; Chinnamastā, literally "she whose head is cut off," stands holding her own decapitated head. Three streams of blood spurt out from her neck, one streams into Chinnamastā's mouth, and the other two into the mouths of the two naked females standing at either side. Dhūmāvatī is a widow, often accompanied by a crow and wearing white. Bagalā or Bagalamukhī, "she who has a crane's head" is often depicted battling with a demon whose tongue she holds. However, not all of the Mahāvidyās possess a fearsome appearance or represent reversals of mainstream values. In fact, other goddesses of the group have auspicious associations. Kamalā, "she of the lotus," is often depicted in ways typical for Lakṣmī, the Hindu goddess of prosperity and the devoted (and orthodox) wife of Viṣṇu. Mātaṅgī, though she has low-caste connections according to some representations, is Sarasvatī, the goddess of culture and learning and so she holds a *vina* (a stringed instrument) across her lap. Ṣoḍaśī and Bhuvaneśvarī are also often depicted as benign and/or auspicious females, dressed according to mainstream standards, and seated on a lotus or a throne.

The account of the Mahāvidyās origin from Satī/Kālī suggests that the Mahāvidyās collectively are an expression of the Goddess's compassion and specifically her desire to protect and free her devotees from fear. In the story, Śiva's initial reaction to the Mahāvidyās illustrates the effect that the Mahāvidyās are widely understood to exert against worshippers' enemies. These effects and the rituals that activate them are sometimes collectively labeled *ṣaṭ karma*, the "six acts." Though some sources (mainly Tantras, tantric digests, and ritual texts derived from them) list more than six acts, a relatively standardized list is as follows: pacification, including curing of disease and exorcism of harmful spirits, exerting control over others, paralyzing, provoking dissension or hatred, inducing flight, and killing. Furthermore, in practice, the Mahāvidyās are worshipped in the pursuit of a wide variety of goals from worldly success to meditative insight and liberation. The *Mahābhāgavata Purāṇa* (8.72) also says that to those who devoutly make offerings, the Mahāvidyās give virtue (*dharma*), power (*artha*), pleasure (*kāma*), and liberation (*mokṣa*).

One area of practice that neatly ties together many of the threads that are offered as explanations for the Mahāvidyās as a group is the practice of creating and wearing a *kavaca*, an armor, or talisman. In textual form, *kavacas* are presented as a long set of invocations of divine beings through which deities, often goddesses, are asked to protect the worshipper from each of the cardinal directions and at zenith and nadir and also all over the practitioner's body. Protected by this armor, which is either visualized or made into a physical talisman, one can proceed fearlessly with further worship, meditation, or with the tasks of daily life and be assured all manner of worldly success (*dharma, kāma, artha*), freedom from danger, conquest of enemies (through *ṣaṭ karma*), perfection in the empowerment of a mantra, and even oneness with the Goddess herself.

Figure 4.4 Dold at Kāmākhyā

Sanskrit texts of and about the Kāmākhyā site (including the *Mahābhāgavata Purāṇa*, and the *Kālikā Purāṇa*,) also suggest that at a *pīṭha*, at Kāmākhyā Pīṭha in particular, one is always surrounded by a living armor of goddesses who protect worshippers from any and every danger. A local protective divine presence is emphasized also by the people of Kāmākhyā, from the women whose singing of Nām invokes the beneficial presence of deities in their neighborhoods or helps make gods and goddesses present in the bodies of Deodhas, to the worshippers who make offerings to deities in the temples of the site or to the Deodhas as living human embodiments of the gods and goddesses of Kāmākhyā. As the Goddess speaking in Taru Devi's Mahāvidyā Nām says: "Do not be afraid! In the form of a shadow I remain in your heart."

Readings

The single most extensive study of the Mahāvidyās as a group and as individual goddesses is David R. Kinsley's *Tantric Visions of the Divine Feminine: The Ten Mahāvidyās* (Berkeley: University of California Press, 1997). Elizabeth Benard's study, *Chinnamastā: The Aweful Buddhist and Hindu Tantric Goddess* (Delhi: Motilal, 1994), contains significant data and analysis of this goddess as a Mahāvidyā. June McDaniel, in *Offering Flowers Feeding Skulls* (New York, Oxford University Press, 2004, especially chapter 4), offers discussion of the Mahāvidyās in popular forms of goddess-worship in west Bengal. For further discussion of the Mahāvidyās at Kāmākhyā, according to Sanskrit texts connected to the site and also data from my visit in 1992, see my essay, "The Mahavidyas at Kamarupa: Dynamics of Transformation in Hinduism," in *Religious Studies and Theology: Hybridic Hinduisms* 23:1 (2004): 89–122. On *ṣaṭ karma*, see Gudrun Bühnemann, "The Six Rites of Magic," in *Tantra in Practice*, David Gordon White (ed.) (Princeton: Princeton University Press, 2000), pp. 447–62. For an example of a tantric textual treatment of the Mahāvidyās, see Sanjukta Gupta, "The Worship of Kālī According to the *Toḍala Tantra*," in *Tantra in Practice*, David Gordon White (ed.) (Princeton, NJ: Princeton University Press, 2000), pp. 463-88. For a summary of the *Mahābhāgavata Purāṇa*, (as well as the Sanskrit edition of the text referenced in this essay), see Pushpendra Kumar, *The Mahābhāgavata Purāṇa: Ancient Treatise on Śakti Cult* (Delhi: Eastern Book Linkers, 1983).

Author

Patricia A. Dold (PhD) is an assistant professor of religious studies at Memorial University of Newfoundland. Her publications to date focus primarily on Sanskrit texts of the Kāmākhyā site and include "Tantra as a Religious Category in the *Mahābhāgavata Purāṇa*," in *Studies in Religion: Special Issue on Tantra in Indian Religions* 38:2, 2009: 221–45) and "Kālī the Terrific and Her Tests: The Śākta Devotionalism of the *Mahābhāgavata Purāṇa*," in *Encountering Kālī: in the Margins, at the Center, in the West*, Rachel Fell McDermott and Jeffrey Kripal (eds) (Berkeley, CA: University of California Press, 2003 pp. 39–59). She is presently developing a book based on her PhD dissertation, "The Religious Vision of the Śākta *Mahābhāgavata Purāṇa*" (McMaster, 2005).

Chapter 5

The accidental pilgrim

Vaiṣṇava tīrthas and the experience of the sacred

Jason D. Fuller

Preamble

A *tīrtha* is a Hindu holy site. The term derives from the idea of a "point of crossing" or "ford," a shallow area that enables one to traverse a body of water at a point of least difficulty. The symbolism is particularly significant for it evokes the idea of a crossing point between the mundane world of ordinary, everyday, profane existence and the spiritual world of extraordinary, special, sacred existence. *Tīrthas* are those geographical spaces where human beings can most easily make contact with the divine. These Hindu holy sites may be associated with the earthly activity of deities or holy men. They may be places of particular geological interest like mountaintops and sacred lakes. Or, they may be places of architectural interest, as when magnificent temples or memorials are built on special locations. As such, *tīrthas* are often the geographic goals of pilgrimages.

In the following chapter, I explore the experiential dimensions of pilgrimages to *tīrthas* through the consideration of my own participant-observer experiences at two Gauḍīya Vaiṣṇava *tīrthas*—one in the United States and one in India. Over the past 20 years I have been to the two *tīrthas* many times. For the sake of consistency and focus the narrative that follows deals with my first experiences at New Vrindaban, USA and Mayapur, West Bengal, India. The two visits were separated by a period of 10 years. The first one, at New Vrindaban, occurred when I was an undergraduate student, and the second encounter took place a decade later when I was a graduate student conducting research on Gauḍīya Vaiṣṇavism in India. Gauḍīya Vaiṣṇavism is a particular form of Viṣṇu worship, which originated in Bengal.

New Vrindaban is a spiritual center in West Virginia. It is a consecrated holy site (*Tīrtha*) that attracts thousands of pilgrim-visitors every year. According to the devotees who travel to New Vrindaban it is, as the name suggests, a living and fully potent replica of the earthly home of Kṛṣṇa (Krishna) in India. The Indian *tīrtha* that the American New Vrindaban replicates is known as Vrindaban and the geographical area of Vrindaban in Uttar Pradesh, India, is itself considered to be an earthly reflection of the celestial home of Kṛṣṇa in heaven. According to the homological thinking of Gauḍīya Vaiṣṇavas in the lineage that recognizes New

Vrindaban as a legitimate pilgrimage destination, the three Vrindabans are "non-different." Similarly, Mayapur, a pilgrimage site in West Bengal, India, is considered by many to be the birthplace of the sixteenth century founder of Gauḍīya Vaiṣṇavism, the saint/God-man Śrī Kṛṣṇa Caitanya Mahāprabhu who was himself considered to be an incarnation of the deity, Kṛṣṇa. Thus, like New Vrindaban, Mayapur embodies, for Gauḍīya Vaiṣṇavas, the spiritual potencies of the eternal home of Kṛṣṇa in the cosmic Vrindaban.

Narrative

I do not remember the first time that I heard about the concept of a Hindu *tīrtha*. I suppose that it was the same spring that I made my first journey to New Vrindaban, the local Hare Krishna commune in Moundsville, West Virginia.

I was 19 years old and in my second year at college. Having been raised by a conservative Catholic mother and a laissez-faire Presbyterian father I was not quite sure what to make of my "Non-Western Philosophy" professor's suggestion that the class take a fieldtrip to a Hindu temple in the mountains of rural West Virginia at the end of the second-semester course. We had spent most of our time that spring plumbing the metaphysical depths of the classical Hindu philosophical systems (*darśanas*) but our professor felt that our education would remain incomplete if we did not get a sense of what Hinduism looked like "in practice," even if in a somewhat idiosyncratic Appalachian diasporic context.

At that time in my life, I was in no mood to engage in a face-to-face conversation with anyone religious, let alone anyone who would self-identify as a Hare Krishna. Even my enrollment in a non-western philosophy course was an anomaly born of a university distribution requirement. My adolescent anti-religious hubris was in full bloom during the spring of that field trip. Although I considered myself to be openly (and maybe even defensively) Christian in high school, a few courses in evolutionary biology, ancient history and philosophy at the college level had quickly and efficiently turned me into that most hoary yet cliché of all academic institutions—the militant undergraduate atheist. A proud new convert, I triumphantly declared to my mother that her religious beliefs, which due to her physical disabilities consisted of watching Mass occasionally on the Catholic television network, amounted to little more than existential thumb sucking. She openly wept. But I was unflappable in my newfound Nietzschean stoicism.

Now I was being asked to return to the land of the repressed by a philosophy professor who, I thought, should have known better. He stood calmly at the front of our class, leaning with his weight on one leg as he announced his odd proposition. He gestured with his hands, wearing his standard hippy uniform of Birkenstocks and a Hawaiian shirt. The lecture hall was unusually quiet; the second-year students shot glances at each other. His voice rang out steadily, issuing a summons to something entirely unknown and thoroughly peculiar: a pilgrimage to a Hindu holy site. I was being asked to venture outside of the insular and tidy anti-religious cocoon that I had spun for myself in college by joining a group of besandaled and tie-dyed seekers on a veritable forced march to a Hare Krishna commune—in West Virginia! My experience of sacred spaces was very circumscribed; my own family never went to church, and I rarely accompanied friends to the various Protestant churches their families attended. The idea of actually going to a temple to witness what Hinduism looked like "on the ground" seemed quixotic to me. I had seen more than my share of late night comedy skits openly mocking the tonsured airport flower vendors. If I had little patience for Christianity that spring, I had even less interest in this particular variety of Hinduism. However, after making the three-hour trip to the temple that May, I realized that my initial reservations about the educational usefulness of the trip were deeply misguided.

Although I did not become a Hindu that day, nor on any subsequent day, my trip to the *tīrtha* of New Vrindaban did awaken something in me. It elicited an experience that can only be described as religious—not mystical, but religious. The change that occurred in me is somewhat hard to define but it might best be characterized this way: prior to being confronted by the beauty and sacredness of New Vrindaban and its inhabitants I did not understand the attraction of Gauḍīya Vaiṣṇavism. After having experienced the *tīrtha,* I did. It is no exaggeration to say that my accidental pilgrimage to New Vrindaban changed my life. I left the commune with a relaxed antagonism toward religious people and institutions but even more importantly I came away from the experience with a profound sense of curiosity and a burning passion to learn more about the rich, engaging form of religious belief and practice that I had met by chance. That first trip to New Vrindaban would not be my last. Nor would New Vrindaban be the only Vaiṣṇava *tīrtha* that I would visit over the years with similarly confounding results.

My educational journey toward understanding what I had experienced that day lead to doctoral study in Hindu religious traditions at the University of Pennsylvania and to fieldwork in India. Eventually my sojourn led me to Mayapur, West Bengal where, ten years after my initial exposure to the uncanny in New Vrindaban, USA, I had similar experiences in a distinctly Indian context. In many ways, my academic studies in Gauḍīya Vaiṣṇavism are the reflexive field notes of one trying to make sense of the wondrously transformative possibilities of Hindu *tīrthas* in India and the United States.

So what exactly did I find that day when I traveled to New Vrindaban? And what would I continue to find religiously exhilarating about Gauḍīya Vaiṣṇava *tīrthas*? Let me attempt to explain.

My introduction to Vaiṣṇava *tīrthas* began with a tour of Prabhupada's Palace of Gold at the Hare Krishna commune in Moundsville, West Virginia. After a three-hour drive on the interstate highway system our class trip concluded with a 20-minute expedition down long winding rural lanes, over hilltops, and alongside of Appalachian dales bright with sunlight, as we made our way to the heart of the Hare Krishna community just outside of Wheeling. When, at long last, our university van pulled up onto the temple property the first thing that we saw was a sign pointing to the "Palace of Gold." Students shifted as the small bus settled into place.

The commune was initially founded by a small group of Hare Krishna devotees from the International Society for Kṛṣṇa Consciousness (or ISKCON for short) who wanted to begin a "Kṛṣṇa Conscious" farm in the late 1960s. Shortly thereafter they began to build Prabhupada's Palace of Gold. A.C. Bhaktivedanta Swami Prabhupada (1896–1977), the founder of the Hare Krishna movement, left India for the USA after decades as a disciple in the Gauḍīya Vaiṣṇava tradition in Bengal. In a remarkably successful mission, he eventually established the International Society for Kṛṣṇa Consciousness (ISKCON), which now has centers worldwide. The palace was originally intended to serve as an occasional home for Swami Prabhupada. However, after his death in 1977, the palace became a memorial for the leader of ISKCON. Taking over a decade to build, the palace served as a focal point for communal action in New Vrindaban in the 1970s and 1980s.

What immediately struck me about the most visible building on the 500-acre property was the compelling, otherworldly architecture of the palace. Scholars of religion do not often properly appreciate the aesthetics of religious experience. Luckily, they are almost always understood by religious devotees themselves. In the case of Gauḍīya Vaiṣṇavas the importance of aesthetic impression is paramount in the designing of temples and buildings. The Hare Krishnas use the term "transcendental" to describe the pleasant sensations that arise within the soul (*jīva*) upon experiencing the divinely inspired moods (*rasas*) associated with sacred architecture. The term seemed especially appropriate in the context of the palace.

Lush green fields of immaculately manicured lawns engulfed Prabhupada's Palace of Gold. The undulating terraces, which defined the carefully attended landscaping, receded from the small hill upon which the palace sat and were dotted with dozens of bulbous, exotically carved terracotta flowerpots spilling over with award-winning red roses. Walls ten feet high painted in fuchsia pastels surrounded and framed the palace precincts. The multi-storied palace emerged out of the hillside like a great pink Indian ziggurat punctuated in its center by a large black and gold filigreed tower with a golden spire on top.

The inside of the palace was even more arresting than the outside. A large square perimeter of expansive hallways surrounded a smaller "house" within which Prabhupada's living quarters were situated. The outer hallways allowed devotees to circumambulate the house, which served as an architectural representation of the departed guru himself, its spatial precision suggesting divine perfection. The halls were easily 15 feet wide by 15 feet high, with ornately designed marble floors and heavily brocaded walls of stained glass and gold leaf filigree. The 40-foot long halls contained ceilings made of wood and mirrors, which reflected the green, pink, amber, blue, gold and red of the stained glass windows. Crystal chandeliers accentuated the regality of the palace ceilings every 10 feet.

The magical feeling that I felt when touring the Palace of Gold was reinforced when our class walked down the hill to the "Sri Sri Radha Vrindaban Chandra Mandir." The temple looked a bit like a wooden barn on the outside and was therefore much less impressive than the very costly and ornate architecture of the palace. But once inside of the temple I was again overcome by the sense of

Figure 5.1 The Palace of Gold at New Vrindaban

attraction that I had experienced earlier. The wooden double-doors of the temple opened onto a large meeting hall. At the far end of the hall sat an enormous partitioned altar, which housed the sacred statuary of New Vrindaban. The main 20 by 15 foot altar was shaped like a small house with the front wall removed so that a typically private space was open for public viewing. It was made of carved dark wood and had ornately decorated gold thrones to house the deities. A long colonnade of gigantic wooden columns with lions' heads on top supported the beams of the roof and led from the main temple entrance to the altar-like rows of redwoods in a sacred forest. A gold railing kept visitors at a safe distance from the statues. Rādhā and Kṛṣṇa were the central deities flanked by Narasiṃhadeva; Gauraṅga and Nityānanda; Jagannātha, Subhadrā and Baladeva; and Nāthaji. The physical deities were dressed in shockingly bright royal clothing and garlanded in brilliant flowers. The deities (*mūrtis*) themselves were magnificently constructed and mysteriously compelling—an uncanny mixture of childish and adult doll-like features, innocent yet seductive, patient and knowing. In a place of honor to the far right of the temple sat an eerily lifelike wax rendering of Prabhupada who, *in absentia*, watched over the temple proceedings on his crimson throne.

I was astonished by the beauty of the temple. Devotees dressed in traditional outfits of multi-colored cotton kurtas and dhotis and saris sat around the giant columns communing with the deities. Some of them covered their heads but I could make out the distinctive vertical lines of sandalwood paste on their foreheads (*tilaka*), which marked them as Vaiṣṇavas. Many of them recited round after round of the Hare Krishna *mantra* on their prayer beads. The glorious smell

Figure 5.2 Rādhā-Kṛṣṇa on main altar in New Vrindaban (1988)

of sandalwood incense filled the air. After a few minutes the temple hall filled with devotees and a devotional ceremony (*ārati*) for the sacred deities/statuary was performed. Offerings of food, incense, flame, water, and music were made to the deities. Before I knew it the hall was thrumming to the cadence of the Vaiṣṇava drums (*mṛdaṅgam*) and the trance-inducing drones of the harmonium with devotees dancing ecstatically, eyes closed, calling out to Lord Kṛṣṇa in devotional hymns (*kīrtanas*) that I had never heard before but nevertheless sounded vaguely familiar to me.

After the service the class was invited to have lunch with devotees in the dining hall of New Vrindaban. Various devotees interspersed themselves among the students' tables. A young devotee in her mid-20s sat at my table. She spoke to us with a subdued confidence, her light blue eyes meeting ours patiently, the bracelets decorating her arms tinkling softly with each movement she made with her hands. Her easy grace demonstrated in abundance the type of behavior that I encountered again and again that day. She was humble and quiet, but full of a passionate joy for her religion. I found her steadfast enthusiasm infectious. Unlike the Hollywood stereotypes, she made no effort whatsoever to proselytize or to argue theology with those of us who tried to bait her with the usual philosophical objections to theism. Instead, she seemed quite happy to acknowledge that opinions varied on metaphysical matters but she nevertheless remained resolute in the ecstatic God-centered life that she had chosen for herself.

The vegetarian food was delicious and a few of us were surprised to learn that so many ingenious things could be done with vegetables. Some of the students who had come on the trip were already vegetarians but their diets consisted mainly of raw salads, cheese, tomatoes, pasta, and breads. To discover the amazing tastes of exotically spiced lentil soup, fried vegetable fritters, whole wheat flat bread, and sweetened yogurt was enough to convince a few of the students to change their diets forever.

The incongruity of the fantastic Indian architectural and cultural cues (part Bengali, part Walt Disney) with the rural farm community in West Virginia made the experience of New Vrindaban marvelously strange to me. Over the years I have felt drawn to the palace and the temple much like the many thousands of pilgrims who visit there each year. The feeling that I experienced in New Vrindaban can be described as religious or aesthetic, but more accurately a combination of both.

After finishing my undergraduate studies, I had the good fortune of visiting many Hindu *tīrthas* in India and America. Although I had similar experiences of fascination and wonder at several of these places, the Gauḍīya Vaiṣṇava *tīrthas* continued to hold a special fascination for me. One particular incident that occurred almost ten years after my initial encounter with the magic of New Vrindaban is particularly worth mentioning.

I had been living in Kolkata, India, for a couple of years conducting doctoral dissertation research when I decided that I needed a break from my studies. My life, the dreary days of the displaced, impoverished graduate student, consisted of a monotonous cycle of sleep and meals and visits to sweltering reading rooms, musty volumes cracking open in my anxious dissertating hands. I had heard about the Vaiṣṇava pilgrimage center of Mayapur many years earlier from devotees in America. In the spring of 1999 I decided that I would go to Mayapur for a retreat from the smothering heat and dusty claustrophobia of the Kolkata archives.

The best way to reach Mayapur from Kolkata is to take the ISKCON bus from the Śrī Śrī Rādhā-Govinda Mandira on Albert Road in the center of the city. Arrangements can be made easily and the staff at the temple is used to dealing with international travelers. So, one afternoon I made my way to the temple (*mandira*) and booked my ticket to Mayapur for a several-day stay in the ISKCON guesthouse. The bus ride from Kolkata takes a few hours. The bus leaves early and arrives at Mayapur in the late morning. Rising up against the pollution and bustle of the city, the village of Mayapur arches across the horizon, an oasis of clean air, blue skies, palm trees, and beautiful pastel buildings bespeaking a time long since past.

As soon as I stepped off the bus in Mayapur I was greeted with that warm sense of belonging that I had come to associate with Gauḍīya Vaiṣṇava *tīrthas* ever since my first trip to New Vrindaban a decade earlier. The "guest house" was really more of a mini-hotel than any sort of house. Painted in the familiar sandy-pink color of so many Vaiṣṇava buildings, the clean floors and walls of the minimally decorated rooms welcomed the visitor with an austere simplicity. Over the next few days I explored the village, meeting and interviewing pilgrims from Germany, Japan, France, England, and the United States. Most of the pilgrims were, however, Bengalis. As had always been my experience with Gauḍīya Vaiṣṇavas, I found the devotees to be the friendliest and most open people that one could ever hope to meet. They sat and talked with me for hours about politics, religion, music, and scholarship. Their eyes were earnest and expressive, and their gazes intent, as our conversation ranged from The Beatles and the band's fascination with Eastern religion to Western ideas about South Asia. But mostly we talked about Mayapur and the powerful grip that it held upon all of us. I tried to explain that each step I took there felt sure, as though I were tracing the same path, again. This strange sense of a familiar "presence" challenged my uncomplicated atheistic convictions.

The pilgrimage town itself is a recent phenomenon. In the late nineteenth century a brilliant middle-class intellectual named Bhaktivinoda Thakura had converted to Vaiṣṇavism and after having had a vivid dream one night he discovered that the small village was the actual birthplace of the founder of Gauḍīya Vaiṣṇavism, Śrī Kṛṣṇa Caitanya (1486–1533). Over the years the village was built up through the loving care of devotees until by the turn of the twenty-first century it was a thriving pilgrimage complex that could house a thousand visitors at any given time.

While I was there I spent a good deal of time meditating and observing in the impressively large Prabhupada Samādhi Mandira. The temple was built to memorialize Prabhupada in much the same way as the Palace of Gold in New Vrindaban commemorated the founder of the movement. The experience of being in the Samādhi Mandira (memorial temple) is much like that of being in the gardens of the ISKCON compound in Mayapur. Rows of trees and bright red flowers line long pathways, which bisect the monumental architecture of the village. In addition

Figure 5.3 Temple at Mayapur, West Bengal

to the imposing edifices, outlined against the sky, there are also grass and earth huts, bowers and groves and gardens teeming with holy basil (*tulasi*) bushes, mewing peacocks, blooming roses and gently swaying palm trees.

Like New Vrindaban, the devotees of Mayapur have attempted to recreate the feeling of a "Vedic Village" on the banks of the Bhāgirathī river in West Bengal. As with my experiences in New Vrindaban, it is hard to describe my feelings during my initial and subsequent stays in Mayapur but adjectives like magical, numinous, uncanny, and sacred point in the right direction. In Mayapur, I felt the full aesthetic impact of visiting a place where the ordinary rules of the mundane world are rendered inapplicable. The devotees had created for themselves their own Vedic theme park where devotees could live in a world of their own fantastical construction.

My observations showed me that many of the devotees felt particularly attached to Mayapur for reasons very similar to those that appealed to me. In conversations, devotees used words like "magical" and "sacred" and "holy" to describe both the place itself and their experiences of it. Several spoke of being transformed by the ambience of the location. In Mayapur, they were able to put aside the mundane concerns of their ordinary, everyday existences and live in a friendly community of like-minded individuals who also appreciated the otherworldly architecture, rituals, routines, clothing, and food of the Gauḍīya Vaiṣṇavas. In Mayapur, as in New Vrindaban, the days revolved around the liturgical hours of the temples and the deities that resided there. Linguistic space matched the wonder of the physical space; talk of worldly endeavors gave way to prayer without ceasing.

Over the years I have returned to Mayapur and New Vrindaban on numerous occasions and I have to admit that I never fail to experience the same sorts of feelings that I had on my initial encounters with the *tīrthas*. No doubt others who have visited these places do not share my romantic (religious?) impressions. That fact, a banal inevitability, neither interests nor concerns me. More intriguing to me has always been the possibility that many, maybe even most, of the devotees who make pilgrimages to these holy sites *do* recognize the feelings, moods, and observations that I mention above. They have told me so again and again. And I have acknowledged these events, similar yet strange, time and again myself when I have visited these *tīrthas*. The question that continues to perplex me as a scholar of religion is this: just what is it about these two Gauḍīya Vaiṣṇava *tīrthas* that continues to exert such a profound influence upon me and the many devotees who describe spatially-evoked experiences of deep belonging and transcendental bliss?

Discussion

Rudolf Otto, Mircea Eliade and C. S. Lewis might refer to the feelings that devotees and some participant observers (*c'est moi!*) experience at holy sites as "numinous" or "sacred" feelings. Although these categories of analysis have fallen out of favor in the competitive post-modern marketplace of the academic study of religion they nevertheless continue to prove useful as interpretive devices in the consideration of religious "experience" as such. Of course, one must acknowledge the caveat that when dealing with the category of "experience" in the consideration of religious cultural production, analysis can become muddled easily because it is, by definition, difficult to talk objectively about subjective states of consciousness. Then again, does not one irresponsibly limit one's interpretive horizons by gratuitously ignoring the resonances between the insider's understanding and the outsider's experience?

In any case, the simple fact remains that when I visited New Vrindaban for the first time I felt a deep sense of belonging. When I talked to devotees I felt as if I had met some of them before and several of them even went so far as to ask me the same question: "Have we met before?" For those who have never experienced this kind of uneasy phenomenon, my description may sound whimsically romantic at best or delusional at worst. I accept this. But for those who have had the experience of a prolonged *déjà vu* experience that lasts for hours on end the description will not seem so exotic and they will have some understanding of what I am describing. In short, the feelings that I experienced that day were uncanny, maybe even "sacred." In fact, the uncanny impressions of that day were so many and prolonged that they were transformed from feelings into a mood (*rasa*)—a mood that can most identifiably be described as religious.

After much reflection upon this issue over the years I have come to believe that the magical world that the Gauḍīya Vaiṣṇavas in West Virginia had created for themselves was, in part, what evoked the uncanny feeling of the numinous in me and in so many devotees. In the early years after I was first moved by the ambience of New Vrindaban I began to wonder about the extent to which my experiences might have been caused by a simple romantic feeling for the novelty of the place. Maybe my feelings toward the community had to do with the foreignness of the Indian architecture and the exotic food and the colorfully draped devotees? Maybe they had something to do with a latent religiosity that I had tried too forcefully to repress while at college? Maybe the rich visual culture and ritualistic emphases of Gauḍīya Vaiṣṇavism resonated sympathetically with the Catholicism that I had inherited from my mother? Maybe all of these things combined? Maybe something entirely different? Who knows?

One should not underestimate the utility of political, psychological and sociological reductionist interpretations in the consideration of a sudden attraction of a professedly anti-religious member of one culture to the spiritual practices, ideas and institutions of another. However, subsequent conversations with Indian, non-converted, non-Catholic devotees who described similar experiences at New Vrindaban and other Gauḍīya Vaiṣṇava *tīrthas* indicate that my own observations cannot be too easily reduced to any form of idiosyncratic neurosis or latent cultural Orientalism. Put differently, my thoughts and feelings could not easily be dismissed as deriving from some personal psychological aberration, or an Eastern stereotype that I was unconsciously projecting onto my experience.

It was precisely the sense that the rules (architectural, cultural and otherwise) of the mundane world did not apply within the sacred space of the *tīrtha* that gave New Vrindaban its appeal. The initial experience for me was not entirely different from the sorts of experiences that people report when they spend a day at a utopian theme park like Disneyland. I say this not to denigrate the religious feelings associated with *tīrthas* but rather to suggest the possible elevation of theme-park experiences to the realm of the sacred. In my experience, the *tīrtha* of New Vrindaban worked on the visitor much like a theme park that maintains its attraction by appealing to the human thirst for the otherworldly, the fantastical, the magical and the eerie. The visceral experience of Prabhupada's Palace of Gold and the communal temple was, for many, one of otherworldly, transcendental inclusion. Although I was not able to put my finger on the exact nature of the experience I was having at the time, I was not surprised to learn later that the leaders of New Vrindaban were, at the very time that I was visiting the palace for the first time, planning to turn the community into a religiously focused theme park called "Krishna-land."

So too, my experiences in Mayapur were indicative of the sorts of moods and feelings associated with theme parks in the United States. Mayapur, self-consciously created on the model of an imagined "Vedic village" on the banks of the Bhāgirathī river in central West Bengal, is not so much an ancient Vedic village as what the cultural theorist Jean Baudrillard would call a fantastical *simulacrum* (simulation) of an ancient village, a *hyper-reality* which has been intentionally designed to elide the distinctions between the "real" world and the world of imagination and fantasy. Although Baudrillard is most interested in the *hyper-realities* produced by the *simulacra* of theme parks, and he holds a very dim view of the ways in which modern day theme parks like Disneyland reproduce and repackage the "real" world in sanitized forms for a bourgeois consuming public, I see no necessary or logical need to link his anti-capitalist polemics to the idea of the *simulacrum* as such. Nor do I see the production of religiously inspired *simulacra* as a particularly novel phenomenon in the history of world civilizations.

The concept of the *simulacrum* is helpful in the consideration of sacred sites like New Vrindaban and Mayapur because it reveals something about the ways in which real and imaginary worlds can come together in the minds of pilgrims and devotees. In both of these places the poetic stories of ancient deities and the aesthetic values of exotic and incredible medieval religious traditions are brought to life in concrete form. I mention the ideas of *simulacrum* and *hyper-reality* to suggest that there is continuity between the sorts of "magical" adventures that many of us have had as children and/or adults when visiting the value-added simulations of reality at places like Disneyland, and the experiences of devotees and pilgrims who encounter the sacred through the value-added simulations of paradigmatic cultural forms at two modern-day Gauḍīya Vaiṣṇava *tīrthas*. By visiting a contemporary recreation of an ancient locale, a Vaiṣṇava pilgrim can participate imaginatively, yet physically, in a sacred reality otherwise encountered only in religious media such as books, music, plays and storytelling. A pilgrimage to a *tīrtha* enables the devotee to live within the context of a sacred narrative. Although there are many, one of the most profound ways that the age-old distinction between sacred and profane spaces can be made manifest to pilgrims in contemporary religious contexts is through the transformation of human consciousness by exposure to fantastical architectural forms, playfully designed landscapes, inspirational or meditative music, hyper-friendly residents, etc.

Tīrthas are, by their very nature, polders, or places of crossing. They are points where the world of the sacred intersects with the world of the profane. The Gauḍīya Vaiṣṇava pilgrimage sites of Mayapur and New Vrindaban are quintessential *tīrthas* in the sense that they open up the sacred realms of Kṛṣṇa's pastimes by evoking religious experiences peculiar to the sacred sites. In the Gauḍīya Vaiṣṇava tradition there are multi-layered schematic rubrics for the various emotions (*bhāvas*) that might be experienced at a *tīrtha*. But the most common English term used to describe the experience of devotees and participant-observers is "transcendental." Theologically speaking, when the grace of Kṛṣṇa has touched the heart of a pilgrim he or she will experience the bliss of participating in the cosmic drama while still on the earthly plane.

Although I am not able to say for certain exactly why it is that I am attracted to New Vrindaban and Mayapur, or just what I experience when I visit them, I have

Figure 5.4 Fuller in India, 1997

grown comfortable with the fact that when I go to do research at either *tīrtha,* I am not just an observer; I am forever, reluctantly and accidentally, a pilgrim as well.

Readings

Diana Eck's short and accessible volume is still the most reliable and down-to-earth introductory text to deal extensively with the concept of *tīrtha*—see Diana L. Eck, *Darśan: Seeing the Divine Image in India* (Anima Books, 1981). Ann Grodzins Gold's *Fruitful Journeys: The Ways of Rajasthani Pilgrims* (Oxford University Press, 1988) is a classic in the field of pilgrimage studies. See also Victor and Edith Turner's coauthored volume entitled *Image and Pilgrimage in Christian Culture* (Columbia University Press, 1995). For more on Gauḍīya Vaiṣṇava aesthetics and the various moods associated with religious experience see David L. Haberman's *Acting as a Way of Salvation: A Study of Rāgānugā Bhakti Sādhana* (Motilal Banarsidass, 2001). E. Burke Rochford's *Hare Krishna Transformed* (NYU, 2007) is the most up-to-date discussion of the Hare Krishna movement in America and India. Hayagriva Dasa's *The Hare Krishna Explosion* (Palace Press, 1985) is still the best first-person account of the building up of New Vrindaban in the late 1960s and early 1970s. Jean Baudrillard's *Simulacra and Simulation* (University of Michigan, 1995) is a good place to turn for a general discussion of his cultural theories. For discussions of sacred space and the idea of religious experience more generally see Mircea Eliade's *The Sacred and the Profane: The Nature of Religion* (Harcourt Brace Jovanovich, 1987) and Rudolf Otto's *The Idea of the Holy* (Oxford University Press, 1958). For a more detailed discussion of the idea of sacred sites in Gauḍīya Vaiṣṇavism, see my article in the fall 2009 edition of the *Journal of Vaishnava Studies,* "Bengali Vaishnava Homelands," *Journal of Vaishnava Studies,* Vol. 18, No. 1, pp. 39-52.

Author

Jason D. Fuller (PhD) is Associate Professor of Religious Studies and Asian Studies at DePauw University in Greencastle, Indiana. In 2005, Jason received his PhD in religious studies from the University of Pennsylvania. He is a South Asianist who specializes in the study of modern Hinduism. He has conducted fieldwork and archival research in Kolkata, India. His areas of research interest include Gauḍīya Vaiṣṇavism and nineteenth-century Bengali social history. When Jason is not teaching, writing or doing archival research in the India Office Reading room at the British Library, he can often be found riding his Indian motorcycle on the back roads of rural Indiana.

Chapter 6

Dance and Hinduism

A personal exploration

Anne-Marie Gaston

Preamble

In 1964, I went to India with Canadian University Service Overseas (CUSO) to teach in Chennai, then known as Madras. At that time I began to study Bharata Natyam, the style of classical Indian dancing characteristic of that region. In this chapter I describe how learning the dance led me to an understanding of certain elements of Hinduism, both as a religion and as a social system. I have drawn on my personal experiences over 40 years of studying the dance in India and performing and teaching it in India, Canada, and other countries. This chapter focuses on the early years when I was unfamiliar with, but very open to, what India and its culture offered. Because I have studied, performed, and taught the dances of India for a very long time, I have, of necessity, concentrated on a few incidents and interactions that exemplify my gradual awakening to the philosophy of Hinduism, to its customs and artistic expressions, and to social changes that I continue to experience.

Narrative

On arrival in India I first went to Chidambaram, Tamil Nadu, where I spent two months studying Tamil at Annamalai University. There, I lived in the girls' hostel of the university, sharing a room with three other students. We regularly visited the Nataraja Temple, an enormous walled sanctuary dating from medieval times, famous both for the worship of Śiva as Naṭarāja ("Lord of the Dance"), and for its elaborate carvings of dancing postures, known as *karaṇas*. These 108 *karaṇas* are described in a fifth-century text on dance, theater, and music, the *Nātya Śāstra*. For me, seeing dancers as important elements of decoration depicted at a place of worship was unusual and intriguing. The women, bare-breasted, scantily clothed, lavishly decorated with jewels, arms and legs flying in gay abandon, were fascinating. The rich music of the *nāgasvaram*, a reed instrument like a large oboe, and the rhythmic beating of the *tavil* and *mṛdaṅgam*, two different kinds of drums, accompanied by the clanging of cymbals, all resounding in the huge temple corridors were awe-inspiring. This early exposure to the interconnectedness of Hindu temple art, dance, music, and rituals entered my consciousness and subsequently became an essential part of my life.

After Chidambaram I transferred to Chennai where, for the next two years, I taught at a government school. I lived at the school in one room which initially did not have a fan; it was almost unbearable in the intense, humid heat of a city situated close to the equator. I had studied dance in Canada, and was naturally curious about what Indian dance might be like. So, without ever seeing an Indian dance recital, I decided to combine teaching with studying Indian dance. By studying Indian dance, in this case, Bharata Natyam, I was given an entrée into traditional south Indian Hindu culture and an introduction to the diverse social and religious structures that comprise Hinduism.

Beginning Bharata Natyam

In India, introductions are very important. Y. G. Doraiswamy, an art connoisseur, brought me to the home of Ellappa Mudaliar, a traditional dance teacher and musician, who had, for many years, accompanied the recitals of one of the most famous hereditary dancers, T. Balasaraswati. I was very excited when Ellappa agreed to take me on as a student, but classes had to be started on an auspicious day and at an auspicious time. An almanac was consulted. I was told that the moment of beginning determined the success of any activity.

I soon got used to the idea that it was necessary to pre-plan important events in relation to the stars and planets. I realized that when you asked someone, "Is this a good time for you?" it did not mean, "Are you free at that time?" but rather, "According to your stars, will this work for you?" From the actual time that I started to take class, to each time I began a new dance, the almanac was always consulted in order to avoid *rāhu kalam*, a specific period each day that is regarded as inauspicious. An activity started during *rāhu kalam*, which occurs when the nine planetary bodies (*nava graha*) of the Hindu astrological scheme are not in proper alignment, is believed to have little chance of success.

My first class took place in the central room of Ellappa's house. My tuition fee was first offered to an image of a deity, probably Murugan, son of the god Śiva, as this is the preferred deity for Ellappa's caste. At that time I could not identify the Hindu deities whose pictures adorned his walls. Ellappa sat cross legged on the floor and beat out the rhythm on a block of wood. He then motioned for me to raise first my right foot and slap it down and then the left and then to approach him and touch the block of wood and stick with both hands. He then blessed me by touching my bowed head. This indicated that I had been chosen to receive an oral tradition for which the teacher's goodwill is essential if real knowledge is to be imparted.

Ellappa showed the hand gestures and indicated the foot movements by beating his hands on the ground and I would imitate him. Only on rare occasions would he get up and dance, moving with grace and precision even though he had never performed publicly as a dancer. This was the traditional teaching method followed by most masters.

Bharata Natyam is a classical art and so has a rigid grammar of movement that must be perfected. Once the basic structure of the body and the steps became familiar, during a period of about eight months, I progressed to what is considered the most important and difficult to master, the descriptive repertoire. It was these descriptive dances that developed my awareness of Hindu myths, philosophy, aesthetics, and poetry.

Ellappa's home (and those of my later teachers) was always welcoming and I became part of the family. After class I would be given a hot rice cake (*idly*) and coffee. This hospitality provided some continuity with the earlier practice of the student living in the teacher's house. The system, known as *guru-śiṣya paramparā*, involved the student living at the teacher's home and doing *seva* (work in the teacher's home). In return, the student was taught free of charge. Tuition fees had replaced *seva*, but there was still an intimate connection with the teacher. I really looked forward to the coffee and snacks because at that time there were very few public restaurants and this was one of the few chances I had to eat socially.

My class lasted an hour and was over by 8:30 a.m. and I would then go off to teach school. In the evenings I attended as many dance recitals as I could. Often these recitals would involve performances by some of my students. Preparing for the stage is a whole art in itself. I discovered that mastering how the costume was assembled and how the jewelry was attached was crucial for a successful performance. How well I remember recitals when things went astray: a pleated fan unfolding as a dancer performed, an earring falling on the floor and injuring the dancer's bare feet.

The dancers were dressed in elaborate gold-trimmed saris, stitched into a costume (the best examples in sculpture can be seen from the king's throne at Hampi in the state of Karnataka, and in the Parvati Court in Chidambaram. The voluptuous women, often bare-breasted, were covered in jewelry, including necklaces, earrings, and bangles. Around their ankles they wore rows of bells. The make-up was very heavy with large kohl-rimmed eyes, red pouty lips and red cheeks. Costumes were and still are very expensive and made only by specialists. The jewelry specialist had his workshop and shop near the Kapilesvara temple in Mylapore. Here you ordered the same type of jewelry used to decorate temple deities. Fake rubies and diamonds were set into ancient patterns, their shape designed to accentuate beauty. For example, the earrings looked like upside down umbrellas and would shake as a dancer moved the neck from side to side, thus accentuating the movement. The costumes accentuated the hips, making them look large and full, while the waist was intended to appear small; real jasmine adorned our hair. Attending live recitals was essential to hear different musicians, and to become familiar with the themes of the classical repertoire.

Descriptive dances and devotion (bhakti)

The descriptive dances revealed many fascinating aspects of Hindu philosophy and myth. The text of the songs to which we dance alludes to the attributes of the deity to which they are addressed. As an example, the god Śiva is depicted in dance very often as he is generally seen in sculpture and painting. One of my favorite dances is addressed to Śiva. It is known as *Rupamu Jootsi,* and is a *varṇam*, where lines of the song alternate with fast rhythmic sections. It begins: "When the door of the temple was opened I saw your wondrous form." During a performance I visualize and then depict in gesture Śiva's different aspects: "radiant as a galaxy of suns," "the deer in one hand the axe in the other," or "with matted locks flying." I include the *liṅgodbhava* story in which Śiva claims that his form as the phallus (*liṅga*) is limitless. Two other gods, Viṣṇu and Brahmā, attempt to disprove his assertion. Viṣṇu takes the form of a boar and digs into the earth while Brahmā, on his swan, flies upwards. All of this is shown in gestures. When neither finds the end of the *liṅga*, thus confirming Śiva's supremacy, I show a gesture of despair, to represent the bafflement of the other gods, and then homage, awe, and adoration to the all-powerful Śiva. The connection between sculpture and dance is evident in this *varṇam*, as the choreography draws inspiration from the rich iconography of the many manifestations of Śiva on the temples.

I soon learned that the descriptive repertoire of the dance is multi-layered. First comes the literal and easily identifiable recreation of the actual song. This is followed by elaboration that touches on other mythological elements and often recreates what we see in stone sculptures. It is the descriptive repertoire and its poetic rendering that makes Indian dance unique: hand signs, facial expressions, neck movements, and body positions are all carefully integrated to relate the many facets of Hindu thought, philosophy, and art. While teaching these descriptive dances, Ellappa and my other traditional teachers would rarely use the same gestures twice, such is the wealth of mythological references that can be employed.

Many of the traditional themes are highly erotic, often culminating in sexual union. These are presented using a codified vocabulary which Ellappa demonstrated for me without any embarrassment. When he extended his thumb, very much like a hitchhiker, then cupped his other hand to show a circle and inserted his thumb, he indicated that I should imitate him. "Joining in love," he explained. This was my introduction to the most important metaphor in Hinduism for expressing the love of God. At that period even a kiss was forbidden in Indian movies, so suggesting the sexual act through mime surprised me, even though it is a very appropriate metaphor for complete surrender. The same metaphor permeates the writings of Christian mystics and Sufi saints.

Many of the metaphors of classical Sanskrit poetry, Indian painting, and dance are shared. For example, to suggest the ideal mature woman, they include showing breasts, full and ripe as mangos, which allow only one or two strands of pearls to pass between them. Highly desirable women have small waists, big hips and move with the slow swing gait of an elephant. They are adorned with heavy ornate jewelry, and have long thick hair, liquid eyes like a fish or a deer, an aquiline nose, and lips as red and plump as ripe fruit. All these metaphors are common to Sanskrit literature and are given physical form in carvings of celestial dancers and goddesses on Hindu temples.

The Naṭarāja image of Śiva as "Lord of the Dance," posed in a circle of fire, combines beauty with energy. Ellappa taught me a dance (*Naṭanam adīnar*) that describes Śiva's dance of creation and destruction. The poetry in this dance brought to life the Naṭarāja image and introduced me to the meaning of the iconography. It linked Śiva's cosmic dance in south India in Chidambaram, and in north India in the Himalayas. During the early part of my career, when I danced mainly Bharata Natyam, this piece was a regular part of my performing repertoire. As performed, the Naṭarāja pose recurs periodically throughout the dance. With my left hand I mimed the hour glass drum (*ḍamaru*), which provided the first rhythm in the cosmos, initiating creation; the right hand, with extended fingers (*alapadma*) symbolized the fire of destruction. As Naṭarāja has four hands, I followed this by mimicking the inner pair of arms, with a combination of the left hand extended across my body (*gajahasta*) and pointing at my raised foot, suggesting "do not be afraid and take refuge at my feet," while my right hand was held at shoulder level facing outward (in *patāka hasta*), indicating that Naṭarāja would protect his devotees. In this way, I became familiar with some of the literal and philosophical meanings of the bronze icon of Naṭarāja.

As I became more interested in the descriptive dances, I wanted to work on my expression (*abhinaya*) and in the 1970s began to study with Swarna Sareswati, who

Figure 6.1 Anjali (Gaston) as Śiva Naṭarāja

was a former *devadāsī*. She had been based in Chennai and after the ban on *devadāsīs* performing in temples she married a Brahmin (a man from the priestly class), who managed her career, initially as a dancer in Chennai and later as a teacher in Delhi. At that time I did not fully appreciate the honor of studying with someone who, as a dancer, was an important part of the hereditary tradition. I was privileged to have daily classes with her. She taught me some of the most important songs in the traditional dance repertoire. When she chose a song to accompany my dance she would demonstrate how to express the various secondary emotions (anger, jealousy, amazement) that would emerge when the dominant emotion was erotic love (*śṛṅgāra*). She would suddenly come alive and very animated as she sang and enacted the gestures. For the abstract elements of the dance Swarna would only accept very contained movement. She was extremely scathing of contemporary developments where dancers covered a lot of space by jumping and running around the stage. If I showed any tendency to make large movements she firmly corrected me. Using a lot of space was not part of her aesthetic. For her, the dance was intended to be an intimate expression and should not be altered just because large theaters had replaced intimate drawing rooms for performance.

Odissi: learning Daśāvatār and Gita Govinda

In 1970, I began to study Odissi with Mayahdar Raut. Odissi is another classical dance style, which originated from the state of Orissa. The movements are less angular and more fluid than those of Bharata Natyam and the accompanying music more lyrical. The body postures are different, too. Odissi allows the hips to deflect, in a posture known as *tribhaṅga*, and the poses are more reminiscent of those of dancing girls on the walls of temples throughout India. Both styles are based on the same vocabulary of hand gestures, but each has its own manner of rendition.

During my initial training in Bharata Natyam my knowledge of Vaiṣṇavite iconography, as shown in the dance, was limited to the discus and conch for Viṣṇu and the flute for Kṛṣṇa. However, *Daśāvatār* (the ten incarnations of Viṣṇu) was one of the first pieces I learned in Odissi. The ten incarnations are: *Matsya* (fish), *Kacchapa* (turtle), *Varāha* (boar), *Narasiṃha* (half man, half lion), *Vāmana* (dwarf), *Paraśurāma* who carries the axe, *Rāma* with the bow, *Balarāma* with the plough, *Buddha*, and finally *Kalki*, who is expected to come at the end of the current age, riding on a white horse. Each of these incarnations has an associated story, which forms the basis for the choreography and illustrates the salient features of the feats performed by each avatar. While nine avatars have appeared on earth, there is some controversy over the identity of the ninth avatar. The *Gīta Govinda* includes Buddha as the ninth incarnation of Viṣṇu, a clear indication of how it absorbs other faiths. In some other accounts, the Buddha is not the ninth incarnation of Viṣṇu. This was pointed out to me several months later when I was about to go on stage to perform *Daśāvatār* in Delhi. Much to my surprise, the announcer for the recital, a Kṛṣṇa devotee, rushed into the dressing room to inquire why his notes made no mention of Kṛṣṇa as one of the ten incarnations. "Surely Kṛṣṇa and not Buddha should be the ninth and most recent incarnation," he insisted. While putting on make-up and tying my costume, not to mention trying to compose myself to perform, I was forced to have a lively discussion on the inclusion of Buddha and/or Kṛṣṇa as an incarnation. Jayadeva, the composer of the song for *Daśāvatār*, was from Orissa, where Buddhism flourished up to the eighth century, and he regarded Kṛṣṇa as the supreme form of divinity.

I became more familiar with Kṛṣṇa *bhakti* (devotion) when I came to study the music of the Pustimarg Sampradaya, a sect of Kṛṣṇa devotees *(bhāktas)* based in Nathadvara, in the north-western state of Rajasthan. Through association with Guru Purushottam Das, a drummer and member of the hereditary caste of musicians who play in the temples of the *sampradāya*, I had the unique opportunity to be invited to perform on two occasions for the Tilkayat, the head of the Vallabha Sampradaya, the senior branch of the Pustimarg sect. The Tilkayat is regarded by them as the embodiment of Kṛṣṇa on earth and as such he enjoys the same entertainments as did Kṛṣṇa: music and dance. The first time I performed for him was as part of the celebrations for the marriage of his eldest son in 1980. This was held, appropriately, in Brindavan, the mythic birthplace of Kṛṣṇa, where he spent his youth as a cowherd and later distinguished himself as a divine lover, capable of replicating himself thousands of times to dance the *ras,* or circle dance, with all of his devotees.

The marriage festivities in Brindavan went on for several days and included recitals by many important dancers and musicians. Several stages were built especially for the outdoor event. Thousands of devotees and local villagers attended. I performed several dances in the Odissi style from the *Gīta Govinda*, which described the relationship of Kṛṣṇa and his beloved Rādhā. For the locals and other devotees, seeing the dances of Kṛṣṇa was like *darśana*, a glimpse of divine play (*līlā*). I can remember that many uttered "*vah vah*" at a moment in the story which moved them, such as when Rādhā, who had waited the whole night for her beloved Kṛṣṇa to return, is enraged when he arrives in the morning, his body covered with the marks of having made love to another woman. These stories are open to many interpretations. However, inherent in this story is that Kṛṣṇa's love is all inclusive and cannot be kept for one alone.

Dancing in these situations brings home the importance of the dance as a religious metaphor. As my dance led the audience through the familiar stories there was a genuine feeling of rapport. For them, to be in *Braj bhūmī* (the land of Kṛṣṇa's play), and for me to perform in Kṛṣṇa's "home," underlined that Brindavan is not a place but a state of mind. Wherever Kṛṣṇa goes there it is eternal spring. Kṛṣṇa is forever with his devotees.

In 1985, I was once again very fortunate to be invited to perform for the *muṇḍan* (first hair cutting) ceremony for the Tilkayat's grandson. It was held in the Tilkayat's private apartments in his palace in Nathdvara. I can remember walking through the town in full Odissi costume, heavily laden with silver jewelry, carrying my ankle bells so as not to attract too much attention. I entered the Moti Mahal (the Tilkayat's palace) via the back door to the temple, its huge elephant-deterring spikes looming sinisterly over my head. Pushing open the tiny inner door, I found myself in a small courtyard, dark except for the lights that blazed from the Moti Mahal. I left my shoes with the guards, many of whom had bedded down for the night in the narrow passageway of the gate, and walked across the courtyard. The sky was clear and the stars provided sufficient light. I climbed the winding staircase, past the portraits of previous Tilkayats and paintings of Kṛṣṇa, and eventually emerged into the Tilkayat's private apartments.

The occasion was quite medieval. A large crowd waited in expectant silence. The Tilkayat sat on a chair but everyone else was seated on the marble floor which was covered in rugs, except for the spot where I was to dance. I walked over, prostrated myself in front of the Tilkayat, touched his feet, and asked his permission to begin. Entering the performance area, I dropped flowers in front of the Tilkayat, to show that I sought both his blessings and those of mother earth, the Goddess Bhūmī. This was followed by invoking the eight guardians of the cardinal points (*dikpālas*) to protect the recital from any evil that might be lurking and then concluded with a final salutation to God, to my teacher, and to everyone present. After the invocation, I presented *Govardana Giri*, a Bharata Natyam piece which relates the story of Kṛṣṇa raising Govardhana Mountain so that his devotees could take shelter from a terrific rainstorm caused by the storm god Indra. This is one of the most important stories surrounding the miraculous child Kṛṣṇa and is central to the Sri Nathji image (*svarūp*) around which the teaching of this group has been built. Sri Nathji's pose alludes to Mount Govardhana by holding the right hand aloft as though supporting the mountain. I also presented several songs from the *Gīta Govinda*: Kṛṣṇa the divine lover with his magic flute, playing with the milkmaids in Brindavan and his special relationship with Rādhā. The recital culminated with *Moksha*, the traditional finale for an Odissi recital, expressing liberation of the spirit.

In Bharata Natyam, the traditional dance repertoire was mainly about the love of the dancer for her lord, a male God. I cannot remember Ellappa's repertoire referring to female deities at all, except in their form as a consort to a powerful male figure: Śiva and Pārvatī, Viṣṇu and Lakṣmī, Kṛṣṇa and Rādhā. I can remember being amazed at the number of names to be learned and the complexity of their interrelationships. Many gods have more than one wife (e.g. Kṛṣṇa with Satyabhāmā and Rukminī), or the same wife who is reborn but with another name (e.g. Śiva with Pārvatī, Satī, etc). Durgā, the slayer of evil in the form of a buffalo-headed demon, a theme that is very popular in temple sculpture, was not in Ellappa's repertoire.

I had to search hard to find repertoire that related solely to a Goddess, but eventually learned *Siṃhāsana Sthite* (seated on the lion throne), a composition about Durgā. Inspired by a dance about the Goddess that I saw performed by one of the greatest non-hereditary dancers, Yamini Krishnamurthy, and with the help of one of my Bharata Natyam teachers, K. N. Dakshinamurthy and the singer, Akhila Krishna, we created this wonderfully powerful expression about the various feats performed by the Goddess who sits on the lion throne. The fecund goddess has shapely breasts, a slim waist, large hips and large eyes. She is beautiful, strong, and terrible. In the dance my postures are peaceful and composed, but when I show the goddess's weapon, the trident, and stride about the stage I represent her fearful aspect. This change in moods—from languid and passive to angry and strong—is an essential part of the Goddess's portrayal.

Discussion

Ritual pollution

Bharata Natyam was an essential part of temple ritual until 1947, when it was banned by the government of the then Madras Presidency. Up until then, many of the same dancers who worked in the temples also performed at private parties and in theaters. Most dancers, teachers, and musicians, who traditionally were employed by the temples as artists and musicians, had a special connection to the dance, as they had actually performed in the context for which the dance was created. I appreciated this better when another hereditary teacher, K. N. Dakshinamurthy, choreographed a dance for me which included recreating the various temple rituals he had seen and participated in as a young man: the circling of the pot light, waving a yak-tail fan, and rotating a light clockwise while ringing a bell, all important rituals used by the priests.

Ellappa's daughters, who in earlier days might have become *devadāsīs*, were always present when I had my class but they did not participate in any artistic activities, either music or dance. At that time I was never able to get a satisfactory answer as to why he did not teach them to dance. It was only later that I learned that in those days, for women in their caste, any association with the dance would mean that they would be unable to get married. Thus they stayed at home and learned how to cook and manage a home, while waiting for an arranged marriage. All this has changed in the past 30 years and females from this caste now teach and perform the dance.

Because my association with Tamil Nadu began over 40 years ago and the classes were taught in homes, many traditional Hindu practices were revealed that might not have come to my attention otherwise. I was made aware on several occasions that, as a foreigner and a non-Hindu, I was at the very lowest level in the caste hierarchy; my presence, my touch, or even my shadow had the potential to pollute. Once, when on a picnic with the family of a Brahmin friend, my friend, looking very agitated, pulled me aside and told me that her Granny must eat first and that I should not go near her while she was eating. She explained: "Granny is very orthodox and your shadow could fall on her." I ate later with the rest of the family for whom my presence was not an issue.

On another occasion, in Delhi, after my dance class, I drank a glass of water and left it on a table. When I returned the next day I noticed that it was still in the same place. Although he was a non-Brahmin, the teacher insisted that I must personally remove the glass of water as he and his family would be polluted by touching it.

Caste is not the only source of ritual pollution. Menstruation is a time when, according to Hindu tradition, a woman is impure. I saw instances of this in my teachers' homes and other homes I visited. At that time, when they were menstruating, the women sat alone for several days, often in an area on the porch, and did not bathe, ate separately, and could not cook, go to the temple or touch anyone or anything, as then that person or object would be polluted. Initially I was ignorant that I could be causing pollution by dancing at that time of the month. I only learned of the taboo later, from one of my Brahmin teachers, who pointed out that "at that time," theoretically, I should not take dance classes. While he did not forbid taking classes he cautioned me to not touch the wooden beating block (*tattukal*), regarded as a sacred instrument, during that period, as it could be polluted.

Rasa and bhava

As a classical dance form, there are standards by which each movement in Bharata Natyam can be judged as either good or bad. All teachers have their own unique dance repertoires set to classical Carnatic music. None of my early teachers referred to the Sanskrit texts that formulate the dance, such as the *Abhinaya Darpaṇa* or *Nāṭya Śāstra*, or taught me the verses (*ślokas*, the Sanskrit recitations) that they provide. After several years I felt it was necessary to do this and so studied with several graduates of Kalakshetra, a school where the teaching was in a more systematic way. Under Gayatri's guidance I memorized the codified verses in the *Abhinaya Darpaṇa* and several other Sanskrit texts that describe and give the uses for different hand gestures and movements.

There is a concept in all Indian dance that derives from the idea of *bhava* (the feeling projected by the dancer in performance), and *rasa*, the spirit and essence that is apprehended by the audience and that is, in formal terms, the true realization of the performance. Intrinsic to this is mastery over the nine moods (love, humor, anger, sorrow, fear, amazement, heroism, disgust, and tranquility), or *nava rasa*.

The formalized teaching of these *rasas* is best achieved in Kathakali, another style of dance which I studied for many years with P.V. Balakrishnan. Eyes, cheeks, eyelids, mouth and nose, everything must move according to the texts. I sat opposite my teacher for hours while he supervised my training: moving my eyes in circles, figure eights, etc., in an attempt assist me in controlling my muscles.

The dominant *rasa* in Indian classical dances is *sṛṅgāra* (desire). For example, most of the *Gīta Govinda* is devoted to the romantic relationship of Rādhā and Kṛṣṇa. Rādhā, a young woman, can be interpreted as personifying the individual soul. The *Gīta Govinda* charts Rādhā's love for Kṛṣṇa and her progress through various moods of anticipation, despair, and anger, to eventual fulfillment with him. The poem forms an important element in Odissi and each mood is presented as an individual dance. Hence, this style requires the full exposition of the *aṣṭā-nāyikā* (eight heroines) repertoire: *Yahe Madhava* shows the *khaṇḍita-nāyikā* (angry), *Kuru yadunandana* shows the *svādhīnapatikā-nāyikā* (satisfied), and so on. I was fascinated by how capricious Kṛṣṇa could be. The songs of the *Gīta Govinda* are known all over India and it is a foundational text for Kṛṣṇa *bhakti*, a form of worship very prevalent in north India.

Conclusions

Through studying and performing the dance, I learned about the complexity and fluidity of Hinduism. I became fascinated with the mythology, as depicted in the dance and represented on the temples in sculpture and paintings. The dances bring to life the many stories and their variations which are found all over India. In particular, I absorbed the various ways of expressing devotion, with God, the beloved, taking the form of various deities (Śiva, Viṣṇu, Kṛṣṇa) and myself as the dancer representing or becoming the universal seeker, always trying to please the lord and receive his attention. The idea of surrender, of yearning, and of self-realization through devotion expressed through a very human form of love became second nature for me.

I also began to connect the expressive portions (*abhinaya*) with the images in stone and bronze of different deities: the various items that the deities hold, such as the deer, allude to philosophical concepts (e.g. the deer is the flitting mind, etc.). Such allusions (the deer and the axe for Śiva, the conch and discus for Viṣṇu) appear directly in the iconography and connect the dance with the symbolism associated with different gods. Through the descriptive portions of the dance I learned a great deal about Hindu myths. This inspired me to look at how these myths were shown in sculpture. The dance revealed links to different aspects of Hindu artistic culture: literature, sculpture, paintings, and mythology. As my understanding of dance progressed, the rich fabric of Hindu philosophy unfolded. The whole process seemed natural. In the beginning I was not looking for anything special, but I now know that I am blessed to participate in this unique art. Learning about Hinduism became an inevitable part of the journey, because the dance itself is deeply embedded in Hindu mythology and imbued with Hindu philosophy.

Figure 6.2 Anjali (Gaston) at Mahabalipuram, Tamil Nadu

Readings

For a comprehensive introduction to Bharata Natyam, see my *Bharata Natyam: from Temple to Theatre* (New Delhi: Manohar, 1995), while pages 15 to 34 in "Secularization and De-secularization of Indian Classical Dance," in *South Asian Horizons – Enriched by South Asia*, edited by E. Tepper and J. Wood (Ottawa: Carleton University Press, 1994) touches upon the transformation of classical Indian dance in the post-colonial period. Two other good resources on dance are Kapila Vatsyayan's *Indian Classical Dance in Literature and the Arts* (New Delhi: Sangeet Natak Academy, 1968), and Indira V. Peterson and Davesh Soneji's *Performing Pasts: Reinventing the Arts in Modern South India* (New Delhi: Oxford University Press, 2008). As the title suggests, my article "Men in Bharata Natyam," in *Interfacing Nations: Indo/Pakistani/Canadian Reflections on the 50th Anniversary of India's Independence*, Rita Chowdhari Tremblay *et al.* (eds) (Delhi: B.R Publishing Corporation, 1998), pp. 61–68, discusses the role of men in this dance tradition, while the place of women is explored in "Dance and the Hindu Woman – Bharata Natyam Re-ritualized," in *Roles and Rituals for Hindu Women*, Julia Leslie (ed.) (London: Pinter, 1991). I examine the relationship of Śiva to Indian classical dance in *Śiva in Dance, Myth, and Iconography* (New Delhi: Oxford University Press, 1982) and *The Dancing Śiva*, (DVD and booklet, University of Ottawa, Cultural Horizons and Inter-Culture, 2006). Saskia C. Kersenboom-Story discusses *devadāsīs* in her book *Nityasumangali: Devadasi Tradition in South India* (New Delhi: Motilal Banarsidass, 1987), and a good study of the Odissi dance tradition is Dinath Pathy's *Rethinking Odissi* (New Delhi: Harman Publishing House, 2007).

Author

Anne-Marie Gaston holds an M.Litt. and D.Phil. from Oxford University. Portions of the work in this chapter have been published as three books: *Śiva in Dance, Myth and Iconography, Bharata Natyam: from Temple to Theatre*, and *Krishna's Musicians: Music and Music Making in the Temples of Nathdvara, Rajasthan* (Manohar). She is an internationally recognized performer in several East Indian dance styles: Bharata Natyam, Odissi, Kuchipudi, Kathakali, and Chhau. All of her training has been in India over many years and she is invited regularly to perform there. Also a choreographer and photographer, she creates mixed media theatrical events: dance, video, images, and text using a variety of universal themes: environment (*Buddha and the Tree of Life*); Greek stories (*Athena-Brahmini, Demeter and Persephone*); Japanese Noh plays (*Tree Soul, Rain Dragon, Lady Aoi*); as well as cross-disciplinary work *Dancing Śiva, Rāmāyaṇa, Revealing the Goddess*. Her interdisciplinary work explores the inter-relationship between dance and art and has prompted her visits to most of the major artistic sites in India from the Hindu, Jain, Buddhist and Islamic traditions. She has spent a lifetime researching the artistic and performing the arts and traditions of India. She is a member of InterCulture, at the University of Ottawa and was a member of their cultural delegation to Yunnan, China in 2007. She is the artistic director of Cultural Horizons.

Chapter 7

Just my imagination?

Puzzling through a Duryodhana festival near Dharmapuri, Tamilnadu

Alf Hiltebeitel

Preamble

What is the role of imagination in fieldwork? What are its limits? When do we bracket it? There are plenty of times where the fieldwork situation is a cooperative and artful venture among researchers and the people who are being studied. But what about the times when the researchers and those being studied both want, for perhaps different reasons, to leave things unspoken? These questions are all compounded in a situation where the fieldwork is about a festival whose rituals refer to a story everybody knows, but knows in different ways. This chapter is about such a situation. The "principal investigator," namely me, knows the "great epic of India," the *Mahābhārata*, both as a classical Sanskrit text and as a story ritualized. I have seen it reenacted in festival dramas in a genre called *terukkūttu* ("street drama"), and narrated by storytellers at Tamil festivals for Draupadī, the epic's chief heroine, whose temples and festivals celebrate her as a goddess. My two fieldwork companions and Tamil interpreters, whom you will meet, also know these "versions" of the *Mahābhārata*, both from their own background and from reading on the subject. What kind of imaginings come into play when this trio seeks to learn about a festival not for Draupadī but for Duryodhana, the villain of "the same" *Mahābhārata* story? More puzzling, who would imagine telling the *Mahābhārata* around Duryodhana as Cāmi, [a] God? Incidentally, a nominal familiarity with the story of the *Mahābhārata* is useful when reading this chapter. As has already surfaced in its title, this essay has a refrain from a song by The Temptations. While doing this stint of fieldwork, the tune and words—Is this "just my imagination, running away with me?"— ran repeatedly through my head.

In April and May 2002, after four years of preparatory fieldwork, I finally got to see the Duryodhana festival at T. Kuliyanur village near Dharmapuri town in northwestern Tamilnadu. My narrative centers on fieldwork events during this festival, which is held around Duryodhana's outdoor temple in the cane fields of an estate in fertile lands that extend up into a horseshoe-shaped valley ringed by mountains. The village, called T. Kuliyanur, is adjacent to, east of, and uphill from P. Kuliyanur, and these two village units function interactively for Duryodhana's festival. P. Kuliyanur has two Draupadī temples—for present purposes, the old and the new. The older one supplies the location or proximity for several of the Duryodhana festival's main ceremonies. Duryodhana seems to traverse the two Kuliyanurs as if they were one. As is typical of rural Hindu festivals, they may draw on cooperation involving a network of villages.

Narrative

My narrative, which takes up the bulk of my article, is structured in three sections. I begin by writing about looking for Kauravas, and then I move on to my description of Kaurava Country and its King for a Day. Finally I discuss the Periyantavar-Duryodhana Festival. That last section presents an extensive description of the Periyantavar-Duryodhana festival subdivided into many parts. Because of the thrust of the chapter, I embed discussion within the narrative, sometimes in the form of glosses. As the title of my chapter indicates, I describe how I frequently encountered comments by religious practitioners, or witnessed ritual activities that evoked, in my mind, symbolic connections to episodes in the *Mahābhārata*. Some set me, and my field-assistants, on wild-goose chases. At other times, I simply could not get from the religious specialists or participants any confirmation of my interpretive hunches. Was it "just my imagination?"

Looking for Kauravas

I headed toward the house in P. Kuliyanur of Perama Goundar, a man I had learned would be knowledgeable on the Duryodhana festival. Along the way what should I see but the unmistakable early-morning preparations for the culminating rites of a Draupadī festival: the construction of a big prone mud effigy of Duryodhana on the ritual battlefield called the "dying field." As a heroine, Draupadī is the wife of the five Pāṇḍava brothers, the epic's heroes, who defeat and kill Duryodhana and his Kaurava brothers (the Pāṇḍavas' cousins) to recover their kingdom from them. Draupadī festivals reenact the epic story around her, and typically culminate in these rites. Since Draupadī wants revenge against Duryodhana for humiliating her, Duryodhana's effigy is fashioned to represent him in his dying posture so that an actor or icon impersonating Draupadī can mount triumphantly on his chest and put up her hair. Draupadī will thereby rebraid her hair after wearing it disheveled for thirteen years since the Kauravas dragged her by the hair when they abused her. I had seen numerous such rites before, and did not expect anything new. But since the celebration was gathering steam, I opted to see the ritual sequence of the "dying field" and subsequent firewalk for the first time in 12 years—before, that is, trying to find Perama Goundar.

Once the ceremony started, I met with a surprise. Alongside Duryodhana's effigy on the west was a group of about 30 women performing "dying field" dances like nothing I had ever seen before. In yellow saris, hair mostly loose, some bore garlands across their chests in the way young men do at Draupadī cult sword-pressing rituals. Carefully interspaced and each rooted, as it were, to her spot, the women moved in rhythms of possession. They moved their hands above their heads sometimes joining one hand's palm to another woman's back, sometimes striking aggressive postures with hands thrust ahead. And they seemed to be lamenting. My field assistant S. Ravindran asked a Dalit girl named Devi who was standing next to him on the edge of the crowd (where she may have felt excluded from participating), "Why are the women possessed?" And Devi answered, "They are all women of the Kaurava household." This simple response set me on a long, intriguing, and not entirely futile, exploration.

Now, at that time, I was interested in the women of the Kaurava household as the subjects of a kind of surreptitious subplot in both the Sanskrit *Mahābhārata* and the Draupadī cult *Mahābhārata*. As the epic text tells it, the Kauravas, led by Duryodhana, are all slain in the war, but their widows had not entered the cremation fires of their deceased husbands to become *satīs*. Thus Vyāsa, a significant character within the epic (and its author), devised a strategy to relieve them of their grief and relieve the victorious Pāṇḍava king of having these widows of his slaughtered enemies complicate life in his capital. Vyāsa invited the widows and others to proceed to the river Ganga, and from its waters he resurrected all the slain warriors, with celestial bodies and apparel. Husbands and wives enjoyed each other's company for a single

Figure 7.1 Dancing 'women of the Kaurava household'

night, as if in heaven. When the night ended, Vyāsa dismissed the dead back to the river, and to the worlds from which they came. He told the women (mainly the Kaurava widows) that if they plunged into the Ganga, they would rejoin their husbands in the worlds that they had attained. The "chaste women" did as they were advised, and (in a sort of watery *satī*) vanished into the waters to join their husbands.

Some Draupadī cult storytellers tell a comparable story about the firewalk in which the god Kṛṣṇa, a friend, ally, and advisor of the Pāṇḍavas, is credited with a similar ruse to deal with the Kaurava widows. He had Draupadī, who was mythically born from her father's fire sacrifice, lure them into the firepit, through which Kṛṣṇa knew she could walk unscathed. As the widows danced through the fire, they saw their deceased husbands calling them, saying, "Come here. Don't be in karmapuri. Come to dharmapuri." However, when they entered the fire, they all perished. Since this story is told in an area southeast of Dharmapuri, I assumed that it would also be known in the Dharmapuri District. When I heard that Devi had described the dancing women at the ritual as "women of the Kaurava household," I took this as confirmation of my hunch. But since then, I have found nothing to support my idea. My narrative illustrates repeatedly how one can doggedly pursue mistaken notions during fieldwork, meet with several dead ends, and yet come upon valuable, albeit different discoveries. No one in Dharmapuri District seems to know a story of the Kaurava widows following Draupadī across fire. Neither the town nor the district named Dharmapuri is the dharmapuri that is not karmapuri.

Yet Devi's words surely meant something. If people didn't know the myth, perhaps it had resurfaced in this Draupadī ritual with the myth displaced or forgotten? But this line of inquiry led nowhere: no one involved in the Draupadī festival, other than Devi, it seemed, considered the women to be the Kaurava widows. But perhaps I would find the Kaurava widows at the Duryodhana festival? Even if the hypothesis about the Kaurava widows was being uncooperative, I was determined to pursue it no matter my misgivings as to the value of doggedness. There will be more on this idea in closing.

Even though I have not found the myth of luring the Kaurava widows over fire in Dharmapuri District, the presence of a temple there for Duryodhana is enough for us to keep another question alive: Is this Kaurava country? I wish to be clear that I mean no disrespect to the district or its inhabitants by that question. Kaurava country would merely suggest a place that celebrates not only the winners' epic but the losers' epic. Would one find more sympathy there for the defeated? From here on, my narrative is a strategy to describe features of the Duryodhana festival through various interpretations that I imagined were suggested by features in the rituals. Though I would not find Kaurava widows, imagining them would still have some productive results.

Kaurava country and its "king for a day"

After seeing the "dying field" and firewalking rites at the new Draupadī temple in the morning, I found Perama Goundar that afternoon and learned that Duryodhana is his clan deity. He thinks the Duryodhana temple was founded by his third or fourth grandfather. Further information was provided by Murugan, the priest and founder of the new Draupadī temple, who also serves at the old Draupadī temple and the Duryodhana temple, and is actually a member of the clan worshipping Duryodhana. According to Murugan, the old Draupadī temple *was* in P. Kuliyanur when Draupadī gave the ancestors permission to worship Duryodhana and instructions in how to do so: They should worship him, she said, for only a day since his laws last only a day. This description of Duryodhana as "king for a day" also serves as a joke about him in Dharmapuri area *Mahābhārata* folk dramas. There Duryodhana sits dispensing justice in his court when two plaintiffs come to him about a land case, and the jester character tells them his laws last only for a day. Duryodhana is thus someone like the Asura Bali in Kerala, who likewise rules for a day during his festival of Onam.

Whatever his laws may be that last only for a day, Duryodhana has more lasting qualities as well. The drama troupes that circulate in Dharmapuri District are a rich source on this subject. At T. Kuliyanur, one or another of these troupes typically concludes the Duryodhana festival with a one-night engagement to perform the play "Eighteenth-Day War," in which Duryodhana's death ends the *Mahābhārata* war. According to two of the actors who had just concluded this play at the 2002 festival, "Duryodhana is not a bad person. He just listened to others. He had wealth. He was never bad. Even if you give fire to his hands, he doesn't know how to throw that away"—that is, according to my associate in this fieldwork, Perundevi Srinivasan, even if you do something bad to him, he will not return it. He is known for his *dharma* and for a "line of giving" in the palm of his hand. As the actors explained further, with reference to an episode in the epic, "Duryodhana takes heaps of treasure giving them away to people, thinking that if he gives them away to three or four people the treasure would dwindle. But it did not happen. As he was taking heaps of treasure with his hands, the treasures were growing. Duryodhana doesn't know fraud. He's a just person."

Duryodhana's birth and death also take on features that seem unique to Dharmapuri District. About his birth, dramatists and others tell a story that I have not heard outside this district. They describe how Duryodhana emerged at birth with a bronze body, and would have been indestructible. But Kṛṣṇa intervened to get Duryodhana's mother, Gāndhārī, to put a cord around his waist. This left everything below that point to grow only as flesh. Kṛṣṇa would eventually reveal this "vital point" to the Pāṇḍava hero, Bhīma, who delivers the blow to Duryodhana's thigh that kills him. In the enactment of Duryodhana's killing on the "dying field," the Bhīma actor clubs Duryodhana's earthen effigy's right thigh with his mace to release the blood that is used to rebraid Draupadī's hair. But what about Duryodhana's torso and head: is it still of bronze? Is it still immortal? At the new Draupadī temple's "dying field" there is a lovely touch, which, if it does not point in this direction, suggests something similar, namely the immortality or longevity of Duryodhana. Sometime since my first visit in 1998, Murugan had planted a banyan sapling to grow exactly beside Duryodhana's—that is his effigy's—left shoulder. Asked whether it has any correspondence with Duryodhana, Murugan replied, "His family is a big one! His crowd asked him, 'Being the "chief" of the family, can you tell us how many of you there are in your family?' Duryodhana replied, 'You can even count the shoots of a banyan tree but you cannot count us. To that extent the country belongs to me.' " As we have seen, Murugan belongs to Duryodhana's "crowd" and is now his priest as well as Draupadī's. Although his answer linked the banyan to the longevity of Duryodhana's lineage, it did not forge an explicit connection with Duryodhana's immortal upper body.

Meanwhile, once the drama troupe that performs "Eighteenth-Day War" at Duryodhana's festival has taken its intermission at daybreak and moved the audience from the stage to the "dying field" behind the *old* Draupadī temple, Duryodhana is given a last request, one that is pertinent essentially to his own temple and festival only, and to his identity as Periyantavar. As Perama Goundar first described this boon to me, "When Duryodhana was about to die, he asked Kṛṣṇa, 'What about me? You always favored the Pāṇḍavas. What happens to me after I die?' Kṛṣṇa says, 'You will be worshipped in Kali Yuga under the name Periyantavar, and if you accept that, you will have a place as a deity.' He comes back as a god." This story explains how Duryodhana becomes a god, and everyone involved in his festival seems to know some version of it. All of Duryodhana's main celebrants are members of the Vanniyar caste, which uses the surname "Goundar." Broadly, Vanniyars are classified as a Śūdra caste: the lowest of the four castes, but above Dalits. But they claim originally to have been warriors (Kṣatriyas). They are the Draupadī cult's main adherents, and in this locale, they worship both Draupadī and Duryodhana in recollection of their martial heritage.

Periyantavar-Duryodhana festival

Periyantavar is thus not Duryodhana *per se*, but Duryodhana having returned as a god. We know that he is a god by Kṛṣṇa's blessing, and that he rules only for a day by the consent of Draupadī because his laws last only that long. What laws these are we may be better able to imagine after looking at his festival. I limit myself to two things: first, an outline of the key features of the T. Kuliyanur Periyantavar festival in the month of Cittirai; and second, an approximation of my mental fieldwork notes in the form of a gloss on points where Periyantavar persists in reminding us of Duryodhana. Fifteen days of fasting are mentioned between Cittirai 1 and the well-digging on Cittirai 15, and one can count three days on which the main events of the festival occur, which begin on Cittirai 15 in the evening.

Day 1 (Cittirai 1 [late April]): Coming of Cāmi and closing of the village

1. ***Coming of Cāmi.*** Cāmi ["God," that is Duryodhana] comes in a dream to a potter and some men in certain Goundar families and tells them that the festival has to be celebrated.
2. ***Closing of the village.*** After this no one may wear shoes in the village. No SCs ("Scheduled Castes" or Dalits) are allowed inside it. According to a Goundar

woman named Saroja, some SCs participate in the firewalk at the new Draupadī temple, but they will not enter the village from the first day of Cittirai until the Periyantavar festival is over: "It is only our people," she explained. After that, they may come to worship Periyantavar at his temple. Vow-takers begin fasting: they have no relations with women. The two lead ritualists, Manoharan and Raja, emphasize that even the smallest violation will result in the vow-takers being cut during the sword-pressing. There should not be impurity, and they should not take non-vegetarian meals during this period.

Sunday evening after nightfall (Cittirai 15)

1. ***First sword-cutting.*** Near the old Draupadī temple is a boundary site for Periyantavar's temple marked by a tree. According to Murugan it is Periyantavar's "first place," but there is nothing special about the tree. Murugan invites Cāmi for sword-cutting. Three swords are used. One is the village's general sword and is kept at the old Draupadī temple, and the other two belong hereditarily to specific families of the Vanniyar clan involved in these rites. Keeping pure for the 18 days, the "sword-cutters" press the sword blades to their chests and shoulders, and must receive Cāmi's grace to keep from injury. Eventually, three men break out, each with one sword, and race through the dark fields to stab the sword in the ground at the spot where Cāmi leads them—a spot in the cane fields about 30 yards northwest of Duryodhana's temple. The lead well-finder is Manoharan, whose family is in charge from this point to the eye-opening rite.

   Gloss: There is, according to Manoharan, no connection between the sword pressers and the *Mahābhārata*. They are not—it was just my imagination—Duryodhana's resurrected army, or any three warriors thereof. Cāmi simply desires the new water to be used in cooking the sweet rice pongal for the offerings that will be made to him.

2. ***Well-digging.*** About 20 men who should have fasted by not eating "non-veg," sleeping away from their places, and having no relations with women since Cittirai 1, begin to dig the well that will yield natural pure water. Since women menstruate, none may be at the site.

Gloss: Is it just my imagination that the well could have anything to do with the lake in which Duryodhana hides himself before emerging for his final duel—a scene that would be familiar from the next night's drama?

Monday (Cittirai 16)

1. ***Mud cones for the Kauravas, a shed for the Pāṇḍavas.*** Behind the Periyantavar temple, still that night but counted as early the next morning (at about 4 a.m.), ground is cleared and string measurements are made for the precise geometric

construction of two east-facing "houses": one southwest of Periyantavar for the Kauravas, the other northwest of him for the Pāṇḍavas. The Kaurava house is then made of rows of small mud cones called *pommai* (effigy, puppet, or doll) freshly formed and arranged into two east-opening square rooms. Expecting 148 pommai from talking to Perama Goundar, I counted 169. Asked about these numbers, Murugan said, "I didn't say 148. It is 108. They build a house. After 108 they draw a line. People will say, 'They have left someone out.'" Questioned further, he continued, "Their number cannot be counted. Up to 99 they are counted and a line is drawn. If it is asked, it is replied that the others are sons or grandsons or granddaughters. It cannot be said how many were born to how many." A hundred and eight is a conventional totality number, while 99 would seem to suggest Duryodhana's brothers. Four years earlier, in 1998, Murugan had mentioned 108 when explaining about Duryodhana. He said that Duryodhana is Rāvaṇa, the notorious demon of the Rāmāyaṇa epic, reborn. However, he is now with 10 times Rāvaṇa's 10 heads in the form of the hundred-headed Kauravas, and thus—whatever the number of *pommai*—"they are all Periyantavar." Still holding to that story, he now comments, "The mud forms are made and destroyed on the same day. And this festival is nothing but first creating him and then destroying him the same day." Alternately, the *pommai* are Duryodhana and his brothers (according to Perama Goundar).

Meanwhile, the shed for the Pāṇḍavas is sided and roofed with thatched palm, with five small stones inside representing the Pāṇḍavas *and* Draupadī (in Perama Goundar's words, the Pāṇḍavas "include Draupadī") and an offering stone in front.

Gloss: As noted, the Pāṇḍavas and Kauravas now get along at the Periyantavar temple. The indeterminacy of the *pommai* indicates that there is room in the

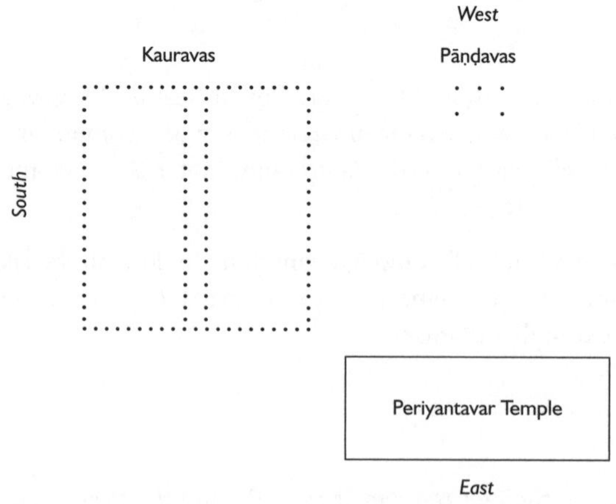

Figure 7.2 House of the Kauravas, represented by a hundred or more earthen cones, a shed for the Pāṇḍavas, and platform of the open-air Periyantavar temple.

Kaurava house for both the Kauravas (i.e., Duryodhana and his brothers) and their descendants (the lineages of Vanniyars that worship Duryodhana as Periyantavar, and who are also now represented in the leaves of the banyan tree at the new Draupadī temple). Daughters, or at least granddaughters, are mentioned as well, and wives "are included," as with Draupadī, but only if one asks about them. Once again, it was just my imagination conjuring up the symbolic presence of women of the royal households (Pāṇḍava and Kaurava) in the surplus *pommai*. Evidently, this is not a place to look for the Kaurava widows.

2. ***Further sword-cutting, baskets, and Periyantavar possesses Manoharan.*** Between about 9 and 11 a.m., the three swords are worshipped: first, the two of them at the houses in P. Kuliyanur where they are kept through the year. Then they are brought out and handled again for more sword-cutting before the tree near the old Draupadī temple. There, clan families bring large offering-baskets containing coconuts, rice flour, plantains, and sweetened water in fresh pots, all covered by margosa leaves, and place them on the ground. Again there is sword-cutting, which this time culminates in Periyantavar's possession of Manoharan: a vivid and exceptional empowerment in which Manoharan slithers low to the ground dragging one leg behind him before doing his own sword-cutting. The baskets are then taken about a mile across the fields to the Periyantavar temple. A VIP, an important Goundar of the village, leads, carrying the basket of the village, and is followed by the chief person who presses the swords, Manoharan. At each scene, when the sword-cutting is finished, and in particular at the tree representing Duryodhana's place near the temple, when the baskets are carried off on heads, people—mainly women and, at the tree, infants—lie face down on the ground to allow the procession to cross over them. This is done for relief from illnesses.

   Gloss: I found it irresistible not to think that Manoharan's leg-dragging movement would recall Duryodhana's broken leg. This impression was reinforced by a report I knew of from Kerala where, at a Quilon temple at which the Kauravas are "Mountain Gods," the priest, possessed by Duryodhana, dances on one leg for hours at the annual festival, recalling the fracturing of Duryodhana's leg by the Pāṇḍava Bhīma. Yet as interpreters, we were determined not to let our expected findings affect the outcome of the inquiry. It was thus important not to prompt such an answer, and in this my fieldwork companions had greater discipline than I. Here are the two main conversations that resulted.

PERUNDEVI: Someone walked very slowly at last. Why? Who descended into him, was it Periyantavar or Draupadī?

MURUGAN: It is Periyantavar. Periyantavar is a spirit, and these people belong to him. They are from his family. They desire to cut swords and for that they fast. Periyantavar descends into them one by one. The one who came last, if he cuts the sword, then we can all start to the festival place. That man is very important to Periyantavar.

Figure 7.3 Manoharan dragging his leg when possessed by Duryodhana-Periyantavar

PERUNDEVI: Does he always come last?

MURUGAN: Always. His father also came like that. His name is Manoharan. Everybody cuts swords with enthusiasm, but everybody who cuts swords cannot just run like that. This man who comes last does that.

ALF: Is there any relationship between the slow way he walked and Duryodhana?

MURUGAN: It is the spirit, and Periyantavar and Duryodhana are one and the same. He was just watching how other people cut swords. When he slowly came towards the tree, maybe another person who has the spirit should descend and slowly invite him to the place. And when he walks slowly, the crowd makes a lot of noise.

PERUNDEVI: And who descended into those who were inviting this man to the tree?

MURUGAN: It is also Periyantavar. If some 10,000 come to our place, we can make them sit down. But do we ask 10,000 to talk? We ask only one to talk to us.

One could go no further. When S. Ravindran interviewed Manoharan himself along with Raja Goundar, we seemed to get closer:

RAVI: When you do this sword-cutting, one of your legs is in a different fashion, but others don't do that. Your grace is different. Is there any reason?

MANOHARAN: To me the grace is huge and nobody can go like that.

RAJA: Cāmi comes like that and takes him along like that.

MANOHARAN: Cāmi stands on his single leg.
RAVI: Oh, is that so?
MANOHARAN: When that situation comes, it changes from two legs to one leg.
RAVI: Is there any specific reason for that?
MANOHARAN: No such reason.
RAVI: Oh, the Cāmi looks after that. You said you get huge grace. Did your father also get this much grace?
MANOHARAN: Yes. In my family it is like that.

This time, I can only ask: is it once again just my imagination that when, as Manoharan puts it, "Cāmi stands on his single leg," Manoharan would have behind his thoughts "that situation" or "place" where the Duryodhana actor "changes from two legs to one" on the "dying field"? That situation would be when, in various "dying field" enactments I had witnessed, Duryodhana, his thigh broken, stands on one leg while learning that the Pāndavas had not been killed as they slept soundly after their victory celebration, as Duryodhana had hoped. Instead, it was the Pāndavas' children, his own nephews, who had been slain. If so, Manoharan simply cannot or will not admit it. As Perundevi remarks, Manoharan may not be able to admit consciously what he does unconsciously. Or perhaps he is playing the same ethnographic game of avoiding interpreter effect that we are. That is, one often has the sense that both parties to an ethnographic exchange know what each other is up to, and that our interlocutors may sometimes structure their responses to leave certain matters unstated. When we sense that possibility, it is best, of course, to respect it.

3. *Eye-opening of horse at the "village shed."* Only after the baskets are brought to the Periyantavar temple can the horse now come into the festival. Halfway from P. Kuliyanur to the Periyantavar temple is a spot called the "village shed," although there is no shed there—just a deep open well and a grove with a neem tree. To this spot the potter brings the festival's chief clay horse, sets it facing east, ritually opens its eyes with a knife behind a cloth screen, and then goes away. The ritual is called "calling Cāmi" or "giving life." Manoharan helps to decorate the horse for the eye-opening, but from here on Kunji Goundar—the person Periyantavar possesses, enabling him to carry the heavy horse on his head—takes over as chief ritualist. Again, once Cāmi is given life and his eyes are opened, there is sword-cutting, now led by Raja Goundar, and again mainly women lie face down to allow Cāmi to walk over them—with Cāmi now for the first time in the form of a horse: he is the rider, horse, and possessor of Kunji Goundar who carries the horse. According to one understanding, "Cāmi (i.e., Duryodhana) will roam the village and the temple area and no one should be there in the vicinity of the temple or the field. Thus once a year he roams for one night; he just goes and sees the village, and comes back. And that is what I was told by my grandfather."

Gloss: Duryodhana is free for a night to roam the village, and now does so ritually by possessing a horse. Should we imagine some kind of residual connection with a Vedic horse sacrifice, in which a horse set free to wander for a year represents the king, for whom it will then be sacrificed after it is returned to the capital? Perhaps, but again there is no explicit confirmation of that imagined connection. According to Murugan, Duryodhana's connection with the horse signifies that "he is the king of Hāstinapuram"—the city where he ruled. Embodying his rule for a day, and thus the power to enact his one-day laws, the horse enables Duryodhana to roam for a day that runs through the night of the play named "Eighteenth-Day War," in which he dies again, and at which, unlike all other places in the village, it is a good and safe place to be—the drama is performed at the old Draupadī temple. The calling of a deity in connection with a horse—often a real horse—is common at rural Tamil festivals.

4. ***Running off ghosts.*** Having been taken briefly to a nearby Hanumān temple, Cāmi (that is, the horse) is carried only about 50 yards southwest to the stretch of field where his most centrally framed and most dramatic ritual now takes place. It is Cāmi's culminating action before he reaches his own temple. The action is called "running off ghosts." There is no name for the stretch of field on which it takes place. But since people—again, mainly women—lie face down on the ground and form a way or path for Cāmi (his horse) to cross over them, it was natural for me to think of it as analogous to the Draupadī cult "dying field." The stretch of field, bare and left unsown, is about 70 yards long and 10 yards wide. The ground has been prepared on the previous night by Murugan and his entourage, who spread sacred ash along its boundaries "so that," as he puts it, "whoever comes inside the boundary, if she or he has any 'black or dark wind' (a term for 'ghost,' suggesting the 'wind of a dark spirit') it will go away." The ghost will be literally nailed to the trunk of a large tamarind tree that stands in a thicket about forty yards east of the stretch's north end. If a woman gets possessed while the horse crosses over her, the ghost will reveal itself in a lock of her disheveled hair that she may grab out from the rest. That lock—the ghost—will be nailed to the tree trunk and then cut off and left there by the exorcists who have led the possessed woman to the tree, often with a good deal of coercion, by whipping and pulling her by the strand of hair in which the ghost has thus revealed itself.

According to Murugan, the hair comes into the picture because "it is the hair that dances/moves." He adds that although the ghost resides throughout the body and drinks its blood, causing anemia, "The spirit that is inside the body comes up in wrath and resides in the hair. The lock is not picked up by the exorcist; it is picked up by the woman herself. The hand is part of the body and only the hand picks the lock of hair. *We* don't pick it up … ." I was told that as many as 500 women come for this ceremony, and there were certainly at least 200 in 2002.

Gloss: This stretch of unnamed field can be imagined as a kind of inversion of the Draupadī cult's ritual "dying field." There Duryodhana's effigy lies face up, dead, for Draupadī to cross over, stand on, and tie up her hair. Draupadī's icon, as her chariot, may actually cross the Duryodhana effigy from foot to crown, crossing over the groin. Here, in reverse, is a kind of battlefield on which Duryodhana, reborn, combats ghosts by walking over face-down women (and some men) to relieve them of being haunted and to improve their lives. Moreover, whereas Draupadī ties up her disheveled hair into a knot on Duryodhana's death effigy using his thigh blood as her hair oil, his ribs for a comb, and his intestines for her garland, here a reborn Duryodhana chases off ghosts when his exorcists nail knotted locks of women's disheveled hair to a tree trunk. We could call it Duryodhana's revenge. But that is not the rite's spirit. Duryodhana is Cāmi, God, and his exorcisms are a blessing. Once possession is relieved, Cāmi's grace can descend on those who have been possessed as they make their way to his temple. Moreover, this grace has already descended on Kunji Goundar carrying the horse, on men who continue to perform sword-cutting in front of the horse, and on the priest and male exorcists. Asked by Perundevi, "Oh, so people (lying down) don't get grace there, is that right?" Murugan replied, "No, *only we* get grace there. Those are only ghosts."

Clearly, there are questions not only of direct but of indirect coercion of the participants. It is widely acknowledged that male ghosts bother women, particularly pretty women. They also especially bother girls who become problems to their parents before marriage by wearing makeup and other allures, and wives who become problems for their husbands and the houses into which they marry. Similarly for men, if a ghost catches a man, according to Murugan, "It is called Mohinī; it charms males and makes them mental cases; these are all matters of black magic; the men resort to beating their wives and creating trouble in their family."

In general, it is denied that anyone is forced to undergo these rites. Perundevi alludes to such matters in this way:

PERUNDEVI: The question is, women are being walked over. How can their bodies stand all this?

MURUGAN: At that time, they don't have self-consciousness.

PERUNDEVI: They walked for a long time. The horse didn't go all at once at a stretch. It was walking over some 10 people, then it would come back.

MURUGAN: They won't be aware of the weight. They won't know that they are being trampled on. Only if there was any spirit or spirit-wind, it will come out as the body is trampled. After coming out of the place, they would ask, "What happened? What did they do? My legs are aching, my arms are aching, my chest is aching ..."

PERUNDEVI: Does the pain then go away?

MURUGAN: It gets better after an afternoon or two. After a good sleep. If there is no "black wind," they will not be trampled, right? People do not lie down only for "black wind." Some do it because of tiredness, or the evil eye. They lie down because they think, "If it is a ghost, let the horse trample! Even not, then also let it trample." It is the peoples' wish to lie across.

"Tiredness" references a particular source of possession that may come from Mūtevi, a sleep-goddess who makes people yawn, get irritable, and grow lazy and useless around the house.

It is crucial to emphasize that all the women I saw taken to the tamarind tree had other women—friends and usually older family members—moving beside them, keeping watch on them, helping them from the side, and eventually guiding them as they made their first steps away from the tree back to their "real" social world, beginning with the temple. Clearly, it is especially at this segment of the festival that Duryodhana's laws of the day are most in evidence. They are laws by which the clan works out interpersonal problems. Two statements best reflect this. As Saroja put it to Perundevi in explaining the closing of the village to Dalits, "It is only our people." And as one man angrily put it to me in what was a difficult but also revelatory moment while I was watching these ceremonies (indeed, recording them with a videographer and photographing them myself), "You are seeing our women." Blundering on as the categorical outsider, the fieldworker can be reminded that he is an intruder.

Finally, this is evidently another place not to look for the Kaurava widows. The exorcisms are for unmarried girls and younger married women. But logically, would there not be affinities in the ways they, like the Kaurava widows, are brought into line?

5. ***Celebrations at the temple and the Kaurava and Pāṇḍava "houses".*** For about an hour and a half in the late afternoon, it is a scene of considerable commotion and high energy, with varieties of food preparation and preliminary eating. According to Murugan, "Food is offered and the baskets are placed in front of Duryodhana, for he is the king." The food is at once offered to the king and offered for him as well for him to gift it away. Near the Kaurava house, goats, pigs, and cocks are sacrificed to be eaten later at home. And using new water from the freshly dug well, 10 headmen cook pongal (sweetened milk-boiled rice) inside "the Kaurava house." The Pāṇḍavas receive pongal and a gourd. In front of their shrine or house, numerous men and women come to be whipped across their upraised arms: an act of devotion through which grace may come. According to Murugan, the Pāṇḍavas "are the just ones, and they will remove our sickness and sin" (the last word, in English). That is, the Kauravas and Pāṇḍavas now work together, and people circulate between their two houses for complementary reasons. Worshippers also come to the temple to receive sacred ash. Another feature: mortars, pestles, conch shells, and a kind of hand bell or rattle are placed on the ground in the Kaurava house.

Gloss: According to Murugan, these things are for Duryodhana as king, and are emblematic of his authority. The conches and rattles are musical instruments: "that is how as a king he goes inside the town." Perhaps they prepare him for his appearance that night on the drama stage. And the mortar and pestle he uses for divine cooking: "Cāmis also eat, right?" Murugan also noted that the mortar and pestle are often cited in an adage that temples should be built in places where their sounds are not heard. Again, it was just my imagination that the pestle could have something to do with the Tamil story of the Kauravas' birth, in which the interminably pregnant Gāndhārī, their mother, finally beat her womb with a pestle to give birth to them.

6. *Tonsure and ear-piercing.* While all this is going on, in and around the temple children receive tonsure and ear-piercing, as is typical at "clan deity" festivals. Boys are named temporarily after Periyantavar and girls after his wife Periyantacci.

7. *Beginning of "Eighteenth-Day War".* The play starts that evening, around 10 p.m.

Tuesday (Cittirai 17)

Conclusion of "Eighteenth-day War" and "dying field" rites for the death of Duryodhana. It is the Draupadī icon from the old Draupadī temple whose hair is knotted on his effigy. Basically, this is the end of the festival.

Concluding discussion

As we have just learned, Duryodhana reborn as Periyantavar ("the Big God") has a wife named Periyantacci ("the Big Lady"). In April 2001, T. Kuliyanur was the venue not of a Periyantavar festival but, for the first time in 60 years, a Periyantacci festival, and since then, the two festivals have alternated from year to year. Periyantacci is the "clan deity" of Vanniyar branches in nearby villages who have an intermarrying relationship with Periyantavar's people.

Figure 7.4 Hiltebeitel outside T. Kuliyanur Draupadī temple, with Perundevi in foreground to his right, and with Murugan's father and Murugan immediately to his left.

Periyantacci is Duryodhana's wife once he has become Periyantavar. But Duryodhana was always a married man, and his wife's Tamil name is Peruntiruvaḷ, not Periyantacci. Draupadī festivals in the Dharmapuri area place a much stronger emphasis on Peruntiruvaḷ's lamentations for Duryodhana than is done elsewhere. Elsewhere, the scene is parodic: a mock lament accentuating the reversal of fortunes between Peruntiruvaḷ and Draupadī. But in Dharmapuri District, it can be performed as a serious expression of Peruntiruvaḷ's grief that enlists the sympathies of local women who come forth to give the Peruntiruvaḷ actor money.

Now if Periyantacci is Peruntiruvaḷ, she would have her prior identity as a Kaurava widow! At last! But for now, even this remains an inchoate story: I have heard that Peruntiruvaḷ became a *satī*; I have also heard that she lived out the rest of her life. But I have not heard that Draupadī led her across the fire, and I no longer expect to. I no longer expect to find the Kaurava widows in the places I had imagined. That is because I believe I now understand what the young Dalit girl Devi had in mind when watching the possessed women dancing on the "dying field" at the new Draupadī temple. When she said, "They are all women of the Kaurava household," she probably meant women of the group of families that have Duryodhana as their family deity—and not women portraying Kaurava widows: a simple solution that eluded us for over four years. If the former interpretation is what Devi actually meant, it would have been a shrewd observation. As a Dalit, Devi would not have been excluded from the subsequent firewalk at that temple. But she would have been excluded from all the ceremonies for Duryodhana as Periyantavar. Standing on the edge of the watching crowd at the new Draupadī temple's "dying field" dances, where we encountered her, she would not have been excluded technically from these funerary rites for Duryodhana. The new Draupadī temple observes no exclusions by caste or religion. But she probably still felt excluded. This is because the "dying field" is more a place for rites hereditary to participating Vanniyars than is the firewalk, where some Dalits, like herself, and Muslims more easily join in. To her, the "dying field" thus probably felt somewhat akin to the Dalit-excluding rites done for Periyantavar.

As is clear by now, we were never able to do a follow-up interview with Devi to enable us to find out what she really meant. For better or worse, some things must be left to the imagination—and it is for the worse, I suppose, if we want to leave no loose ends. But it is also for the better because it keeps us coming back to the heart of the fieldwork experience: learning more and more from research on the ground through repeated visits, and then making of it what we can in writing.

Readings

For the "interpreter effect in fieldwork," see Gerald D. Bereman, *Behind Many Masks: Ethnography and Impression Management in a Himalayan Village* (Ithaca, NY: Society for Applied Anthropology, 1962). See Madeleine Biardeau, *Stories about Posts: Vedic Variations around the Hindu Goddess,* Alf Hiltebeitel, Marie-Louise Reiniche, and James Walker (trans.), Alf Hiltebeitel and Marie-Louise Reiniche (eds) (Chicago,

IL: University of Chicago Press, 2004) regarding the horse sacrifice as reflected in both the *Mahābhārata* and Tamil ritual. On Tamil Draupadī festivals, consult Alf Hiltebeitel, *The Cult of Draupadī, vol. 1: Mythologies: From Gingee to Kurukṣetra*; *The Cult of Draupadī vol. 2: On Hindu Ritual and the Goddess* (Chicago, IL: University of Chicago Press, 1988, 1991). My article "Hair Like Snakes and Mustached Brides: Crossed Gender in an Indian Folk Cult" in Alf Hiltebeitel and Barbara D. Miller (eds) *Hair: Its Meaning and Power in Asian Cultures* (Albany, NY: State University of New York Press, 1998), pp. 143–76, deals with the deity Mohinī. A preliminary discussion of our opening and closing question about the Kaurava widows is found in my article, "Looking for the Kaurava Widows" in James Blumenthal (ed.) *Incompatible Visions: South Asian Religions in History and Culture. Essays in Honor of David M. Knipe* (Madison, WI: University of Wisconsin-Madison, 2005). An exploration of similar exorcism rituals to those done for Duryodhana is available in Isabelle Nabokov, *Religion against the Self: An Ethnography of Tamil Rituals* (New York: Oxford University Press, 2000), while Giles Tarabout's *Sacrifier et donner á voir en pays Malabar* (Paris : École Française d'Extrême Orient, 1986) discusses a festival in which Duryodhana is worshipped in Kerala.

Author

Alf Hiltebeitel's publications and research have taken him back and forth between the *Mahābhārata* and fieldwork on the south Indian Draupadī cult. From this tandem project, his work branches out into related texts, most notably the *Rāmāyaṇa*; other cults, including other Tamil *Mahābhārata* cults and ones related to other regional Indian oral epics similar to the Draupadī cult *Mahābhārata*; and into an attempt to understand the Indian concept of *dharma*, the subject of his most recent book: *Dharma* (Honolulu, HI: University of Hawai'i Press, 2010). Meanwhile, forthcoming are *Reading the Fifth Veda: Studies in the Mahābhārata, Essays by Alf Hiltebeitel*, Vol. 1; *When the Goddess Was a Woman: Mahābhārata Ethnographies, Essays by Alf Hiltebeitel*, Vol. 2 (Leiden: E. J. Brill); and *Dharma: Its Early History in Law, Religion, and Narrative* (New York: Oxford University Press, 2011).

Chapter 8

The wisdom of Kapila's cave

Sāṃkhya-Yoga as practice

Knut A. Jacobsen

Preamble

Sāṃkhya-Yoga is an ancient philosophy but also a living tradition, although currently a minor one. The most important Sāṃkhya-Yoga tradition that is active today in India, and perhaps the only one, is centered at the Kāpil Maṭh in Jharkhand in north India. Since 1991 I have met with associates and disciples of the Kāpil Maṭh who have shared their understanding of the Sāṃkhya-Yoga traditions with me. Here I describe the Kāpil Maṭh and some aspects of Sāṃkhya-Yoga as a living practice and some basic principles of the Sāṃkhya-Yoga system of religious thought. The Yoga system of religious thought originated as a school of Sāṃkhya philosophy, and the significance of the Kāpil Maṭh is that it preserves the tradition of the "original Yoga." My narrative derives from notes, memory, texts, and photographs.

Narrative

The Kāpil Maṭh

When I arrive at the Kāpil Maṭh the first sight that meets me is the brown and reddish colored gate, like a piece of art shaped as a person in meditation in the lotus position (*padmāsana*), and the mantra *ādividuṣe kapilāya namaḥ* ("homage to Kapila who was the first knower") written in Sanskrit with *devanāgarī* letters above the gate. Underneath the mantra the words *nāsti sāṃkhyasamam jñānaṃ nāsti yogasamaṃ balam* ("there is no knowledge comparable to Sāṃkhya, there is no power comparable to Yoga") are written. Although I knew enough Sanskrit to figure out its meaning, I would later discover that it was derived from the great Hindu epic, the *Mahābhārata* (12.304.2), a text which held Sāṃkhya-Yoga philosophy in high regard. In this otherwise open landscape, the gate is in a narrow street with walls on both sides. There is a gate on both walls. The gate with the mantra that pays homage to Kapila, the ancient sage who is considered the founder of the Sāṃkhya philosophy of religious thought, is the one on the left side and leads to the *kuṭi* (hut) where one or two monks stay, to the Kāpil Mandir ("temple of Kapila"), and to a building that is an artificial cave called the Kāpil *guha* ("cave of Kapila"). I already knew that the one and only entrance to the cave is permanently blocked and the swami, the leader and teacher, of the Kāpil Maṭh actually lives inside this sealed enclosure. I learn that the Kāpil cave was the first building at this holy site, while the Maṭh was built afterwards. The other gate, on the right side, leads to a building called Kāpilāyan, where lay followers of Sāṃkhya-Yoga and other visitors can stay for a shorter or longer time. A lay disciple takes me to a room where I will be staying. The room contains only a hard wooden bed and some blankets as is common in *āśramas* (places of meditation and homes of ascetics).

When I go through the gate on the left side I enter a picturesque garden. The aesthetic beauty of red, yellow and white flowers and trees giving shade characterizes the area. The garden reminds me of the description of the beautiful nature of *āśramas* found in so many Hindu texts, such as in the works of the renowned Hindu playwright and poet, Kālidāsa. In the Kāpil Maṭh's garden the same mantra *ādividuṣe kapilāya namaḥ* ("homage to Kapila who was the first knower") has been written with dark flowers in a bed of white flowers.

Several statues, monuments, and pieces of religious art surround the temple and the cave. The largest statue is of the person considered to be the founder of Sāṃkhya-Yoga, the sage Kapila. The large statue shows Kapila with several animals resting peacefully in his vicinity. I knew from previous studies that animals surrounding him signify that Kapila was perfect in *ahiṃsā*, the practice of non-injury. According to the teaching of Yoga and as is stated in the *Yogasūtra* 2.35, when a yogin is perfect in the practice of *ahiṃsā*, his surroundings also become

Figure 8.1 Entrance doorway to Kāpil Maṭh

peaceful. All beings coming near him cease to be hostile; even the animosity of animals who are natural enemies disappears, and all rest peacefully together. Kapila is also represented in a painting on the wall of the temple. Here Kapila is portrayed sitting in a teaching mode instructing another person whose back alone is visible. The disciple's position immediately orients me with him, so I feel that I too am among the students receiving instruction from Kapila. I would later learn that the painting shows the discourse (*saṃvāda*) between the sage Kapila and his student Āsuri. According to the Sāṃkhya philosophical tradition, Kapila gave his teaching to Āsuri and this marked the beginning of the Sāṃkhya *paramparā*, the lineage of Sāṃkhya teachers. The concept of *paramparā* is quite significant in the Hindu tradition, because it indicates that the current head teacher (*ācārya/guru*) holds a direct lineage of transmission of knowledge from the original founder of the philosophy. These two representations of Kapila point to the two most important dimensions of this sage: Kapila as a yogin perfect in virtue (*dharma*), knowledge (*jñāna*), detachment (*virāga*), and power (*aiśvarya*), and Kapila as a teacher of the philosophy of Sāṃkhya.

In the garden I also see two *samādhisthānas*, places of entombment of persons who have been liberated from rebirth. The *samādhisthānas* are of the founder of the Kāpil Maṭh, Swami Hariharānanda Āraṇya, and his successor Swami Dharmamegha Āraṇya. *Samādhisthānas* are constructed in memory of deceased sages and mark the places where they are buried. *Samādhisthānas* are often considered sources of power, but this is not a predominant belief at this *maṭh*. Hariharānanda Āraṇya disliked the sometimes exaggerated focus on yoga powers (*siddhis*) among many yogis, sādhus, and lay people he encountered, and he prohibited his disciples from writing his biography. One reason he gave for this prohibition was that he feared supporting the creation of a hagiography, a reverentially embellished biography, which would focus mostly on yoga powers and his person instead of the philosophy of Sāṃkhya-Yoga.

The Kāpil cave was built for Hariharānanda Āraṇya (1869–1947) by a volunteer who wanted to provide a suitable house containing an artificial cave as Āraṇya's permanent home. Hariharānanda Āraṇya spent the last 21 years of his life (from 1926–47) in the cave. The current *ācārya* took his permanent abode in the Kāpil cave in 1986 where he maintains the same lifestyle of seclusion and solitude of the two previous *ācāryas*. He has continued to spread the teaching of Sāṃkhya-Yoga. I was told that the beauty of the flower garden with its statues and monuments is to a large degree the result of his aesthetic vision.

For the gurus and the disciples of Kāpil Maṭh, Sāṃkhya-Yoga is a living philosophy, originally founded by Kapila and with a tradition of teachers from Kapila, and Āsuri, to Pañcasikha (but with no record of a continuing tradition after Pañcasikha, although names of many teachers are given in Hindu texts). However, despite this concern to affirm their lineage, the *ācāryas* have been quite detached about the propagation of Sāṃkhya-Yoga. Hinduism is mostly not a missionary religion. As I continued my research there, I noted that the early *ācāryas* also had shown little concern for the material prosperity of the monastery. Material prosperity is often seen as a cause of spiritual decline, and the establishment of monasteries is not considered necessary for the practice of spirituality. Rather the demands of the administrative functions of a monastery are detrimental for spiritual practice, argued Dharmamegha Āraṇya.

These values of solitariness and renunciation were reaffirmed when I read *A Unique Travelogue: An Allegorical Exploration of Spirituality and Yoga*, a book that is partly fiction and partly autobiographical, written by Hariharānanda Āraṇya. In it, he made a case for the value of solitude and describes Sāṃkhya-Yoga forms of meditation and various wisdom producing experiences as the narrator of the book progresses towards *samādhi* and salvific liberation (*mokṣa*). In this book Hariharānanda Āraṇya described some of his ideas about solitude, which can partly explain the Maṭh's tradition of their *ācārya* dwelling permanently locked up in a cave. One figure encountered in the book, an ascetic who dwells in a cave, is quoted saying:

> for those who are engaged in spiritual practices and have not yet reached the goal, solitude is absolutely necessary. . . . In fact, only those who are pure in mind can stay in solitude. Ordinary people lose their balance of mind under such circumstances. Ignorant people believe that greed disappears in solitude. But it is not that. In solitude only those with power of introspection can successfully fight to eradicate the roots of all desire. (p. 16)

The Kāpil *guha*, the cave of Kāpil Maṭh, and the temple appear as one building from the outside, but I soon found that the building is made of two structures, the artificial cave itself and the temple built adjacent to the cave. The entrance to the cave is permanently closed, but in the temple there is a small opening in the wall between the two structures through which the *ācārya* can interact with the devotees once a month. The *ācārya* never leaves the artificial cave. This is the tradition of the *maṭh*. Food is brought to him every day from the *maṭh* kitchen. The opening is small and only the head and a part of his upper body can be seen. The temple contains two small rooms. The larger is the one facing the opening of the cave and it is here the few devotees gather for worship; the smaller is a rectangular room facing the garden and the *samādhisthānas* behind the temple on the outside. The worship room is centered on the small opening of the cave where the *ācārya* meets the devotees for a few hours five days in a row every month. I later learned that he appears regularly on the first to fifth day of the Bengali months except for the four months before the month of Kārttika (October/November) when he always lives in complete isolation. A few devotees gather every month when he comes out of seclusion.

The first time I gathered with a very small group of devotees to witness this event was memorable. I learned that most had come from Kolkata (Calcutta). Males were seated on the right side of the guru and women on the left as we waited for him to appear. The males were dressed in white clothes, the women in beautiful saris. The instant the guru appeared several surged forward to receive his blessing. He was dressed in orange clothes as are most Hindu *saṃnyāsins*, and he was shaved and an orange cap covered the top of his head. He looked tired, but that was perhaps because it was winter and it had been quite cold. One woman who was here for the first time asked something that I could not understand. Fortunately, it and the other Bengali conversations were translated to me by the person beside me. The woman asked if the guru could bless her by touching her head, to which the guru replied that since he had had no physical contact with a woman for many years, he was not about to start now, and so that was not possible.

The atmosphere of the meeting with the guru and disciples were friendly. All kinds of topics were discussed. Some asked for advice. The guru asked the disciples about the welfare of their relatives and children, about their ailments and health. There were lively conversations about the value of yoga, the meaning of Sāṃkhya, the value of solitude, the wisdom of the guru, different traditions of medicine, and other such topics. I particularly remember one story that the guru told. It was about Guru Nānak, the founder of the Sikh religion. Once, while walking with some devotees, Guru Nānak came upon a corpse covered by a sheet of textile. Guru Nānak told the devotees to go there and eat. Since corpses are regarded as ritually impure and inauspicious, they all refused except for one obedient student. He went up to the corpse, lifted the cloth sheet and discovered a pile of fruit there instead of a dead body. The story illustrates the idea that obedience to the guru is vital, because the guru always knows what is best for you. Such lively conversational exchanges continued for hours, especially on the first day.

When I first witnessed these encounters I was struck by the calm atmosphere and the quiet and friendly conversations that took place between the lay members of the *maṭh* and the guru. It reminded me of a meeting of family members with a

Figure 8.2 The current *ācārya*, Swami Bhāskar Āraṇya, through the opening to Kāpil cave

respected senior member who had been away for some time. But it was also different because of the devotion shown towards him, and the *prasād*, the blessed offerings, the visitors, devotees, and disciples received from the guru when their meeting with him was over. The guru institution itself, the authority of this lineage of gurus, the memory of Hariharānanda Āraṇya and Dharmamegha Āraṇya, and the ascetic feat of living isolated in the cave for so many years seem to me to be main sources for the admiration of the guru.

Above the opening in the cave are pictures of Kapila, Hariharānanda Āraṇya, and Dharmamegha Āraṇya. On the right side of the room on the wall there is a human skull. A plaque below it has a Sanskrit *śloka* written on it with a Bengali translation. The *śloka* reads: "I was once covered with a lovely skin and what have I not done to preserve it! Look at this hard reality and concentrate instead on the eternal realities." The message of the skull is common to many ascetic movements in South Asia, but in the Sāṃkhya-Yoga interpretation it means that human beings, and also all other living beings, are constituted by two fundamental principles: the *puruṣa* principle which is pure contentless consciousness, eternal and unchanging, and the *prakṛti* principle which is the material principle and made up by the three constituents (the three *guṇas*: *sattva*, *rajas* and *tamas*) which are constantly changing. The skull points to the teaching of Sāṃkhya-Yoga that the true identity of human beings is *puruṣa*, which is different from the mind and body. Every person has an immortal principle of pure consciousness that does not die when the body dies and the realization of which leads to salvific liberation. The mind and body will die, but the *puruṣa* is eternal unchanging and is neither born nor does it die. All that we usually consider ourselves is in fact not our true identity, but belong to the material principle.

Daily life in the Kāpil Maṭh is very quiet. The *ācārya* is most of the time in seclusion and solitude in the cave. One or two monks who practice Sāṃkhya-Yoga meditation live in the *āśrama*, in houses in the garden. One person takes care of the garden, another the kitchen, and a few lay persons may be present staying at Kāpilāyan. The monks regularly practice the four month vow (*cāturmāsyavrata*) of austerity with emphasis on control of body, speech, and mind. Keeping silence is an important aspect of the vow, which adds to the quietude and peacefulness of the place. The *cāturmāsyavrata* may also include the study of texts (*svādhyaya*) and silent recitation of mantras (*japa*). Yoga is understood to mean concentration, *samādhi*, which is the definition of yoga (*yogaḥ samādhiḥ*) in the *Vyāsabhāṣya* commentary on *Yogasūtra* 1.1. Solitude, mental restraint, concentration, and knowledge are considered the means to salvific liberation. However, mental restraint and concentration have to be practiced steadily over a long time. Many monasteries are like large households, but Kāpil Maṭh is not. It is very quiet, and mostly silent. Silence (*mauna*), tranquility (*śānti*), dispassion (*vairāgya*), and fondness of solitude (*ekāntaśīla*) characterize Sāṃkhya-Yoga in practice. The goal of Sāṃkhya-Yoga is peace, the guru emphasizes to me.

However, once a year a larger number of persons come to the Maṭh. This occurs during the three-day Kapila festival, or *pauṣa utsava*, in the month of Pauṣa (December/January). This festival in no way represents a total reversal of the everyday situation. One supporter of the Maṭh commented that this festival "was held in such a Spartan manner that it did not seem like a festival." This is because in Sāṃkhya-Yoga, yoga practice (*samādhi*, concentration) is considered superior to ritual worship. According to the teaching of the Maṭh, worshipping Kapila means following the ideal set by him. Kapila set the path of peace, *śānti*. A two-hour program of singing and reading of sections from sacred texts is the most important part of the festival. A few other festivals are also celebrated but with few participants. On the last day of the month of Pauṣa (on January 14), *pauṣa saṃkrānti* or *makara saṃkrānti* is celebrated at Kāpil Maṭh with the singing and chanting of verses in Sanskrit (*ślokas*). While many Hindu religious festivals are noted for their energetic swarms of devotees, bathing or crowding together at temples, I was struck by the calm atmosphere of monastic life that marks this festival, as I experienced it. The *makara saṃkrānti* festival is also celebrated at Ganga Sagar Island south of Kolkata, which is the largest annual religious festival in Bengal in terms of people participating. It occurs at the location of one of the most important Kapila temples in all of India. According to the well-known sacred narrative of the birth of the river Gaṅgā, Kapila burned to death the sons of King Sagara, who were destroying the earth while looking for the sacrificial horse of their father's *aśvamedha*, a Vedic rite in which a stallion roams the countryside for a year before being sacrificed. Since Sagara's sons had been killed by the sage Kapila, only water from the sacred celestial river Gaṅgā could bring their souls to Heaven. This made it necessary for the river Gaṅgā to be brought to earth. The followers of Kāpil Maṭh seem less concerned about this mythic tale attributed to Kapila. They either consider that sage to be a different Kapila or explain the myth metaphorically as the conquest of passions, and where the fire is the blaze of discriminative enlightenment which alone can wipe out the last trace of ignorance. At Kāpil Maṭh the festival closes with the mantra *ādividuṣe kapilāya namaḥ*, which is also used sometimes to greet people.

The main communal activity in the Kāpil Mandir is the gathering in the temple for the singing of hymns composed by Hariharānanda Āraṇya. The singing of hymns is a practice that was introduced by Dharmamegha Āraṇya who also introduced a special melodic way of reciting them. When at home, the devotees sing these hymns as their daily morning meditation. At home they sing the hymns alone, but when at Kāpil Maṭh they are sung together, early in the morning and usually lasting about 30 minutes. The same hymns are sung every morning, and this combination of routine, repetition, and rhythm induces a meditative mood. The verses sung or recited are composed in Sanskrit. In the Kāpil Mandir as I experienced this for the first time I was handed a booklet with the hymns with the Sanskrit printed in *devanāgarī* and with a translation in Hindi. In this way I could sing along. All the others, however, knew the songs by heart since, I learned later, the singing of them is part of their daily meditation practice. I seldom saw a person who would use the written text to help his memory. After a while, sitting on the stone floor my body started to ache, but the hymns kept the mind focused, and helped to divert the mind from the pain. The hymns describe the Sāṃkhya-Yoga teaching and the Sāṃkhya-Yoga gurus. I did not understand everything when I

Figure 8.3 Entrance to Kāpil Mandir (temple)

was reciting in the Kāpil Mandir the first times, but I have since translated them into English. Some of these are included in the Discussion section below.

As is the case with many contemporary monastic organizations in India, philanthropic activities, *sevā*, have also become part of Kāpil Maṭh. Philanthropy is a regular activity connected to the Maṭh and also an aspect of several festivals. *Sevā* is hard work. One form of *sevā* is the offering of free medical consultations by doctors who are lay members or other qualified persons. A charitable medical unit is associated with the Maṭh, placed at Sādhu Mā Mandir, called Biram, which is a five-minute walk from Kāpil Maṭh. Various types of treatments are organized by Kāpil Maṭh, and free allopathic and homeopathic treatments are offered regularly. A general physician is present, and sometimes specialists from Kolkata, such as pediatricians, dentists, orthopedists, heart specialists, or gynecologists are brought to the charitable medical unit of Kāpil Maṭh for specialized treatments of patients. Free medicines are also distributed to the patients. On December 21, the second day of the Kapila festival, blankets and books are offered as gifts to the poor. On that day everyone who comes to Kāpil Maṭh—usually around 3,500 to 4,000 people seated around in the garden around Kāpilāyan—are offered a free meal as *prasād*. *Sevā* is understood as *karmayoga*, yoga of action, and appropriate mainly for lay people, but has gradually gained in importance. However, the highest value according to Sāṃkhya-Yoga as it is practiced by the *ācārya* and the monks of Kāpil Maṭh is ascribed to the solitariness of meditation.

Discussion

Hindu systems of religious thought and renunciant traditions

Indian philosophy is a theoretical and historical subject taught at the universities in India and is explained in numerous scholarly books, but attainment of the salvific goal of the systems is not the concern in these academic contexts. There are, however, several aspects to Hindu systems of religious thought in contemporary India and some systems are also part of a living religious practice. Kāpil Maṭh is unique as a contemporary Sāṃkhya-Yoga institution, but the Maṭh illustrates the way philosophies of salvific liberation (*mokṣa*), renunciation, and monastic organizations often have been, and to some degree still are, closely related in Hinduism.

Hindu systems of religious thought have since medieval times been classified into six schools (*ṣaḍ-darśana*), and Sāṃkhya and Yoga are two of these schools. However, it should be noted that Sāṃkhya and Yoga are just two interpretations of the Sāṃkhya system of religious thought. The Yoga system of religious thought is also a school of Sāṃkhya philosophy. Yoga is Sāṃkhya-Yoga! These six Hindu systems of religious thought are defined by having one foundational text (a *sūtra* or *kārikā*) and a tradition of commentaries on these texts that explain and interpret the foundational texts, and further sub-commentaries that explain the commentaries. Thus Sāṃkhya and Yoga have separate foundation text and commentary traditions. Sāṃkhya as a system of religious thought is based on the *Sāṃkhyakārikā* of Īśvarakṛṣṇa (350–400 CE) and a tradition of Sanskrit commentaries on this text. The Yoga system of religious thought is based on the *Yogasūtra* that was composed and compiled and provided with the commentary known as the *Vyāsabhāṣya* around 350–400 CE the *sūtra* and the *bhāṣya* were probably written by the same author and originally as one text and commentaries on these texts. Each system is also associated with a founder. Kapila is considered the founder of Sāṃkhya; Patañjali is considered the author of the *Yogasūtra,* and therefore by some also the founder of Yoga. There is no reliable description of a continuous Sāṃkhya tradition as a spiritual practice, not even from Kapila to Īśvarakṛṣṇa, nor of Yoga. The Sāṃkhya-Yoga tradition might possibly have died out or had very few practitioners and been revived several times in Indian history. The Sāṃkhya-Yoga of Kāpil Maṭh might therefore not be the first revival of Sāṃkhya. The practitioners of Sāṃkhya and Sāṃkhya-yoga (the Yoga school of philosophy) were probably always quite few.

What is known about Kāpil Maṭh's history is a follows. Hariharānanda Āraṇya was from Kolkata, and after a period of university studies, in which he among other subjects studied Sanskrit, he was initiated by a Sāṃkhya-Yoga guru, took *saṃnyāsin* vows (became an ascetic) and devoted the rest of his life to the practice of Sāṃkhya-Yoga. He spent six years in seclusion in the caves of Barabar Hills in Bihar, but did yoga also at several other places before he entered the Kāpil cave.

He visited a number of places in north India and in the Himalayas. A secluded and ascetic lifestyle and the practice of yoga characterized his life, but he also wrote a number of books on Sāṃkhya and Yoga in Sanskrit and Bengali. Āraṇya started a small Sāṃkhya-Yoga renaissance in Bengal. His successor, Swami Dharmamegha Āraṇya (1892–1985), continued the practice of cave dwelling and chose to be locked into the cave some months after the death of Hariharānanda. Dharmamegha Āraṇya did not himself write scholarly commentaries in Sanskrit and Bengali on the Sāṃkhya-Yoga Sanskrit texts as had Hariharānanda Āraṇya, but he continued to disseminate the philosophy of his guru to the disciples of the Maṭh in articles, letters, and sermons (in Bengali). He was the spiritual advisor of the disciples that Hariharānanda Āraṇya had initiated and he also himself initiated new disciples.

Sāṃkhya and Yoga are paired together because of their similarity, thus the term Sāṃkhya-Yoga. There are only minor differences between the two. They are based on the same philosophical foundation: the same three means of knowledge (*pramāṇas*): perception, inference, and authoritative testimony; the same number of fundamental principles (25 *tattvas*), the same doctrine of two ultimate principles (*puruṣa* and *prakṛti*); and the same salvific goal (*kaivalya*) of the realization of *puruṣa* as separate from *prakṛti*. Some of the vocabulary used in *Yogasūtra* is different from *Sāṃkhyakārikā* but that vocabulary is found also in Buddhist texts. The vocabulary might have been common to several philosophies of meditation in ancient India. However, scholars think that Buddhist influence or a Sāṃkhya controversy with Buddhism was one reason for the formulation of the Yoga school of philosophy and this explains the difference in vocabulary between the Sāṃkhya and Yoga schools. This means that Sāṃkhya and Yoga are just two interpretations of Sāṃkhya. Before these distinct Sāṃkhya schools developed there were probably many Sāṃkhya centers where more or less parallel doctrines developed.

What characterizes the philosophy of Sāṃkhya and Yoga? Sāṃkhya and Yoga are *mokṣaśāstras*; the purpose of the teaching of Sāṃkhya and Yoga is the attainment of liberation, *mokṣa*, in Sāṃkhya-Yoga called *kaivalya*. *Kaivalya* means the realization of *puruṣa*, the principle of consciousness, as independent from mind and body. Common to a large section of Hindu religious thought is the idea that living beings are reborn in *saṃsāra* because of ignorance, *avidyā*. What kind of rebirth a living being attains is decided by karma, but the attainment of knowledge, *vidyā* or *jñāna*, causes the destruction of karma, the end of rebirth, and attainment of salvific liberation, *mokṣa*. The purpose of the practice of Sāṃkhya-Yoga is to remove the *avidyā*, which means the realization of the difference between *buddhi* (the intellect, the part of *prakṛti* that is most similar to *puruṣa*) and *puruṣa* by means of "the cessation of the functioning of ordinary awareness" (*cittavṛttinirodhaḥ*). The goal of Sāṃkhya-Yoga is realized through practice (*abhyāsa*) and detachment (*vairāgya*). Detachment means withdrawal of the senses and practice means the application of effort for a long time. *Kaivalya*, the salvific goal, means isolation. In the Kāpil Maṭh the cave is considered an ultimate means for this practice (*abhyāsa*) of detachment (*vairāgya*) and withdrawal of the senses. It also mirrors the isolation of *puruṣa* in the liberated state.

Organized ascetic institutions have existed in South Asia at least from the fifth century BCE and there was probably a close relationship between Sāṃkhya philosophy and the institution of renunciation. The early Sāṃkhya and Sāṃkhya-Yoga teachers were probably renunciants. Asceticism was based on the idea that withdrawal from society is a necessary presupposition for salvation. Buddhism and Jainism arose as institutions of renunciants, but in Hinduism the organization of renunciants in large scale organizations happened later.

Inevitably, monastic organizations develop institutional practices. The singing of *ślokas* composed by Hariharānanda Āraṇya set to melodies by Dharmamegha Āraṇya is a daily practice at Kāpil Maṭh and a common pattern of all the festivals such as the day Hariharānanda confined himself in the cave, the days of the death of the gurus, and the celebration of sage Kapila.

I have included here translations from Sanskrit of two of the songs from the booklet that I have heard sung in the daily ritual in the morning in the temple and at festivals and that are among the hymns the devotees sing every day as part of their Sāṃkhya-Yoga meditation practice. They illustrate the philosophy of renunciation and salvific liberation and other aspects of the Sāṃkhya-Yoga teaching described in some detail above. The first song is called "Collection of Four Verses Describing the Desire for Attaining Salvific Liberation (*mokṣa*)" (*mumukṣācatuṣkam*) and the second "Reflection on the True Self" (*ātmasvarūpamananam*):

Mumukṣācatuṣkam

1.
Om.
When shall I get my mind completely purified?
When shall I be free from confusion?
When shall I be free from attachment and anger?
When shall I be free even from that purpose which is served by human and divine birth and by wealth,
so that I can get my mind completely pacified?

2.
Oh God.
When shall I be full of patience
    with the mind completely peaceful
    by having withdrawn my mind
    which naturally runs towards worldly objects
by means of remembering you
    always, without diversions
and realize my mind as completely happy?

3.
When shall I be happy
    by means of concentration,

because the highest bliss shines when all the sense organs
have been withdrawn from external objects,
and thus shall with completely peaceful mind,
be totally free from suffering and greed?

4.
After ignorance is destroyed by discriminative wisdom,
and thereafter having destroyed attachment
including its root cause
and having controlled my mind,
not transforming any more into the form of any worldly objects,
I shall be a person devoid of the threefold suffering.

Ātmasvarūpamananam

1.
The Self is neither the mind (*manas*), nor the intellect (*buddhi*)
nor egoity (*ahaṃkāra*),
which all are internal organs.
It is neither hearing, nor eye, nor the organ of taste or other sense organs,
neither the five elements,
nor the five sheaths (*kośas*),
but the Self is the highest bliss,
a witness to all,
and consciousness only.

2.
In the Self there is no difference between humans and gods,
no difference of the castes
like *brāhmaṇa*, *kṣatriya* and *vaiśya*,
neither hatred nor attachment,
nor even grief and delusion,
but it is bliss,
witness to all
and consciousness only.

3.
Happiness is not the Self, but the Self is the experiencer of that,
and the experience is consciousness only.
Unconscious things are objects of experience,
The Self is the fourth (*turīya*),
beyond the sheaths
beyond even the sheath made of bliss,
Ātman is the experiencer of bliss
and consciousness only.

4.
By means of developing the pure knowledge
that "I am *brahman*",
when the impure notion of body and so on is totally absent,
one has to put full stop
even to the feeling that I am all in all,
then the experiencer of bliss,
being of consciousness only,
is revealed to the person.

Readings

The literature on Indian philosophy is very large. Surendranath Dasgupta's five-volume *A History of Indian Philosophy* (Delhi: Motilal Banarsidass, 1975) covers a large number of schools, philosophers, and texts. An excellent short introduction is Jonardon Ganeri, *Philosophy in Classical India* (London, Routledge, 2001). For the philosophy of Sāṃkhya, see Gerald James Larson, *Classical Sāṃkhya* (2nd. rev. ed. Delhi: Motilal Banarsidass, 1979), and Gerald James Larson and Ram Shankar Bhattacharya (eds), *Sāṃkhya: A Dualist Tradition in Indian Philosophy* (Delhi: Motilal Banarsidass, 1987). For Yoga as a philosophical tradition, see Gerald James Larson and Ram Shankar Bhattacharya (eds), *Yoga: India's Philosophy of Meditation* (Delhi: Motilal Banarsidass, 2008). Summaries of some of the books of Hariharānanda Āraṇya are also given in this book. For Hariharānanda Āraṇya's interpretation of

Figure 8.4 Jacobsen engaged in fieldwork at Kāpil Maṭh, 2010

Yoga, see his *Yoga Philosophy of Patañjali* (Calcutta: University of Calcutta, 1981). In addition, English translations of a number of texts of Hariharānanda Āraṇya and Dharmamegha Āraṇya have been published by Kāpil Maṭh. The religious traditions surrounding Kapila have been analyzed in Knut A. Jacobsen, *Kapila: Founder of Sāṃkhya and Avatāra of Viṣṇu* (New Delhi: Munshiram Manoharlal, 2008). In this book is also found the Sanskrit text and English translation of the conversation between Kapila and Āsuri, the *Kapilāsurisaṃvāda* (pp. 82–132). For an analysis of the cave tradition of Sāṃkhya see, Knut A. Jacobsen, "In Kapila's Cave: A Sāṃkhya-Yoga Renaissance in Bengal," in Knut A. Jacobsen (ed.), *Theory and Practice of Yoga: Essays in Honour of Gerald James Larson* (Leiden: Brill, 2005) pp. 333–50. For a monograph study of the Sāṃkhya-Yoga tradition of Kāpil Maṭh, see Knut A. Jacobsen, *Living Sāṃkhya-Yoga: The Yoga Tradition of Kāpil Maṭh* (forthcoming). The literature on Hindu asceticism and monasticism is also huge. One start is Patrick Olivelle, *Saṃnyāsa Upaniṣads* (New York: Oxford University Press, 1992), and G. S. Ghurye, *Indian Sadhus* (Bombay: Popular Prakashan, 1954, repr. 1995).

Author

Knut A. Jacobsen (PhD) is Professor of Religious Studies at the University of Bergen, Norway. He is author or editor of around 20 books. His latest publications include *Kapila: Founder of Sāṃkhya and Avatāra of Viṣṇu* (2008) and the edited volume *South Asian Religions on Display* (2008). He is the editor-in-chief of the five-volume *Brill's Encyclopedia of Hinduism* (2009–13).

Chapter 9

Tablā, spirituality, and the arts

A journey into the cycles of time

Jeffrey Lidke

Preamble

Hindus recognize an innate connection between their traditional arts, their theological understandings, and the traditions of spiritual practice that link them together. Since the time of the Upaniṣads, Hindus have recognized sound, *nāda*, as divine, as Brahman (Absolute Reality). A profound tradition of classical music has developed over the past 2,000 years that integrates ancient techniques of yoga with the finest technologies in musical practice, instrument design, and performance. The union of art and spirituality reached its apex in the aesthetic reflections of Abhinavagupta, and other geniuses of Hindu Tantra. In this chapter I reflect on my 20-year study of *tablā* and Tantra, both in academic contexts here in the United States, as well as in my field research in Nepal, India, Bhutan, and Bali.

Narrative

Tāna, tāla, *and Tantra: the interwoven cycles of time*

It is the fall of 1988. I am barely 20 years old as I come to the front door of a house that will soon become my proverbial home away from home. Suddenly I hear only the sound of my heartbeat, now excited by my anticipation in meeting for the first time a man who will forever change the way I see myself and the world around me. The buzzing rickshaws and street vendors at the nearby intersection of Gaidi Dhara, Kathmandu, all grow silent as my index finger presses the metal doorbell fashioned just beneath a small painted image of the elephant-headed god, Gaṇeśa. As the door opens, I am greeted by a beautiful young girl who offers *namaste* (a gesture of welcoming made with palms pressed together) and requests me to come inside, sit, and wait in the living room for her father, Pandit Homnath Upadhyaya.

Pandit Homnath Upadhyaya is a court musician for the king of Nepal, and widely regarded as the premier *tablā* player in all of Nepal to this day. The *tablā* is a north Indian percussion instrument used for solo performances and as well as to accompany classical, light classical, and devotional musical. While the current design of the *tablā* drum itself is a little over 200 years old, its roots trace back over 2,000 years to the ancient temple drums called *pakhawaj*. As I sit in Pandit Upadhyaya's living room I recollect the steps that have led me to this moment: my initial encounters with Indian music in high school through my mother's influence, my decision to major in religious studies at the University of Colorado at Boulder, and now my participation in the University of Wisconsin-Madison's College Year in Nepal program. I have come to this house with the intention of pursuing what I understand to be "musical interests." Little do I realize that this initial meeting with my *tablā* teacher will plant seeds that will sprout into a lifetime interest in the connection between spirituality and the classical arts of India.

After several minutes Pandit Upadhyaya enters, introduces himself, and invites me to begin my first lesson. The *tablās* are designed to be played from a cross-legged yoga position called Lotus Posture (*padmāsana*). I am informed at the outset that the connections between yoga and music are deeply abiding. Posture is the foundation of *tablā*. Correct posture is necessary for proper breathing (*prāṇāyāma*) which in turn facilitates the kind of deep concentration (*dhāraṇa*) at the heart of rhythm-mastery. This triadic link between posture, breath, and concentration, Upadhyaya explains, facilitates conscious withdrawal (*pratyāhāra*) from the sensory world and toward the internal pulse of rhythm within one's own body. "There are times when I am playing," he says to me, "that I feel as if a divine rhythm itself is playing through me. The audience disappears and there is just the music. To reach this state, I practice."

The circa fifth-century scripture, the *Yogasūtra*, attributed to Patañjali, states that steady practice (*abhyāsa*) is necessary for success in *yoga*. Without steadiness in practice one cannot enter into the higher states of awareness (*samādhi*) that are the goal of the tradition. In this first lesson, Upadhyaya is already enabling me to begin to see the connections between the arts and spirituality in the Hindu tradition. In this regard, he is exhibiting one of the most important functions of the *guru*, or teacher: illumination. After several minutes of demonstrating the basic sounds of the *tablā*, Upadhyaya looks at me in meaningful earnestness and states, "Never step over these drums. They are gods. Show them respect by walking around them and always taking care of them, treating them as if they were alive."

The idea that inanimate drums could be "gods" is something my 20-year-old mind has never encountered before. Intrigued, I ask him to clarify what he means. He goes on to explain that the drums are like gods in that they exist to show us who we really are at an intrinsic level, to show us the potential that can be cultivated through training in the science of rhythm (*tāla-vidyā*). He goes on to warn me not to think of the drums as inanimate beings (*jaḍa*) but rather as "alive" (*caitanya*). In concluding this initial lesson, he cites the teachings of Kṛṣṇa in the *Bhagavad Gītā*, stating that devotion has the power to win divine grace and noting that the best players, like Kishan Mahārāj, are clearly blessed by grace.

After this initial lesson, I spend the next year attending lessons four times a week and practicing a minimum of two hours a day. Twice a week I travel to my Guruji's home in Gaidi Dhara, and twice a week he travels to my apartment in Bodhanath, which is on the outskirts of town.

Figure 9.1 Lidke on *tablā*

Even in these initial stages, and despite being a foreigner, I am committed to regular practice and desirous of understanding *tablā* in relationship to the cultural logic from which the tradition stems. Seeing this, my Guruji invites me to attend the Ekādaśī musical celebrations at the royal palace in Kathmandu. Ekādaśī means "eleventh" and marks the eleventh day in the moon cycle, a time considered auspicious for worshipping the gods with music. Homnath tells me that the Ekādaśī celebrations are a continuation of a tradition of offering classical music at royal temples that extends back in Nepalese history at least 2,000 years.

As I arrive at my first Ekādaśī celebration I am led by my Guruji past the palace guards into a small open courtyard crowded with small temples to a host of Hindu deities. At the center of the courtyard stands a small circular pavilion, large enough to comfortably seat a small troupe of musicians and an audience of 10 to 15. As I enter the pavilion I follow my teacher's lead in touching the floor with my right hand and raising my hand to my forehead as a gesture of respect.

As I enter the room I am immediately enveloped by the tangible mood (I would later be told that this perceived "mood" is called *Rasa* in the ancient language of Sanskrit) that pervades the room and seems to be naturally blending in with the late afternoon sounds, colors, and smells which waft in gently with the breeze through the barred, open walls that allow inner and outer worlds to meet and dance together to music now being performed by two men whose mastery of their craft had long since become legendary.

Sitting next to my Guruji, I find myself only three feet from two, now-deceased, masters of north Indian classical music: Sambadev Sapkota on harmonium and

Shambhu Prasād Mishra (Shambhuji) on *tablā*. They are both in their late 70s and yet they are as vibrant, alert, and powerful in their playing as any of the younger masters of the arts. Moreover, there is a power to their playing that is truly stunning. As I listen I find myself entering into a serene trance. Within me all becomes still. The world outside becomes non-distinct from the rhythms and melodies being so beautifully created and interwoven by these two dignified elderly Nepalese men, dressed elegantly in traditional clothing.

At a climactic moment in the performance, Shambhuji begins a form of *tablā* composition known as *laya-kāri*, or the "making of measurements." In *laya-kāri* the *tablā* artist creatively manipulates the audience members' experience of time. For example, he might play several bars at three beats per pulse and then suddenly shift to five beats within the same pulse, creating the illusion that time has sped up. Or he might do the opposite: shift from a higher beat count to a lesser beat count to create the illusion of time slowing down. When *laya-kāri* is effectively demonstrated, the audience members will experience the aesthetic state (*bhāva*) of wonder. The purpose of such a composition is to enable the audience to aesthetically taste any one of nine possible cognitive-emotional states, *bhāvas*, made possible through encounter with art. These states are: fear, anger, heroism, joy, pathos, compassion, love, disgust, wonder, and peace.

As the performance comes to a conclusion I find myself feeling an overwhelming sense of strength, wonder, and peace. I feel at home in a way that I had not imagined possible being as I was so far from land of my birth. I realize that I feel as if I have

Figure 9.2 Sambadev Sapkota on harmonium and Shambhu Prasād Mishra on *tablā* (Pasupatinath, Nepal)

been in this very place many times before—that I am returning to a home at a more profound level than I have ever known. As I talk to my Guruji after the performance he explains to me that the feelings I had are the result of the powers inherent in sacred sound. Music, he says, returns us within ourselves to a place of innate knowing. It is a yoga that makes possible an experience and understanding of who we are at a meaningful level.

As we return to his home that evening for supper, walking briskly along crowded streets busy with vendors selling products from all over India and Nepal, I am hesitant to ask Guruji my next question. I had seen in Shambhuji's playing a quality I had never witnessed before, even in the profound playing of my own teacher. It was not just that Shambhuji's physical posture was different—he sat in a yoga posture called Hero's Pose (*vīrāsana*), adopted by placing one's heels on either side of the buttocks and distributing one's weight across the shins—there was something about the quality of his playing. I saw in it that night a power and concentration that seemed nearly transcendent.

When we reach the gate of my teacher's home, I look him in the eyes and ask, respectfully, "Guruji, Shambhu Prasād's playing seems different in some ways. Why is that?"

Guruji looks at me for a few minutes, as if to scan the depth of sincerity in my eyes, and then replies, "Shambhu Prasād Mishra is the greatest *tablā* player of Nepal, perhaps of any century." He continues on, as we sit together in his courtyard watching the setting sun, sharing with me the famous account of Shambhuji's first meeting with the legendary Indian *tablā* maestro, Chatur Lal (1925–65), during the latter's heralded visit to Nepal as a young man in the 1950s. Shambhu Prasād, Guruji explains, is the Royal Court *tablā* player, appointed by the king himself. When Chatur Lal came to Nepal with Ravi Shankar to perform for the king, he met Shambhuji, who was introduced as Nepal's premier *tablā* artist. This introduction pricked Chatur Lal's ego and he dared to challenge the humble and unshakeable Shambhuji to a duel of their respective mastery of the science of rhythm (*tāla-vidyā*). With the guise of politeness, Chatur Lal challenged Shambhuji to clap the rhythmic cycle of Tīn Tāla while reciting the rhythmic pattern (*ṭheka*) for Ek Tāla in medium speed (*madhya-laya*). As I was soon to learn, this is not a particularly difficult task.

Tin tāla is a 16-beat rhythm, divided equally into four sections (*vibhāgas*) of four beats (*mātra*) each. Ek tāla is a 12-beat rhythm divided into 6 sections of two beats each. In Indian classical music—northern and southern—rhythms are not just played on percussion instruments but also clapped and recited, both in practice and, at times, in performance. The clapping and recitation pattern for middle speed Tīn Tāl consists of three claps and a wave subdivided each by four equal counts. Reciting and clapping Tīn Tāla is something even a beginning student—as I was at the point of this conversation with my teacher—can do fairly quickly. The rhythmic pattern for Ek Tāla at middle speed is also fairly simple. One recites: Dhin Dhin | Dha Dhage | Tun Na | Kat Ta | Dha Dhage | Dhin Na |. In order to recite Ek Tāla over the count of Tīn Tāla one needs to overlay a count of four beats per measure upon an already established count of three beats per measure—something Guruji proceeds not only to demonstrate but also to invite me to do with him. While I struggle miserably for several minutes, I finally find myself relaxing in to a place where I can clap Tīn Tāla (which is based on a four beats per measure count) and speak Ek Tāla (which is based on a three beats per measure count). In other words, I have successfully recited the 12-beat pattern of Ek Tāla while clapping the 16-beats pattern of Tin Tāla, dissolving the former into the latter. Time, I begin to see, is indeed relative and transformational.

Returning to the narrative of Shambhuji's encounter with Chatur Lal, Guruji explains that Shambhuji very humbly accepted Chatur Lal's challenge and with an innocence that was typical of his nature, proceeded to demonstrate the technique as requested, naturally and with ease. After doing so, he looked Chatur Lal in the eyes and asked him to please perform the opposite: to keep the count of Ek Tāla while reciting Tīn Tāla. He additionally requested that he do so at slow speed, *vilambhit laya*, making the task more difficult, both because the precise execution of rhythms at slow speed is by nature more difficult and also because the rhythmic patterns at slow speed are in fact more complicated.

Guruji pauses for a moment and turns to look at the Himalayan foothills ascending up from the northern edge of the Kathmandu valley. The sun's fading rays have turned them an exquisite hue of magenta.

He looks at me and says, "Music is an ocean. There is no room for ego. You can never be as vast as that ocean. You are never greater than music itself. You should never try to put someone else down or show yourself as being superior. Just do your practice and hope that one day you will drown in that great ocean."

As soon as his words touch my ears I know I will never forget them. He continues on explaining that Chatur Lal was visibly shaken by Shambhuji's request. As he began his counting of Ek Tāla one could apparently tell that Chatur Lal's previous confidence was starting to give way. What was at stake, of course, was that if Chatur Lal could not execute the challenge, Shambhuji very well could. After several failed attempt at reciting slow speed Tīn Tāla over slow speed Ek Tāla (in musical terms, attempting to subdivide a hand-clap pattern of six equal measures of two beats per measure by a vocal pattern of four equal bars of four beats per measure and thereby creating an overall feeling of four over three at the slow tempo of approximately 30 beats per minute) it became obvious that Chatur Lal was perhaps not as perfect in his abilities as he sought to present himself as being. He looked at Shambhuji in acknowledgment of his failure and asked if he himself could demonstrate his request. Shambhuji, with humility, performed the challenge and all present saw him as clearly demonstrating a superior knowledge and ability to even the great Chatur Lal.

Guruji is quick to caution me against making the mistake of not respecting Chatur Lal's obvious mastery of *tablā*. "All of us," he says to me, "can suffer from pride. Chatur Lal was young and proud, but I believe Shambhuji taught him an important lesson, and I consider Chatur Lal to be one of the greatest masters in the history of the *tablā* tradition."

I am struck by the degree to which the study of *tablā* has taken me into a world of apparently incessant revelation. I had thought I would just be learning an instrument.

I have begun to realize that the "instrument" is itself a door into a deeper universe, a deeper awareness of self, a deeper way of being human. Just as Shambhu Prasād had transmitted a valuable lesson to Chatur Lal, so Guruji was routinely teaching me, not just how to play *tablā*, but how to be in the world in a more meaningful way. In doing this, he was acting in relationship to me in the same way that his teachers, including Shambhu Prasād Mishra, had acted in relationship to him. Through this experience I was learning that lineage is the heart not just of Nepal and India's spiritual traditions, but its artistic traditions—two traditions that are in fact wedded so intrinsically that to distinguish them is to misrecognize both.

Four months later I am in a taxi driving towards an ashram or spiritual center in the village of Ganeshpuri in the Tana district of Maharashtra, India. I am going there to see a female teacher I met at her retreat site in upstate New York when I was a teenager, the Siddha Guru, Gurumayi Chidvilasananda. On the ride to Ganeshpuri I witness the aftermath of a horrific accident on the famed Bombay highway. As we speed towards the ashram, narrowly escaping close calls on several occasions, I reflect on how very thin the line is that divides the living from the dead. And I find myself spontaneously reciting a *tablā* composition Guruji gave me just the day before I left, beginning as follows:

GeḍaNaga   TetekaTā   –ṇa Dhā–   Dhin Na

After reciting the full composition to the point where I can consistently do so without error, I next try to understand what he had told me before teaching the composition: "This composition is called the Dowry Composition because, being so highly valued for its artistic beauty, Shambhuji offered it as a dowry cost for one of his daughters, and the dowry was accepted with deep gratitude."

I know enough about Hindu marriages to know that dowries can be quite expensive, in some cases in the thousands of U.S. dollars (which in Nepalese *rūpīyah* is the equivalent of millions). In other words, the composition he has taught me has a recognized cultural value equivalent to the value of marriage. I reflect to myself, "How can this be? How can a rhythmic pattern have this kind of literal economic value?" At the ashram this question will, at least in part, be answered.

I am staying at the ashram for a month. I arrive just after Iraq invades Kuwait and am at the ashram when all the ashramites are informed that the United States Congress has approved President George H.W. Bush's call to go to war. The news of the first bombings hits me and others at the ashram hard as we learn the Iraqi civilian death totals are high. We have come to this ashram to find peace. The world around us is at war.

It is in this state of reflection on the complex nature of life that I begin to see more clearly the connection between arts and the natural world in the Indian tradition. One of the Swamis at the ashram introduces me to a book about Abhinavagupta written by an American scholar, Paul Muller-Ortega, titled *The Triadic Heart of Śiva*. In this book I read that Abhinavagupta was an eleventh-century yogi and mystic from the northern India state of Kashmir, who wrote works on Indian aesthetics that remain among the most influential writings of their kind in Indian history. This introduction to Abhinavagupta reveals clearly to me that Indian music literally is a yoga, or a means for yoking the potential inherent in the human being. Through the experiences I have at the ashram over the next month I come to see that success in practice requires mastery of yogic techniques such as posture, breath control, and concentration, and that musical performance is the ritual outlet by which the wisdom of that practice is shared with one's community.

The first key experience happens on Christmas Day in 1989. I am sitting in front of my *tablās* inside the Bhagavan Nityānanda temple, dedicated to Gurumayi's grand teacher, the master of Swami Muktānanda. I have been asked to perform as part of a candle offering to the perfect master, Siddha Guru, symbolic of the divine light shining in all, and to the spirit of Christmas, which recognizes the coming of the Light as Christ into the world. I was raised by parents who were actively engaged in Asian meditative practices from an early age. Their own views were highly tolerant and ecumenical in spirit. I was often told to honor the light of truth that shines in all great spiritual traditions. To my parents, Jesus is a great symbol of the greater Truth that includes and transcends all human claims for truth. I have also often been told by them that that Truth exists as light within me as my own soul, but until this day that statement has been little more than words with little reference point to make them meaningful.

It is 4:00 a.m. Having awakened at 3:00 a.m. to bathe, drink a cup of chai tea, and meditate, I am now quite awake and filled with excitement at the prospect of drumming in the presence of Gurumayi and over 100 other members of the ashram gathered together to celebrate this auspicious day. Suddenly, Gurumayi walks into the temple and sits on her chair at the front of the room. Ritually, her presence is understood to embody the divine feminine, or *śakti*, within the temple, thereby signifying the auspicious moment to commence. As the melody of the harmonium commences and the lead singer begins to recite the sacred verses of the morning's prayer I find my body flooding with the energies of simultaneous cavernous exhilaration and unwavering stillness. I am possessed by the mood of devotion and reverence permeating the room.

The moment the tip of my right index finger first strikes the outer edge of the right hand drum, called *dāyāṇ*, making the sound "Na" I feel a direct and very clear connection between the rhythm and melody that seems to link me together with every other self in the room in a web of shared experience and meaning. This experience of multi-layered interconnectedness permeates the length of the hour long musical ritual and continues beyond into the meditation, shaping my mood and reflections for the duration of my time at the ashram.

Returning to Nepal by bus, taxi, train, and airplane, I find myself traveling not first to my apartment but rather to Guruji's house to ask him about my experience playing in the temple. His response is illuminating: "Our music has three primary elements: rhythm (*tāla*), melody (*rāga*), and composition (*tāna*). These three are interwoven through composition (*tāna*) which is by definition the union of rhythm, understood as the divine masculine or Śiva, and melody, understood as the divine feminine or Śakti."

I recognize this explanation of music as a "union" of masculine and feminine as parallel to central ideas in Hindu theology, particular in the traditions of Hindu Tantra, which I have been told represents the continuation of aspects of indigenous Indo-Nepalese culture, society, and religion. When I ask Guruji about these parallels he smiles and asks, "Do you not see the root of Tantra in *tāna*?" Being at this point only a novice in the Sanskrit language I am nonetheless humbled to realize that *tāna* and Tantra both come from the verbal root √*tan*, meaning to interweave, extend, interconnect. In music, *tāna* is the interweaving, the connecting of rhythm with melody through the elaboration of melodic possibilities in rhythmic ways and the elaboration of rhythmic possibilities in relationship to melodically framed time cycles. The result is a union, or intersection, that I now understand to be recognized by the initiates of classical Indian music as embodying the highest ideals of the Tantric tradition.

Discussion

Hindu arts as the fifth veda

This discussion of the spiritual dimensions of the *tablā* tradition must properly be placed within the larger context of Hindu understanding of the classical arts as having arisen from the "fifth veda," the *Nāṭya-śāstra,* or *Scripture on Dramatic Arts*. All classical Indian arts trace their roots back to the *Nātya-śāstra*, and in this way inherit the status of being a sanctified medium for transmitting religious and cultural values. It is open to debate whether as a "fifth Veda" the *Nāṭya-śāstra* has comparable status to the other four traditional Vedas ("*veda*" designates "revealed scripture"): *Ṛg*, *Sāma*, *Yajur* and, *Atharva*. However, even orthodox Hindus accept its designation as "veda" to mean that is a revealed and therefore timeless scripture, having ultimately come directly from divinity. Current editions of the text contain close to 6,000 verses, but oral tradition claims that these verses are what remain of what was originally a 36,000-verse revelation called the *Gandharva Veda*, of which no copies survive. Authorship of the *Nāṭya-śāstra* is attributed to one of India's greatest heroes and sages, Bhārata. As it is for Homeric heroes in the west, so is it the case that ascribing exact dates to Bhārata is not so easy (in no small part because legendary heroes do not always "actually" exist). Traditional scholarship, based on linguistic analysis of the text, places current versions of the *Nāṭya-śāstra* as no later than the second century BCE and no later than the second century CE. However, we have no way of knowing how far back an oral tradition may have preserved the original verses. In any case, it is safe to say that in classical Hinduism, the arts, theology, ritual, and yogic practice have been linked for no less than 1,800 years. In all likelihood, that link was established considerably earlier.

In the *Nāṭya-śāstra*, the creator god, Brahmā, is cited as stating that the purpose of the *Nāṭya-śāstra* is to reveal to humankind the technology by which one can come to understand the nature of the world through its dramatic re-presentation. Towards this end, the scripture devotes considerable attention to the nature of aesthetic sentiment (*rasa*) and its artistic production as eight concomitant states of experience (*bhāvas*): love, joy, sorrow, anger, virility, terror, disgust, and wonder. The *Nāṭya-śāstra* describes an intimate connection among theater, music, and dance grounded in an understanding of the stage itself as an archetypal cosmogram or representation of the cosmos as perfected geometry, called *maṇḍala*. Within the realm of the arts, the mathematical logic of the *maṇḍala* at once guides architectural construction (ritual spaces, theaters, and temples being the primary examples), musical and rhythmic composition, and self-understandings of the body in its subtle and gross physical forms. *Maṇḍala*-logic states that all creation is a manifestation of reverberating light. It is at once photic (a visual field) and phonic (an acoustic field). Light vibrates as sound, which is light's acoustic dimension (just as light is sound's visual dimension). The Word is Light. Light is the Word. And the cosmos, world, and individual are all replications of this light-word which arises from a singular point (*bindu*) as it projects out into infinite space in all directions an ordered, patterned, infinitely reduplicating expression of creative power as essential harmony and balance.

According to the *Nāṭya-śāstra*, art is the best means for initiating the masses into this complex, visionary way of seeing reality. Art is identified by the text as a mirror in which the individual can see reflected the meaningful patterns of the cosmos and thereby acquire knowledge. This gnostic orientation towards art highlights the intimate links between the lineages of artistes on the one hand and the lineage of yogis and philosophers on the other. It is no accident that one of the oldest classical texts on yogic knowledge, the *Sāṃkhya-Kārikā* (circa 500 CE), utilizes the analogy of a male patron witnessing the dance of a female performer as one way of thinking about the relationship of pure consciousness (*puruṣa*) to the environment (*prakṛti*). By the time of the authorship of this text during the Gupta dynasty, there was already established in India a temple tradition in which dance was performed by females for the two-fold purpose of pleasing the deities of the inner sanctums of royal temples as well as illuminating and pleasing the patrons, priests, and devotees of those temples. The deities were pleased through the secret, "inner" dances performed by an elite class of dancers called Devadāsīs (literally, "servants of the gods") who were trained to perform alone for the sacred images at the center of the great temples of that time. In those dances, the Devadāsīs would assume a series of sacred gestures that transformed their bodies into moving prayers, prayers witnessed by the divinity within and beyond the sacred images. When those same dancers danced in the inner courtyards of those temples they would perform for an elite human audience whose collective aim would be to taste profound aesthetic experience for the higher purpose of self-illumination.

The apex of classical philosophical reflection on the connection between spirituality and the arts came during the life of Abhinavagupta, an eleventh century *yogin*, Tantric guru, artist, and aesthete in whose writings we find a systematic synthesis and expansion of orthodox Hindu theology, doctrine, and ritual practice in relationship to classical arts. At the conclusion of his illustrious career

Abhinavagupta had established in his refined, poetically nuanced philosophical writings not only that divinity itself was the Dance, but that art was the most subtle and beautiful way of recognizing that the Witness to the Dance (identified by Abhinavagupta as the masculine principle of luminous being, Śiva) and the Dance Itself (identified by Abhinavagupta as the feminine principle of creative self-reflectivity, Śakti) are two inseparable aspects of one's own infinite being. In other words for Abhinavagupta, art was means for the attainment of spiritual realization.

Abhinavagupta was a leading voice among many who spoke for, represented, and embodied the popular traditions of Hindu Tantra that flowered from the seventh to the twelfth centuries in northern India (interrupted there by the Muslim invasions) and continued unabated in southern India until British occupation in the eighteenth through twentieth centuries. Tantra, which literally means "interweaving," was a religious ideology and practice grounded in the fundamental premise that the body is a microcosm of a universe which is itself the artistic expression of the infinite powers of divinity. Recognizing that this creative potential exists within one's own being, the Tantric practitioner utilizes a variety of strategies for harnessing his or her own innate potencies. This private pursuit of self-empowerment is buttressed culturally through a system of artistic practices grounded in the fundamental tenets of the *Nāṭya-śāstra* tradition. Consequently, there remains today a strong tradition of artists—dancers, *tablā* players, instrumentalists, and poets alike—who understand their craft as a means for expressing the intricate spiritual philosophies of their culture. These artists recognize their respective cultural traditions as having originated from a divine source, a Cosmic Artist/Dancer/Musician/Mandala, whose creative energies generate and manifest as this cosmos and whose nature is best understood through the act of immersing oneself in art as itself a yogic path.

In this chapter, I have sought to illumine the path of the Hindu artist by weaving together my ethnographic and textual studies of the Hindu arts together with my training in the *tablā* traditions of Nepal and north India. While I have emphasized the tradition-specific aspects of the *tablā* tradition (such as the clapping system) it is hoped that the reader understands that classically trained *tablā* players themselves perceive their art as inseparably linked to the web of Hindu classical artistic traditions that traces back to the *Nāṭya-śāstra*. For this reason, they perceive *tablā* practice and performance as one artistic means for expressing and experiencing the fullness and beauty of divinity—a divinity that they understand to express itself as the endlessly returning cycles of life. For them, all of creation is a cycle, a series of turning wheels in which the cyclic rhythms of the breath mirror and are linked to the rhythms of the drum which in performance imitates the gestures of the dancer whose body movements would traditionally unfold within the courtyard of classical Hindu temples whose architectural forms give three-dimensional expression to the *maṇḍala*, that ubiquitous Indian symbol that articulates an abiding Hindu truth: divinity endlessly emanates as the harmonious, interwoven cycles of life. The Hindu artist utilizes his or her body and its creative talents as a means

Figure 9.3 Lidke tuning his *tablā*

for experiencing and expressing these cycles and thereby preserving an artistic tradition whose purpose is the revelation to society of the nature of divinity.

Readings

There is a great deal of writing on Hindu arts and their connection to Hindu spirituality more generally, as well as a few that reference Tantra specifically. Very few works discuss the Tantric aspects of the *tablā* tradition. One noteworthy exception is Jeffrey M. Feldman's *Pranava Tala Prajna: The Tabla Legacy of Taranath Rao* (Venice: Digitala, 1995). There are a number of fine works on Abhinavagupta's Tantric theory of aesthetics, including Raniero Gnoli's *The Aesthetic Experience According to Abhinavagupta* (Varanasi: Chowkhamba Press, 1985). David White's two masterpieces on Tantra, *The Alchemical Body: Siddha Traditions in Medieval India* (Chicago, IL: University of Chicago Press, 1996) and *Kiss of the Yoginī: Tantric Sex in Its South Asian Contexts* (Chicago, IL: University of Chicago Press, 2006) demonstrate the historical synthesis of alchemy, yoga, Tantra, and theories of art. I recommend all the writings of Mark Dyczkowski, but particularly his *Canon of the Śaivāgama and the Kubjikā Tantras of the Western Kaula Tradition* (Albany, NY: SUNY Press, 1988). For insight on the mystical and ritual nature of Indian classical dance and its connection to medieval polity, see Frederique Appfel Marglin's classic *Wives of the God King: The Rituals of the Devadāsīs of Pūrī* (Oxford: Oxford University Press, 1985) as well as Saskia Kersenboom's *Nityasumangali: Devadāsī Tradition in South Asia* (New Delhi: Motilal Banarsidass, 1987). Padmasri Dr. Nataraja Ramakrishna's *Dancing Bells: An Aesthetic and Spiritual Expression* (Hyderabad: Katyayani Arts, 2007) provides illuminating insights on the ritual and yogic dimensions of temple-based contemporary performance dance institutions in India. K. Kunjunni Raja's *Indian Theories of Meaning* (Chennai: The Adyar Library and Research Centre, reprint edition, 2000) offers a solid introduction to the linguistic foundations for classical Indian philosophy of aesthetics.

Author

Jeffrey S. Lidke (PhD) is Associate Professor of Religious Studies at Berry College in Rome, Georgia. His books include *Vishvarupa Mandir: A Study of Changu Narayan, Nepal's Most Ancient Temple* (Nirala Press, 1996) and *The Goddess Within and Beyond the Three Cities: Śākta Tantra and the Paradox of Power in Nepāla-Maṇḍala* (Edwin Mellen, 2011).

Chapter 10

Divine times

Goddess worship in Banāras

Hillary P. Rodrigues

Preamble

Hindus celebrate scores of religious rites through the course of a year. Activities during religious festivals may involve temple visits, devotional worship rites (*pūjā*), Vedic fire offerings (*yajña, homa*), fasting (*vrata*), and pilgrimage (*yātrā*). In the following chapter, I briefly describe some of my experiences during my study of two consecutive celebrations of the autumn Navarātra festival in Varanasi (Banāras). I begin with the period leading to the second year's celebration (in 1991) and flash back to events during the previous year. I spent 18 months in India in 1990–1991, and my narrative derives from a combination of my memories, photographs, video footage, and journal entries. I wish to convey the excitement of discovery, and the challenges entailed when attempting to study a varied assortment of activities that occur in diverse locations during a relatively narrow window of time. I then utilize this description to talk about the festival cycle in Hinduism.

Narrative

Times leading to Navarātra

This time

It was late July and Varanasi was an oven. Temperatures in Śiva's holy city soared close to 45°C in mid-afternoon, and did not sink below 30°C at night. The river goddess Gaṅgā (i.e., the Ganges River) was a clear blue-green trickle, dramatically shallow in contrast to her swollen muddy-brown heights and surging width during the rainy season. The Ganges submerges much of the land on either side of her banks, including small temples, and then recedes as the seasons shift through the autumn, winter, spring, and summer, until the arrival of the monsoon rains. This summer was different from most. The monsoons had not yet arrived, and the hot season had dragged on for more than a month beyond its allotted period of torture. All of the often submerged stone steps fringing the river's west bank were fully visible. If the first rains did not fall by Ratha Yātrā, the upcoming day of the chariot festival, the authorities would officially declare the onset of a drought. The wooden chariots that would hold the gods Jagannātha and Balarāma and the goddess Subhadrā stood decorated, waiting to be viewed by devotees. "The chariots' flags must be drenched with rain," remarked a temple priest, who shook his head despondently. The city waited in heat-exhausted expectation.

I vividly remember the immense sense of joy, as well as relief from the suffocating heat, when dark clouds, like a herd of elephants, rolled in from nowhere. And then the rain fell. The scorching asphalt on the streets seemed to cry out in pain at first, instantly vaporizing the first water droplets, but the rain kept on falling, soothing and cooling the world, filling the air with life-affirming moisture. Children ran out of their houses to get their clothes and bodies soaked, and I wondered if there was anyone in the city who did not step out to actually touch at least a few of those first raindrops. When the downpour had abated, people were visible everywhere, on the front porches of their homes and in the doorways of their offices, with unforgettable looks of contentment on their once-beleaguered faces. The monsoons had arrived. The hues of the damp fabric that covered the chariots were now vibrant, and worshippers went to have their audience with the gods, who were pulled through the streets.

It is on the day of Ratha Yātrā that artisans traditionally begin crafting images of the goddesses Durgā and Kālī that will be worshipped several months later, during the Durgā and Kālī Pūjās. A couple of weeks after Ratha Yātrā, I visited the workshop of Bangshi Pal, the master craftsman who makes the unbaked clay figures for many of the city's Durgā Pūjās, including the image clusters for the Lahiris, a Bengali Brahmin family, and for the Durgotsava Sammilini, one of the oldest Bengali community celebrations. The Pals belong to an artisan caste (*jāti*), some of whose members fabricate earthen images used in the ritual worship of gods and goddesses. The most elaborate of these figures were those made for the Durgā Pūjā. I noted that Bangshi Pal and his fellow artisans had already begun to fashion the skeletal frameworks of the images from bamboo and straw.

On a visit to the workshop many weeks later, I was surprised to see it crowded with dozens of grey-brown mud figures, many larger than life. There were muscled and mustachioed demons, elephant-headed, pot-bellied Gaṇeśas, and powerful life-sized lions. Most amazing were the full-breasted, bald-headed mannequins of Durgā, which stood high above all the other figures, each Durgā with her eight arms radiating outward, like the tentacles of an octopus. I marveled at the artistry of the images, particularly those of the Goddess atop her great lion, Mahāsiṅgha, engaged in the act of slaying the buffalo demon, Mahiṣa. Here, Durgā's snake noose twisted around the demon's thigh as he stared incredulously at the Great Goddess. There, the lion clawed into the flanks of the buffalo, while its teeth sunk into the horned beast's back. Every one of these triads was unique, shaped by the artists without any apparent illustrations as a guide. My astonishment grew as paint, clothing, and ornamentation were painstakingly applied to the images in the weeks that followed, for the workshop was soon a blaze of color and tinsel. The demons writhed frozen in defiant pain. Blood oozed from their wounds and the severed heads of the buffaloes. The minor goddesses wore pink, yellow, or white saris, while Durgā's was most always blood red. The tin weapons and mock jewelry gleamed in the dimly lit studio space.

Excitement in the Lahiri home had been building up for weeks as the autumn Navarātra approached. Navarātras ("nine-nights") are the most widely celebrated festivals to the Great Goddess in the Hindu world, and the autumn Navarātra has long surpassed the spring festival in the exuberance of its celebrations. Married daughters customarily return with their families to their fathers' homes for the festival, and Mr. Manindra Lahiri had four married daughters, all of whom resided with their own husbands' families, some as far away as Kolkata (Calcutta). Mr. and Mrs. Lahiri now expectantly awaited the reunion of their dispersed family members. Meanwhile, hundreds of *paṇḍals* (temporary temple pavilions of bamboo and canvas) were being constructed throughout Varanasi. Diagonally opposite the renowned rust-red Durgā Kuṇḍa temple, whose profile reflects into the waters of the square pond from which it gets its name, the Durgā Sporting Club was setting up one such pavilion. This would be the site of their Durgā Pūjā, organized by young men from the local community, and funded by donations they had gathered in the previous months.

Navarātra: The Nine-Night Festival of the Goddess

That time

On my first Navarātra, the year before, I did not know where and when I ought to carry out observations at the many likely locations of Durgā worship in Varanasi. I knew about the city's Nine Durgās, and so, early on the morning before the first night of Navarātra, I traveled out to the small temple of Śailaputrī Devī, at the city's northern boundary. Śailaputrī (Daughter of the Mountain) is the first of the city's Nine Durgās, who are visited in consecutive order on each of the festival's nine nights. It was no easy task getting there, for the temple is situated beyond the city's major ring road, at the end of a long, narrow unpaved alley, mucky with the autumn rains. When I finally arrived, I was surprised to find next to no activity there, but was assured by the temple priest that things would be "different tomorrow when 50,000 people will visit" or even "tonight," when the first of Navarātra's nine nights would actually begin. I wandered around the site, shot a few photographs, and then returned to the city's downtown, a bit frustrated and confused.

I had arranged to visit the home of the renowned healer Mithai Lal (Sweet Red) later that morning. Mithai Lal often conducted public sessions at the fire-pit in the Durgā Kuṇḍa temple on Tuesday evenings, but had died just before my arrival in Varanasi. In the months following his death, his wife had continued the healing work. I had been granted permission to observe her rites on the first day of Navarātra. Her home was situated along a twisted maze of alleys, better reached from the river bank, and its rooms were dark, dank, and smelly. I was led to a back room, an entire half of which formed the home's shrine section. One wall was covered with framed lithographs of gods and goddesses. Near ground level rested an assortment of small metal, stone, and plaster images of deities, brass ritual implements, flower and food offerings, incense, and so on. Goddess images clearly outnumbered the others. Mithai Lal's wife, clad in a red sari and assisted by a young girl, perhaps her granddaughter, squatted on the ground. She acknowledged my presence but paid me little attention as she attended to the ensuing rite. Mixing water with mud and cow dung she fashioned a small earthen altar, in size and shape like a circular birthday cake, and set an earthen pot upon its surface. As she squatted there, with her own red sari draped over her head, ministering to the pot, now swathed in red cloth, I could not help but notice how in shape it resembled her. By then, I plainly understood that she had been fabricating a figurine of the Great Goddess in the form of an earthen jar with leafy appendages and a coconut fruit head. She then sprinkled the earthen altar with rice and other grains, and began to garland the figure as part of a devotional worship rite or *pūjā* to this goddess, the Goddess, whom she has just assembled before my eyes. Since then, I have seen countless such constructions, but mostly by men, performed during both the spring and autumn Navarātra celebrations. Once established, the Goddess is worshipped regularly for the entire nine days, often through a daily recitation of the *Durgā Saptaśatī*, a highly respected goddess-centered, or *Śākta*, scripture.

Later that day at Daśāśvamedha Ghat, Varanasi's central access point to the Gaṅgā, I observed immersion rites for clay images of the god Viśvakarman. Fairly exhausted by day's end, and dubious about the value of making a midnight research excursion, I nevertheless hesitantly headed back to the temple of Śailaputrī. I was

Figure 10.1 Healer venerating the Goddess, established in the form of a jar (Banāras)

astonished to find the mucky alley leading to it, which was nearly deserted that morning, now lined with stalls selling *pūjā* offerings and souvenir trinkets, and choked with pilgrims. It was 1:30 a.m. before I was actually able to enter the temple premises. I noted that the swarms of worshippers rang the temple bells, and circulated within the courtyard making offerings at the surrounding shrines, before crowding around the small central temple. There they awaited *maṅgala darśana*, the highly auspicious first view of the goddess on Navarātra. The priest had been ministering to the goddess within the sanctum. The sense of expectation intensified among the throng of votaries, who could hear him uttering prayers and ringing bells. At the astrologically calculated exact moment, about 2:30 a.m., the priest flung open the sanctum doors so that the eager devotees could catch their first glimpse of Śailaputrī. The goddess was draped in shimmering silk, covered with garlands, and offered her devotees her metal-masked face upon which to gaze. Devotees folded their palms together, cried out "Mā, Mā," and bowed or fully prostrated. They offered red hibiscus flowers and hundreds of coconuts, which the priest smashed on their behalf. Some remained to participate in a *homa* or *havan* rite, in which offerings are made into a traditional Vedic-styled square fire-pit.

I subsequently performed the pilgrimage to each of the other Durgās located in temples scattered across Varanasi. Their names are evocative of the Goddess's nature, but also enigmatic, and I wondered about how they originated and came to be associated with Durgā. For most of the year, the goddesses in these temples are known by other names and may or may not receive a lot of attention. For instance, the Śailaputrī temple receives only a handful of visitors at most other times in the year. Like desert rains to desert plants, the festivals are crucial for its survival. On the pilgrimage to the Nine Durgās that year, I experienced what was at times a frightening crush of bodies, and it still makes me ponder more deeply the mystery behind such rites, where so many thousands of people are induced to visit sacred sites, at precise times of the year. The swelling and ebbing flow of pilgrims, in accord with the religious ritual calendar, resembles the seasonal changes of the river goddess Gaṅgā.

This time

On the first day of this year's Navarātra I visit the Durgā Saptaśatī Mandir to observe the jar installation rite. The temple developed around an extraordinary Śākta yogi named Sukhananda Mahārāj, who had meditated in what was once merely forest. Since the temple was built, Sukhananda spent most of his time sleeping, eating, and entering into swooning states in front of a large marble statue of a many armed, lion-riding Durgā. He was in one of those states of absorption when I first met him, days earlier, being cared for by an attendant disciple, and when he emerged from it appeared suspicious and reluctant to see me. However, his demeanor towards me quickly warmed. At one point when discussing his intense spiritual practices of the past, he simply opened his mouth and flipped his tongue backwards. The membrane on the underside had been wholly severed so that his tongue could flip back completely, for the performance of what is known as *kechari mudrā*, a rarely seen yogic technique said to grant the practitioner supernormal powers. In particular, the yogi is said to be able actually to taste the nectar of immortality that flows downwards from the uppermost psychic energy centers (*cakra*) if one has perfected the goal of Kuṇḍalinī Yoga. On this Navarātra, the disciples at Sukhananda's temple have commissioned a young ritualist to install Durgā in her jar form. However, at various stages the inexperienced priest seems to be confused, stumbling through the sequence of ritual actions, much to the anxiety of those in attendance, who fear that the window of sacred time will close before he completes the rite. With prodding, criticisms, and assistance, he is finally able to carry out the installation, and *pūjā* worship rites are rapidly performed to the jar and the various other forms of the Goddess in the sanctum premises. At the high point of the devotional rite now centered on the marble statue, Sukhananda, who wears his old, stained, and tattered smock, suddenly peels it off so that he now is virtually naked, but for a saffron loincloth. Grabbing a basket overflowing with small, reddish-stemmed, shefali blossoms, and showing surprising agility for a man of his age and seeming frailty, he swiftly mounts a stool beside the main image in the temple sanctum. Then, at the appropriate moment, he showers the lion-riding Goddess with hundreds of the sweetly fragrant, small white flowers, said to bloom only by autumn moonlight, and to be much loved by Durgā.

Back at the Lahiri home, Pandit Nitai Bhattacharyya is the Brahmin ritualist who will preside over the upcoming Durgā Pūjā, a rite spanning four or five days and situated within the nine days of Navarātra. The Lahiri home is abuzz as each of the four married daughters, their husbands, and children have returned to Varanasi for the celebration. Everyone gathers to watch the polychrome clay image cluster carried from Bangshi Pal's nearby workshop into the home and set up in the place of worship. This takes place on the sixth day of Navarātra. The Bengali-styled image cluster has the entire array of deities placed in a single tableau. However, at the non-Bengali community *pūjās*, such as at the Durgā Sporting Club pavilion, larger than life images in separate pieces are more the norm, in which Durgā's features may resemble those of a Bollywood actress and the demon's physique is like that of a professional wrestler. In the Lahiris' image cluster, Durgā's face is a golden yellow, her eyes lined black with collyrium, and the demon is green skinned. "Durgā has gained a little weight this year," remarks one of the teenage grandchildren in an expression of fond familiarity, as if the Goddess's arrival is just like that of one of the other aunties, who has not been seen for a year.

When I ask him why he celebrates the Durgā Pūjā in his home, a costly tradition that has mostly vanished in Varanasi to be replaced by the more affordable community-styled celebrations, Mr. Lahiri is almost tearful with joy as he answers. "Look at my house, now," he explains. "It is so full of life. Somehow when Durgā is here, my house is unlike any other time of year. Mother is smiling." As he continues, I cannot always tell whether he is referring to the clay image of the Goddess, who has now take up abode in his home, to the female energy embodied in his returning daughters, or to the happiness of his wife and the other women of the household (visiting aunts, cousins, etc.), who have been reunited by this extraordinary festival. I think this ambiguity is uncalculated, and telling, for Durgā somehow represents and simultaneously is all these and more.

Meanwhile at the public *pūjā* celebrations, the mood is both jubilant and expectant. Trucks are dispatched from Bangshi Pal's and other workshops throughout the city, and carry the arrays of large images to their various community *pūjā* sites. One such truck heads to the Durgā Sporting Club's pavilion. Priests, especially skilled and initiated in the performance of the upcoming complex goddess worship rites, have been commissioned by the community groups and are already at work in each of over 200 locations in Varanasi.

The seventh day of the autumn Navarātra, known as the Great Seventh, constitutes the first official day of the Durgā Pūjā. This is the day when Pandit Nitai, through extensive rites that testify to his extraordinary expertise, within the framework of Hindu beliefs actually brings the Goddess and other deities in the clay image cluster to life! Uttering both Vedic prayers and Tantric seed syllables, through elaborate visualizations, and an array of gestures with his hands and body, he transforms his own body into that of the Goddess, and then ritually transfers her into her clay abode. Initially present in the form of the jar, and the Cluster of Nine Plants, Durgā is now present in the household in a human-like form. The family members gather for the long, honorific rites of devotional worship, which give the Durgā Pūjā its name. "When I stare at the image," one devotee confided to me, "I see Mā's face actually move. She seems to smile, or be displeased, and expresses many emotions over the days of the *pūjā*." Like most devotees, he calls the Great Goddess "Mā," which simply means "Mother." The Goddess is presented an assortment of uncooked and cooked foods, is bathed in various waters, anointed, and offered flowers. Since he cannot actually wet the unbaked clay images without damaging them, Pandit Nitai places a mirror before them, and bathes their reflection in it. The devotional offerings culminate in the *āratī*, when flames are passed before the image, and the household members gather to ring bells, shout out praises, and collectively worship the Goddess. The women utter a yelping cry, known as the *ululu*, like the call of a jackal. The intensity of the *pūjā* actually builds up as these rites are repeated on the following day, and peaks on the cusp between the Great Eight and Great Ninth. It was traditional for the Lahiris to sacrifice a goat at that sacred juncture of time, but they have given up the practice.

At the Durgā Kuṇḍa temple, however, such complete restraint is not evident, although the frequency of blood sacrifice has greatly diminished in Varanasi. On a rectangular plot of ground, directly in the line of sight of Durgā in the inner sanctum, a sacrificial post is embedded. I sit chewing *paan*, a betel-nut quid, with my friend, Om Prakash Agarwal, who owns a bangle and *bindi* shop just feet away from the sacrificial pit, when a devotee brings a goat to the temple. The ritualist places the beast's neck within the sacrificial post, a Y-shaped yoke, and tethers it there. He picks up a large sword, curved at its tip, and anoints the blade and the animal's head. An assistant grasps the goat's hind legs. The ritualist utters a quick prayer and, with a single stroke, severs the beast's neck. The head and decapitated

Figure 10.2 Ritualist at a small shrine to Rudrabhairava at the Durgā Kuṇḍ temple (Banāras)

body fall to the ground. Blood oozes from the severed neck, like petals of the hibiscus flower sacred to Durgā, and flows into the earth of the sacrificial pit, strewn with actual flower blossoms. The ritualist then places a small earthen lamp by the goat's head and sets these on a nearby post in offering to the Goddess. Soon both body and head are removed, placed in a basket and given to the devotee who brought the offering. Such blood sacrifices, officially sanctioned in Varanasi only at the Durgā Kuṇḍa temple, take place throughout Navarātra, and with greater regularity on the last few days of the festival. On this occasion I am invited to accompany the Nepali soldier, who had just made the blood sacrifice, back to his home. There, he and his friends first make a fried spiced preparation from the head and some inner organs. "It is especially blessed," I am told. A delicious goat curry is next prepared from the skillfully skinned and dismembered body, all right before my eyes. Many family members arrive, and we devour the consecrated offering, washing down the spicy curry and rice with copious quantities of rum. "I promised Mā that if I came back alive from my dangerous posting in the army, I would offer her the life of a goat in exchange for sparing mine," he informed me.

Life in the city throngs during the autumn Navarātra. Merchants have been doing brisk business as people shop for items for *pūjā* offerings, food for family and guests, and new clothes to wear on *pūjā* days and on temple visits. The Goddess is often given fine saris as offerings, which end up going to the presiding priest's wife. The Durgā Pūjā celebrations of the sort involving the polychrome clay images originated in Bengal among wealthy rulers and landlords. When these celebrations grew too expensive, the *pūjā* was progressively democratized, leading to the communal celebrations, which also originated in Bengal. People throng the city's streets as the nine days progress. Some are performing the Nine Durgā pilgrimage, while some are visiting other goddess temples too. Most are simply curious to visit the temporary shrine displays (*paṇḍal*), particularly those that are reputedly the most magnificent. Communities and businesses engage in friendly rivalries through the opulence of their celebrations, and some of the most renowned pavilions in Varanasi are several stories high, with grandiose tableaux of the Goddess and her accompanying figures.

On the Great Ninth, Pandit Nitai constructs and worships Durgā in the form of an elaborate sacred diagram. This is also the day when pre-pubescent girls, known as *kumārīs*, are worshipped as living forms of the Goddess. The priest first transforms the virgins into Durgā, and proceeds to worship them in the traditional manner, giving them each a plate of food and sweets in the process. I wonder at the notion that Hindu priests (indeed, even female healers) can make a god or goddess manifest in virtually any abode of their choosing, such as an earthen jar or image, but am further amazed that the deity is believed to have just taken up presence in living human beings. As the rite finishes, the elderly female and male devotees gathered there pay homage to the girls; some even prostrate at the feet of these young, living goddesses.

Times after Navarātra

At the end of the ninth day, Navarātra officially ends. However, there are numerous key activities that follow, which keep the festival spirit alive for much longer. On the day following Navarātra, known as Vijāyā Daśamī (Tenth for Victory), Pandit Nitai performs rites to dismiss the Goddess at the Lahiri home, thanking her for her visit. Although sending her off, he asks her to maintain a lingering presence in the earth, water, and this home. The married women of the household now gather for a rite in which they feed each other and all of the figures in the image cluster (including the demon and the lion) with sweets, literally stuffing and smearing their mouths with the offerings. Then, the earthen images are carried by processions of worshippers from the Lahiri home, and from their hundreds of various *pūjā* sites in the city to the Gaṅgā, where they will be delivered into the flowing waters of the river goddess.

At the Durgotsava Sammilini compound, the mood is tense. Many years earlier, as the images were being transported through a Muslim neighborhood, their procession sparked riots that spread through the city and claimed many lives. The organizers at the Durgotsava Sammilini naturally continue to worry this year, and hope that nothing as terrible as the destructive riots that occurred years before ever happens again. Fortunately, this year's immersion procession and procedures unfold without incident. Tens of thousands of curious onlookers line the streets and steps leading down to the Gaṅgā's banks. The Bharat Sevāśrama Saṅgha, an influential religious organization, has staged an elaborate performance on two houseboats at the river's edge. While one of their learned scholars broadcasts a recitation of the entire *Durgā Saptaśatī* over blaring speakers, other members enact the myths that are described in that scripture. The myths tell of the Goddess's manifestation, in which the collective energies of the male gods were pooled together to produce the irresistibly beautiful Durgā, who then wielded weapons drawn from the male gods' own armaments. The performers enact how the Goddess slays Mahiṣa, whose destruction is her most renowned exploit, as well as how she defeated many other demons, and how the male deities extol her praises.

The feelings as the Lahiris gather at the river's edge are mixed. They are exuberant with the joy that the festival season has brought, but poignantly aware and saddened that it is coming to an end. Their family reunion, too, will soon disintegrate like their earthen image of Durgā, whom they tearfully deliver to the waters. After they have immersed their Durgā, I accompany all the Lahiri family members in a houseboat on an unforgettable sunset cruise on the Gaṅgā to watch the celebrations. There is ecstatic singing and dancing on the streets and riverbank by the mostly male worshippers. Some hold earthen pots smoldering with fragrant smoke, and they wave these before the images being carried to the river. Each of the community groups commissions a rowboat to transport their images a short distance from the riverbank and then topple them into the waters. The figures sink quickly and, since they are made of unbaked clay, rapidly dissolve. The Goddess and her entourage, fashioned from clay probably drawn from the Gaṅgā's own banks, now melt back into the watery form of the river goddess. I cannot help thinking how this process of image building and destruction resembles the Tibetan Buddhist procedures of painstakingly building elaborate cosmograms, or *maṇḍalas* of sand, only to destroy them once the ritual of worship has ended. It vividly conveys an awareness of the flow of existence, its constant change, and how all created beauty, like a blossoming flower, is transient and ephemeral. Amid the array of boats on the river, and the throng of people on the riverbank, I also have an unmistakable appreciation for the power inherent in the unified community of Hindu worshippers and their enthusiastic emotional devotion to the Great Goddess, who as their divine mother, Mā, has reunited all her many children into one great family.

The spirit of the autumn Navarātra extends right through to Dīvālī celebrations several weeks later. People send greeting cards, wishing each other the best, for there is a sense of renewal that has occurred through the course of these days. While the goddess Lakṣmī is often the focus of attention on Dīvālī for most Hindus, Bengali families, such as the Lahiris, celebrate Kālī Pūjā on that day. The Lahiris bring an earthen image of the dreadful black goddess of Time from Bangshi Pal's workshops to their home and worship her there with similar but less elaborate rites than those performed on behalf of the Great Goddess, Durgā.

Discussion

Festivals are an integral dimension of the Hindu tradition, and are celebrated throughout the year. Many are localized, taking place only in particular villages, cities, or regions (e.g., south India), while others are widespread across the Hindu world. Festivals might include a variety of religious activities such as pilgrimages, visits to temples, ritual worship at home shrines and temples, the practice of austerities, feasting, and so on. The Navarātra (Nine Nights) is a widely celebrated festival, practiced by Hindus throughout India and abroad. Of course, the styles of celebration vary regionally. There are actually two main Navarātras, one in the spring and the other in the fall. The description above derives from research conducted during two consecutive autumn celebrations. Since I was carrying out research on the goddess Durgā, who is worshipped in a variety of ways during Navarātra, I could not restrict myself to examining just the Nine Durgā temple pilgrimage circuit, or the worship rites at a particular temple, for the course of the entire nine days. Rather I found myself having to move among a variety of locations, making observations, gathering data, conducting interviews, filming rituals, and so on. While I was in one place, evidently something crucial may have been happening somewhere else that I was unable to observe first hand. I often had to rely upon others to describe what I had missed. I stayed in the field for two consecutive celebrations to observe the festival celebration twice consecutively (when social, political, economic and other factors would be relatively similar), and selectively shift my locales to fill in the gaps in my observations. In subsequent

Figure 10.3 Rodrigues with *bhakti* singers at a goddess temple

years I have continued my observations of Navarātra celebrations in India, Nepal, and in the Hindu diaspora.

Although I could have used the foregoing narrative to discuss *pūjā*, pilgrimage, the goddess Durgā, temple worship, women in the Durgā Pūjā, the priesthood, and a host of other elements, I have opted to focus my discussion on the calendrical system. Although I had read about the Hindu calendar before conducting fieldwork, my eyes would glaze over when studying detailed descriptions of it. However, I found that it was vitally necessary to know something about the Hindu calendar to understand certain features in these religious rites. Without such knowledge, it would be difficult to understand why a rite begins or ends at a particular time, why these vary from year to year, why certain times of certain days are inappropriate for ritual celebrations, and so on.

Dividing time

Hindus use a combination of solar and lunar cycles in their calendar. One solar year (about 365 solar days) is divided into twelve lunar months (the time from one full moon to the next), each about 29.5 days. Since 29.5 days/month × 12 months = 354 days, leaving an additional 11 days in each solar cycle, every two and a half years an additional month is inserted in the calendar to compensate for the discrepancy. A lunar day is known as a *tithi*, and these vary in length from about 19 to 26 hours. Thus it is possible for a particular solar day (24 hours) to have two *tithis*, or for a *tithi* to extend over two consecutive solar days. Lunar months consist of two fortnights, 15 day periods known as *pakṣas*. The waning or dark fortnight leads from the full moon, known as *pūrṇimā,* to the new moon. The waxing or bright *pakṣa* is the fortnight from a sliver of a new moon, known as *amāvāsyā*, to the next *pūrṇimā*.

Just as in the Western calendar, the solar week consists of seven days, each ruled by a particular celestial body. Sunday is Ravivāra, ruled by Ravi, the Sun. Monday is Somavāra, ruled by Soma, the Moon. Tuesday (Maṅgalavāra) is ruled by Mars, Wednesday (Budhavāra) is ruled by Mercury, Thursday (Bṛhaspativāra) by Jupiter, Friday (Śukravāra) by Venus, and Saturday (Śanivāra) is ruled by Saturn. Tuesdays and Saturdays are astrologically dangerous days of the week, since they are ruled by the inauspicious planets, Mars and Saturn, respectively, and it is common for Hindus to visit shrines of the celestial forces (*graha*) to appease these forces. Besides the seven celestial rulers of the solar days, Hindus include two other inauspicious *grahas*. These are Rāhu and Ketu, astronomical points on the moon's orbit. The Rāhu Kāla is a shifting inauspicious period of time that occurs every day, and which is regarded as inappropriate for the celebration of certain religious rites.

The Hindu festival cycle

The Hindu annual cycle consists of six seasons, each roughly corresponding to two lunar months. The spring months (March–May) are Caitra and Vaiśakha, the summer months (May–July) are Jyaiṣṭha and Āśādha, the rainy season months

(July–September) are Śrāvaṇa and Bhādrapada, the autumn months (September–November) are Āśvina and Kārttika, the winter months (November–January) are Mārgaśīrṣa and Pauṣa, and the early spring months (January–March) are Māgha and Phālguna. Thus the autumn Navarātra described above began on the first lunar day (*tithi*) of the waxing fortnight (*śukla pakṣa*) of the lunar autumn month of Āśvina (September/October), which in 1990 fell at 2:30 a.m. on September 19. Navarātra continues to the ninth day of the waxing fortnight of Āśvina, although clearly various related celebrations continue to the tenth (Vijāyā Daśamī) and the eleventh (Ekādaśī) of that lunar month. Many Hindus regard Vijāyā Daśamī as commemorating the day when Durgā slew the buffalo demon Mahiṣa, while others hold it as the day when the warrior god Rāma killed the ten-headed demon Rāvaṇa. It marks a climax of the various Rām Līlās, folk dramas that enact the *Rāmāyaṇa* epic, some of which have been running for a month. In Nepal, it is known as Dusshera or Dasain, and marks the high-point of that nation's pre-eminent festival, which is particularly renowned for its spectacle of blood-sacrifices.

During the hot summer season, on the eighth day of the waning fortnight of Vaiśakha (April/May), is the feast of Śītalā, the Cool One, the goddess of smallpox, cholera, and other fever diseases. She is especially worshipped on waning eighths (beginning with the waning eighth of Phālguna), although eighths (waxing and waning) are regarded as especially sacred to goddesses generally. Elevenths of the lunar month are sacred to Viṣṇu, one of the great gods of Hinduism, and he is said to go to sleep on the eleventh day of the waxing fortnight of Āśādha (June/July), at the onset of the rainy season. His four month period of sleep ends at the end of the autumn, on the eleventh of the bright fortnight of Kārttika (October/November).

At the beginning of the rains, on the second day of the waxing fortnight of Āśādha (June/July), one of the most well-known festivals takes place in the north Indian city of Puri, in the state of Orissa. There the deities Jagannātha, Balarāma, and Subhadrā, are dragged in massive chariots, pulled by hundreds of worshippers around the city. This chariot (*ratha*) procession (*yātrā*) led observers to coin the word "juggernaut" (after Jagannātha) for a massive, unstoppable object. Since Varanasi is regarded as a microcosm of Hindu sacred geography, it too celebrates a Ratha Yātrā festival, but on a far smaller scale.

Another festival of pan-Indian fame, but particularly popular in the state of Maharashtra is Gaṇeśa Caturthī (Fourth for Gaṇeśa), which is celebrated on the fourth of the waning fortnight of Bhādrapada (August/September). Popularized by the activist B. G. Tilak, as an effective means of mobilizing national solidarity through a religious symbol during India's struggle for independence, the festival has continued to grow. Paralleling forms of the Durgā Pūjā rites described above, large, colorful clay images of the elephant-headed god Gaṇeśa are constructed, housed in decorated temporary shines, viewed and worshipped by devotees, and then carried off for immersion. The eighth day of the dark fortnight of Bhādrapada (August/September) is designated for celebrating the birth of the flute-playing, cowherd god Kṛṣṇa. Kṛṣṇajanmāṣṭamī (Eighth for Kṛṣṇa's Birth) is celebrated with a moderate fast, permitting foods using milk, butter, and other dairy products, and the singing of devotional songs dedicated to Kṛṣṇa.

The waning fortnight of Āśvina (September/October), known as Pitṛ Pakṣa, is dedicated to the ancestors (*pitṛ*). Widely celebrated throughout the Hindu world, it is a time for rites for departed family members. Hindus may commission special fire rites, or simply make food offerings to the deceased at home shrines or temples.

The month of Kārttika (October/November) marks one of India's most popular festivals, widely celebrated by Hindus and non-Hindus alike, and among many of the Hindu communities outside of India. This is Dīvālī or Dīpāvalī (Row of Lights). People light lamps to invite Lakṣmī (Goddess of Fortune) into their homes and offices and set of firecrackers and other fireworks to appease a host of spirits and demigods. Merchants open new account books, clean and paint their homes, and thus for many this marks a sort of New Year's Day. However, there are numerous regional differences among Hindus for the day designated as the beginning of the annual religious cycle.

In mid-January, the harvest festival of Pongal ("overflowing") is celebrated in south India, particularly within Tamil Nadu, and among Tamil communities abroad. The southern monsoons have come to an end. Old clothes and utensils are destroyed, and sweets made from rice, milk, and cane sugar are prepared in new pots. It is considered auspicious to watch the mixture boil over and overflow, a sign of abundance from which the festival derives its name. Cattle are honored, and women draw elaborate diagrams, known as *kolams*, to decorate the entrances to their homes. The festival marks an important division in Hindu calendric considerations, for the sun has begun its journey north of the celestial sphere and the daylight hours are beginning to get longer. This northern or upward passage of the sun, which is considered to be auspicious, continues for half a year until mid-June, when daylight hours begin to grow shorter.

Mid-month, on the fourteenth night of the waning fortnight of Phālguna (February/March), when there is virtually no moon visible, Hindus celebrate Mahāśivarātri, the Great Night of Śiva. Since it is dedicated to one of the Great Gods of Hinduism, this festival is widely celebrated in the Hindu world, particularly by ascetics who belong to Śaivite renouncer sects. Worshippers visit Śiva temples, bathe the phallic effigies (*liṅga*) with milk, and may themselves consume intoxicants such as cannabis-laced beverages (*bhang thandai*), since such consciousness-altering substances are beloved by Śiva. The advent of spring also brings the exuberant festival of color, known as Holi, which is celebrated on the full moon of Phālguna. Known for its suspension of caste norms and other proprieties, the festival is marked by people liberally spraying each other with colored water and powders. Derived from more ancient spring rites, often dedicated to the God of Love (Kāma), the festival of Holi maintains certain carnivalesque features, where raucous singing and dancing in the streets, the making of lewd gestures and speaking obscenities are permitted. Here, too, the inhibitions of celebrants may be loosened, and their enthusiasm enhanced through the consumption of *bhang*.

The spring month of Caitra (March/April) is when the spring Navarātra is celebrated, although this is less elaborate than the autumn festival, and mostly consists of the establishment of jar forms of the Goddess, and recitation of the *Durgā Saptaśatī*. On the ninth day of the waxing fortnight of Caitra, some Hindus celebrate Rāma Navamī (The Ninth for Rāma), which commemorates that god's birth. This fervor of this festival has grown in concert with efforts to build a temple in Ayodhya on the ruins of a Muslim mosque purportedly built on the ruins of a former Hindu temple that marked the birthplace of the mythic hero-god, Rāma. On the full moon of Caitra, Hindus celebrate the birthday of Hanumān, the beloved monkey god and hero, whose adventures are recounted in the *Rāmāyaṇa* epic.

Readings

It would take an encyclopedic study to enumerate and describe all of the many Hindu religious festivals celebrated through the course of a year. The rationale here has been to provide a simple overview of certain well-known celebrations, in the context of the Hindu calendar cycle. An excellent description of the annual religious cycle of festivals in Varanasi is found in Diana L. Eck, *Banāras: City of Light* (New York: Alfred A. Knopf, 1982). For the festival cycle in south India, see Guy Welborn and G. E. Yocum (eds) *Religious Festivals in South India and Sri Lanka* (Delhi: Manohar, 1985). An engaging treatment of the annual cycle of worship to a host of deities in an Indian village is found in Lawrence Babb, *The Divine Hierarchy: Popular Hinduism in Central India* (New York: Columbia University Press, 1975). The north Indian village festival rotation is described in Stanley A. Freed and Ruth S. Freed, *Hindu Festivals in a North Indian Village* (Seattle, WA: University of Washington Press, 1999). For a discussion of Navarātra and a detailed description of the Durgā Pūjā, see my *Ritual Worship of the Great Goddess* (Albany, NY: State University of New York Press, 2003). On the temple and worship of Vindhyavāsinī, see Cynthia A. Humes "Vindhyavāsinī: Local Goddess Yet Great Goddess," in John S. Hawley and Donna I. Wulff (eds), *Devi: The Goddess in India* (Berkeley, CA: University of California Press, 1996) pp. 49–76.

Author

Hillary P. Rodrigues (PhD) is Professor of Religious Studies at the University of Lethbridge. A former chair of the Departments of Anthropology and Religious Studies, he is the recipient of the university's Distinguished Teaching Award (2000) and the Board of Governors Teaching Chair (2009–11). His books include *Ritual Worship of the Great Goddess* (Albany, NY: State University of New York Press, 2003) and *Introducing Hinduism* (London, Routledge, 2006).

Chapter 11

A Himalayan exorcism

William Sax

Preamble

Somewhere in the middle of my career as an academic anthropologist, I found myself searching for my next research topic. I didn't know exactly what that topic would be – I only knew that I wanted to work on the religion of the lowest castes of the Hindu social system in the Himalayas. In my doctoral research I had concentrated on the cult of the Himalayan goddess Nanda Devi, and done most of my research among the highest castes of Brahmin priests. In my subsequent research on folk theater I had worked closely with the other regional high-caste group, the Kṣatriyas, or Rājputs. And now, in order to deepen my knowledge of local culture, I planned to work amongst the lowest castes, locally known as Harijans. It is difficult to decide which term to use for the lowest castes in the central Himalayas, where I have conducted most of my research. "Untouchable" is offensive to many, and "untouchability" is in any case illegal in India. "Scheduled caste" is an awkward and rather vague term, though it is often used of people of this group. "Dalit" (literally "oppressed person") is preferred by those who are politically active and aware, but the term is hardly known in the central Himalayas. Here I use the term "Harijan," which was coined by Gandhi and means literally "child of god," because it is the most widely used and politically neutral term in the region.

Of course I already knew many Harijans. As drummers and musicians, they were central to all of the religious and theatrical forms of Himalayan Hinduism that I had studied. I had interviewed them, recorded and translated their songs, and visited them in their homes. But I had never done proper anthropological research among them, never lived with them for long periods of time, never focused on their social life and customs, never asked them in detail about their lives. And for a variety of reasons, both personal and professional, it seemed to me that now was the time to do so.

Narrative

These were my (rather vague) ideas when I returned to the village where I had conducted research, on and off, for decades. The village is not far from the town of Karanprayag along the Alakananda River, and lies at an elevation of about 1,500 meters in a wide valley surrounded by forested mountains. Unfortunately I was not quite sure how to put these ideas into practice. I only knew that certain low-caste men, the so-called "gurus," functioned as priests in a local religious cult that was very popular amongst the Harijans. Here the word "guru" refers not to a spiritual master, but rather to a "master of the spirits" – someone who can summon, control, and exorcize ghosts, demons, and local deities. I was trying to find out more about the cult, and its rituals and other practices, but I wasn't having much success. I had taken a long bus trip to the village of one of the best-known local gurus, who had a rather dark reputation as a sorcerer (*sabarī*), and was told that he had gone to the fields. It was there that I found him, a hardy 80-year-old man working alone, planting the spring crop. He was polite but reserved, first inviting me to accompany him during a ritual that he was going to perform a few days later, and then taking back his offer because it was a secret ritual. Perhaps a client had hired him to curse someone, and he didn't want to be seen engaging in such an immoral act.

Then I went with my old friend and assistant Dabar Singh, with whom I was staying at the time, to see a Harijan woman who sometimes acted as the oracle of a local god. Clients would come to her with their problems and she would go into trance. Speaking through her, the god would diagnose the causes of the illness or misfortune, and prescribe a remedy, normally a ritual of some kind. She and her husband told me that they needed to sponsor a lengthy ritual, but did not have enough money to go and summon the guru, so I gave them 100 rupees (less than $3) for their travel costs. I came back several days later at the appointed time, but they had done nothing.

Like other scientists, an anthropologist needs data, but I was not getting any. The invitation to see the secret ritual had been rescinded, the Harijan oracle had taken my money but done nothing, and several other promising leads had also failed to bring results. I was irritated, frustrated, and worried about my lack of progress. But as I left the oracle's village, I ran into a young man on the path. He called himself Satyeshvar Himalaya, but to the villagers he was just "Sacchu," and in the following months and years he became my major informant and a good friend. He charmed and delighted me with his ready smile and quick laughter, his irreverent stories about high-caste people, and his tales of adventures around India. He claimed to have spent some 15 years on and off in Bombay (Mumbai) and even to have done a bit of playback singing there. He seemed to understand my difficulty immediately, and told me that he and his father were gurus themselves, and that they could arrange for me to see one of the rituals in which I was so interested.

Sacchu took me to the house of a man named Makkhan Lal. Like most peasants in the area, Makkhan Lal had grown up in a large, joint family. His childhood household had consisted of his father, his father's elder brother, and their multiple wives and children. But Makkhan Lal's uncle died, and then his first wife died, so that all five of his children were left in the care of his younger wife. Three children were the offspring of the older wife, and two were the offspring of the younger wife. The younger wife took good care of her own two children, but she didn't really look after the three children of her deceased elder co-wife. One day Makkhan Lal's father pointed this out to her and she became furious, and called upon her god, saying, "God, my brother, you alone must look after me!" Makkhan Lal assumed that she had gone to her natal home and uttered a curse. All of this had happened over 14 years previously, but the god had only recently "seized" Makkhan Lal's daughter, in fulfillment of the curse. She was afflicted with such intense stomach pains that she sometimes collapsed, but in a short while she would be well again. I asked Makkhan Lal if he had consulted an oracle, and he answered:

> At least a hundred times. I went to one oracle after another, but different answers emerged. When I took her to the hospital she had no pain, but when I brought her home she seemed as though she would die. So I would take her back to the hospital, and once again there was no pain. But as soon as we reached home, the stomach pains would begin again. We exhausted ourselves consulting oracles, until at last we found out which god it was.
>
> I made a vow to the god. I gave him some money and some other things, and said, "I will worship you if she is cured." And she got well for three months. The god gave us relief for three months. And last winter I was ready to worship, but I had no money, so I couldn't do it. I did the preliminary rituals, but nothing else. And I couldn't worship him in the springtime, either – there was no money! Then my daughter's pains began again, and I thought "It would be better if she died!" Just today I've taken her to the hospital. I spoke to the goatherds [to buy a goat for the sacrifice], made all the preparations for the *pūjā* (ritual), got ready for it … I even split rocks along the roadside to make money to pay for it [this is very hard and demeaning work], but I was unable to sell them. Finally I managed to perform the preliminary *pūjā* and the god appeared again, and we asked for relief. My wife said, "If it's really, truly you, God, then seize someone else!" Then Sapna's elder sister began to have pains in her foot!

As soon as I finished interviewing Makkhan Lal, his daughter Sapna manifested her symptoms. She was about nine years old at the time, and seemed like a typically happy, carefree child. But suddenly she bent at the waist, put her head on her father's knee, and began crying and sobbing for several minutes. "Look, sahib," said her parents, "how can we cure this?"

Makkhan Lal said that if only I would give him 3,000 rupees (around $60), he would be able to purchase the sacrificial animals, pay the guru's fee, take care of all the guests that he would be obliged to invite, and cure his daughter's illness. But I was reluctant to give him the money. First of all, there was the matter of professional ethics: I wanted to be as unobtrusive as possible, and to record only those rituals that were "spontaneously" performed. Certainly, I did not want to start paying for them! On the other hand, Makkhan Lal was clearly desperate to have the *pūjā* done – and I was rather desperate to see one. The cost was nothing to me, no more than the cost of a good meal in a restaurant with my family back home. How could I deny this to him? And then there was the matter of my local reputation: if word got round that

I was being exploited by the Harijans, or even worse, that they had made a fool of me by taking my money and not performing the ritual, then I would be a laughing-stock. I didn't know what to do, so I played for time, and told Makkhan Lal that I first had to confer with my assistant Dabar Singh. Makkhan Lal's father Mathura Lal must have understood my doubts, because he accompanied me on the bus back to Dabar Singh's village, and during the whole trip he kept promising that he would do the *pūjā*. Over and over, he said, "I'm speaking from my mouth, not my asshole! No one eats shit from my mouth!"

That evening, Dabar Singh warned me to be careful. "These Harijans are masters at gaining your sympathy," he said. "They'll break your heart and bring tears to your eyes, but in the end you'll have nothing but an empty pocket." I told him that I had my doubts in any case, and thought that perhaps it was nothing more than a little girl's game, that Sapna was only pretending to be sick because she enjoyed the attention. He looked at me darkly, and said that I should never, ever doubt the power of the god. "Be careful," he said. "That *devta* (god) causes even the healthy and powerful to fall!"

The next day it was terribly cold, with freezing rain and treacherous, muddy paths. On the way down to Makkhan Lal's village I slipped and badly sprained my ankle. I gave him half the amount he had requested – 1,500 rupees – so that he could purchase a male goat and two small sheep. "But there is one condition," I said. "You must promise to do the ritual just as you normally would. Don't change anything on my account. And if you don't do the ritual after I've given you all this money, then you will have to answer to your god!" Makkhan Lal spent the whole day climbing up and down the mountains in the freezing rain, negotiated a price for the animals, and brought them home. But they were in terrible shape, and I wondered if they would survive the night. It grew dark. I missed the bus, and limped back to Dabar Singh's village on my painfully swollen ankle. Next morning it was pouring rain, my ankle was hurting very badly, and I developed a case of diarrhea. I lay in bed and asked myself why I ever left my comfortable home and family to come here and do this fieldwork. I wanted nothing more than to stay in Dabar Singh's house under my comfortable quilt, but nevertheless I made my way to Makkhan Singh's house, only to discover that the large goat, the main sacrificial animal, had died during the night.

Of course, I had to pay for another.

Makkhan Lal had already completed several oracular consultations, and had been told that in order to cure Sapna of her affliction he had to erect a shrine for the god in his house. Most of the ritual activity took place in a tiny room barely 15 feet square. Over the course of the afternoon this room slowly filled until there were perhaps 30 people, sitting knee-to-knee. But I was not used to such cramped conditions, and every few minutes I had to shift my position to take the pressure off my knees, which was very difficult since we were packed so closely together. Finally it was time to begin. Sacchu's friend Dinesh brought two wooden sticks whose tips had been hardened in the fire, inverted a steel platter, and began warming up, playing this platter like a cymbal – rat-a-tat-tat-tat-tat! rat-a-tat-tat-tat-tat! Sacchu tuned his drum by adjusting its leather straps, and a third man took his place next to them, to sing the part of the "bumblebee" (see below). The music started, and soon the gods began to dance.

This musical backdrop was similar to other rituals I had witnessed in this region, where the guru normally plays a *huraki*, a small hourglass-shaped drum with two goatskin heads, the tightening straps of which are attached to a harness which he wears around his back, so that when he plays the drum he can, by pulling on the straps, cause it to make an unusual sound, which is especially effective in invoking the spirits. He is accompanied by the *thakalyor*, who plays an inverted metal platter with two wooden drumsticks, and usually by a third man, the *bhamvar* or "bumblebee," who echoes the final lines of each verse of the song. During my fieldwork, I often performed this third role. Garhwali gurus are also called *jagariya*, that is, ritual experts who lead night-long vigils called *jagar* (related to the words "awake" and "waken"), in which everyone stays awake and/or a particular god is "awakened" by singing his songs and performing his rituals.

I was utterly bewildered by the number of gods who came, possessed their human "beasts," and danced. Sacchu the guru was occasionally puzzled too, as several gods would often dance at the same time, and he would have to quickly recognize who it was, and change his praise-song accordingly. Even the gods' language was difficult to understand, full of shrieks and hesitations, as if they found it difficult to speak. But perhaps my strongest reaction was to see how the guru's music was made for dancing! Sacchu may or may not have been a playback singer in Bombay, but he had a superb voice that immediately captured everyone's attention, while his friend Dinesh played an irresistible rhythm on the platter. On the first night, in the middle of the séance, Makkhan Lal's wife suddenly cries out from the back room. Sacchu stops playing his drum and calls out in a slightly panicked voice, "Is it a ghost? Is it a ghost?" And indeed it is: the ghost of the woman who had placed the curse had possessed Makkhan Lal's wife! They carry her out into the tiny room and Mathura Lal begins to protest his innocence: "What did we do to deserve this? I only said that you didn't feed those children properly, and you went straight to lay a curse on me!" Sacchu sings on:

> Hey ghost, become godlike
> You come to the guru's rhythm
> You hear it and you come
> You've come to our happy ritual of celebration
> This celebration is for you
> The master of this house is making you his support
> He's making you his goddess!

Sacchu stops playing and says, "Why are you crying? We're making a new place for you; we are worshipping you! What else do you want?" Then he sings a song of praise to the god for whom the ritual is being performed, asking him to give milk to the livestock and intelligence to the family, to bless his client who is sponsoring this ritual, to be the mother and the father of the orphans, the support of the poor, to be a tree in which little birds can rest. The god Bhairav possesses Makkhan Lal, who cries out as if in pain. He moves his jaw but no sound comes out (this means that the god is trying to speak, but cannot). Makkhan Lal's wife (Sapna's mother) loses consciousness, and it is clear to everyone that there is now a problem: the ghost will not allow Bhairav to take up residence in his new shrine. They put oil on her forehead and give her milk to drink, and she regains consciousness. Within minutes, more gods arrive and there is more possession, more dancing, and more exchanges with the god that I do not understand. My head is spinning from the drama of the ritual, from the difficulty of comprehending what is happening. Villagers kneel before the gods possessing their human "beasts," asking them the reasons for their illnesses and misfortunes. A young girl suffers from headaches, a retired soldier wants to know who has tipped his new taxi into the ravine, and the guru himself asks why he still has no son. So many problems, illness and misfortune, missing children, barren livestock, financial ruin, earnest faces, beseeching gestures – it is a world full of affliction and pain.

Sacchu explains that the ghost and the god are "joined" and must be separated before the god can manifest himself. It is very late and we stop so that everyone can catch a few hours of sleep before the sun rises. Late in the afternoon, Sacchu's father Darpal comes to perform the ghost *pūjā*. Soon the gods begin to dance, and the ghost again comes over Makkhan Lal's wife, who begins screaming very loudly in the back room. The sound is frightening and my hair stands on end – it sounds as if a soul is howling from the depths of hell! Then the guru begins to sing:

Figure 11.1 A ghost possessing a woman embraces one of her surviving family members

That sinful god of death [Yama: the god of death and lord of the underworld]
took you away while you were still living
He put you in death's net, he put the noose on you
Come here, oh ghost! Come here, oh ghost!
Your curse has come true
Come here, oh ghost! from the house of death
Come here, oh ghost! from the land to the west
Come here, oh ghost! you've come via the oracle
Come here, oh ghost! from the canyons and ravines
Oh ghost, you had no one when you died.

Mathura Lal calls out, "Listen! The children of whom I spoke were your descendants as well as mine! Give up your curse! Take a divine body!" There is more music, dancing, prophesying. Bhairav possesses Sapna's mother, and s/he plucks at her hair. (The villagers say that this has a meaning: when the younger wife laid the curse she tore out a lock of hair and left it at the god's shrine). There is more possession, music, drumming, dancing, more conversation with the gods, more oracular consultations, and then the evening's performance is at an end. Everyone seems content.

The next day, they perform the ghost *pūjā* in the afternoon. Makkhan Lal lights an oil lamp and some incense, and prepares the other ritual materials. Darpal does not bring his drum, but instead plays the inverted metal platter without accompaniment. He recites a long spell, and then began to play the platter while singing:

Awaken, oh ghost! Your lamp is lit
Awaken, oh ghost! We have lit the incense
Awaken, oh ghost! For the head of the family
Awaken, oh ghost! Who dwells far away
Awaken, oh ghost! In the land of death
Awaken, oh ghost! In the children's square
Awaken, oh ghost! In this village of ours
Come, oh ghost! For your children and grandchildren
Come, oh ghost! For the orphans
Come, oh ghost! For the abandoned children
Come, oh ghost! For the descendants of your womb
Your curse came true in the land of death
That sinful Yama took you while you were still living
Come, oh ghost! Yama caught you in his net; time caught you in her noose
Come, oh ghost! That sinful Yama took all your tears, took all your eyes
Come, oh ghost! From the land of death.

(At this point the ghost possesses a woman, who begins to scream and wail, and Darpal shouts out, "Light the incense!")

Come, oh ghost! From the house of Kalangiri
Come, oh ghost! The morning sun has set in the West
Come, oh ghost! Night has fallen, the air is cool

They put a bunch of grass on the "ghost's" head and cut it with a sickle, to free the ghost from the net of death so that she can take a divine form. They feed milk to her, and put milk and oil on her head. Often in such cases the ghost asks about his or her old friends, children, relatives, and other loved ones. This time, however, there is little conversation: the ghost dances awhile, embraces Sapna, the afflicted girl, puts her head on her lap, and departs (i.e. the woman falls unconscious).

The main ritual for Mathiyala Bhairav is completed without further delay. When the god next possesses Makkhan Lal, he is smiling and happy. Everyone seems content and satisfied, and the guru sings of all the things they will offer to the deity. Mathura Lal, whose casual remark to his elder sister-in-law caused the whole affair, says he only wanted to protect the children, that he didn't do anything wrong, and the god replies that this was why he only gave a slight illness, and not too much trouble.

Later that night Dabar Singh and I find ourselves standing in a field at 4 a.m., in the freezing cold. Makkhan Lal has not made the shrine properly, and the Guru must repair it. It is bitterly cold, and my hands are freezing – even more so because

Figure 11.2 A woman possessed by Bhairav performs an oracular consultation

I have been assigned the task of bringing a bucket of water for cleaning the guts of the sacrificed goat. The mood is one of furtive secrecy. There is no dramatic conclusion. They have invited Dabar Singh and me to stay overnight, but he cannot bear the thought of staying with the Harijans, and so we walk back to his home, arriving at dawn.

This fieldwork was very psychologically demanding, partly because the rituals were so exciting and dramatic: the drumming and singing, the ecstatic dancing of possessed people, the awesome appearance of the fearsome deities, and the ghosts from the past, wailing and shrieking in a stuffy, crowded room. And all of this together with the poverty and suffering of the Harijans – it made such a contrast to my own relative wealth and power. At the very beginning of my fieldwork, I wrote this entry in my diary:

> I think it's finally happened: I've found a research topic that is too intense for me … rituals to awaken the dead, performed secretly in the middle of the night at the cremation ground; deities that feed on corpses and filth; long-forgotten curses that cause even the wealthy and powerful to sicken and die; magical herbs and poisons slipped secretly into an enemy's food; violent sacrifices at midnight, the blood of the writhing animal dripped slowly into a red earthen pot filled with thorns, centipedes, worms, and other low and slinking creatures …
>
> For weeks I have been trekking from village to village, meeting with exorcists and magicians, transcribing old manuscripts with secret spells, and participating in these fearsome rituals. The people are so poor, their houses tiny and dirty; they haven't enough to eat; they are beset on all sides by poverty, violence, and disease; their only powerful friends are the fierce beings who inhabit these cold, threatening mountains. They call on these deities to curse their enemies, but there is a price to pay: the worshipper must establish a shrine of the god in his own home, and his descendants must continue to worship him forever.
>
> And so they call the Harijan guru, who comes with his Huraki drum. At midnight the villagers gather, they light a lamp, and the guru calls the spirits down from the high Himalaya, up from the cremation ground. He sings and chants all night, summoning the gods, who possess the villagers one by one. They shout from enthusiasm, agony, or both, then "dance" on the earthen floor on all fours, some barking like dogs, others roaring like lions, the women's long hair unbound, whipping back and forth as they dance in wild abandon. Sometimes the ghosts of the unhappy dead come: they wail and moan, and seek to learn the reason for their unending torment. And all the while the guru smiles and sings and plays his drum, the wild music echoing through the hills.
>
> What is my role here, what is my purpose, my responsibility? To record these peoples' poverty? To subject their suffering to a "scientific" analysis? To display it to my students and readers? How can I help these unfortunate, suffering people?

Discussion

In many parts of the world, "possession" (by a ghost, or a demon, or a god) is a frequent occurrence, but it is rare in North America and Europe. Certain Christian sects speak in tongues or have other ecstatic experiences, but the average student is unlikely to have had much experience with this sort of thing. Certainly I had almost never encountered it before conducting my research in India.

Most people in North America and Europe believe that a "person" is a single personality, an "individual" who changes and grows over time, and is associated with one single body. But in possession phenomena, people claim to be temporarily "taken over" by a completely alien personality. That is why possession is so fascinating and puzzling: like multiple personality disorder, it calls into question some of our basic assumptions about what it is to be a person.

What is the best way to understand this? Some authors have claimed that possession provides the chance for subordinated people such as women, slaves, and others to criticize those who oppress them: after all, if it is not "me" who is speaking, then how can I be criticized for what I say? This argument is most closely associated with Ioan M. Lewis in his 1971 work *Ecstatic Religion*, which is a classic in the field and has been reprinted numerous times. Lewis' thesis, which is much more complex and subtle than I have indicated here, was extensively discussed and debated in the 1970s. The basic idea is that possession provides a kind of "safety valve" for people to express their anger, frustration, and critique in a way that will insulate them from retribution from those in authority. At first glance, this thesis seems to be very appropriate for the kinds of behavior I described above. Certainly, the lowest castes of India qualify as a "subordinated group," and possession behavior like the kind described above has been widely reported among them. Moreover, as I described in chapter two of my book *God of Justice: Ritual Healing and Social Justice in the Central Himalayas*, this behavior is powerfully triggered among the Harijans of Garhwal when certain myths are recited, that tell of grave injustices committed against them.

But things are not so simple. There are many other kinds of possession as well, and not all of them are associated with subordinate groups. For example, members of the highest caste of Brahmin priests are often possessed by gods and goddesses, but their style of possession is quite different. Harijans are typically possessed at night, indoors, and often as a result of some kind of affliction, so that their bodies appear to be contorted and in pain. Brahmins by contrast are typically possessed in the daytime, outdoors, by a deity giving blessings, and typically they stand with hands raised and smiling, as Osella and Osella describe in their chapter in the 1999 edited volume *Possession in South Asia: Speech, Body, Territory*.

In other words, there are many different kinds of possession, both positive and negative. There is negative possession by unwanted ghosts and demons, as well as positive possession by gods and goddesses, who are invited to come and possess the bodies of their devotees. The oracle's possession is positive because s/he seeks to be possessed, often in order to help with the negative possession of others.

What seems to be true around the world, in Europe and North America as well as in India and elsewhere, is that when one finds possession and other trance-related behavior, there is a hierarchy of bodily styles. When members of high-status groups are possessed, the style seems to be more refined and controlled, whereas the trance and possession of lower-status groups tends to be more violent, uncontrolled, and often erotic. Similar ideas were developed extensively by the Heidelberg sociologist Norbert Elias, in his voluminous studies of how the European aristocracy gradually distinguished itself from the rest of society .

Some readers may feel that I have not dealt with the most important question: are oracles and others "really" possessed by supernatural beings? This is a central question, with many philosophical implications, and there is not enough space to deal with it adequately here. On the one hand, my academic, anthropological language does not allow me to make pronouncements about the reality or non-reality of supernatural beings. That would be theology or perhaps philosophy, but not anthropology. On the other hand, as an anthropologist, I am obliged to report faithfully what I have seen, and to respect the beliefs and experiences of those about whom I write. When I do so, it becomes quite clear that possession is a powerful human experience, and that it has to do with deep truths about the human psyche, and about peoples' relationships to each other, their environment, and to the supernatural beings in whom they believe. Moreover, it is sometimes associated with powerful effects: Sapna's stomach pains disappeared after the successful exorcism of her great-aunt's ghost, and I could give many more examples where similar rituals have healed people's bodies, their psyches, and their

Figure 11.3 Sax with friends, co-researchers, and informants (Himalaya)

family relationships. The task of explaining how this all works, without lapsing into theological language, remains both challenging and rewarding.

Readings

Ian Hacking's *Rewriting the Soul: Multiple Personality and the Sciences of Memory* (Princeton, NJ: Princeton University Press, 1995) is an excellent study of multiple personality disorder. A classic on spirit possession is Ioan M. Lewis' *Ecstatic Religion: an anthropological study of Spirit Possession and Shamanism* (Harmondsworth: Penguin Books, 1971). Caroline and Filippo Osella's, "Seepage of divinised power through social, spiritual and bodily boundaries: some aspects of possession," in J. Assayag Kerala and G. Tarabout (eds) *Possession in South Asia: Speech, Body, Territory. Collection Purusartha* 21 (Paris: Editions de l'Ecole des Hautes Etudes en Sciences Sociales, 1999), pp. 183–210, contains a wonderful description of the different castes' possession "styles." On various Himalayan religious practices, see my study of the cult of Nanda Devī in *Mountain Goddess: Gender and Politics in a Central Himalayan Pilgrimage* (New York: Oxford University Press, 1991), on enactments of the Mahābhārata in *Dancing the Self: Personhood and Performance in the Pandav Lila of Garhwal* (New York: Oxford University Press, 2002), and on possession and healing in *God of Justice: Ritual Healing and Social Justice in the Central Himalayas* (New York: Oxford University Press, 2009) – parts of this chapter were adapted from Chapter 1 of this book.

Author

William S. ("Bo") Sax (PhD) studied at Banaras Hindu University, the University of Wisconsin, and the University of Washington, where he received bachelor's degrees (high honors) in South Asian Studies as well as in Asian Languages and Literatures in 1980. From there he went to the University of Chicago, where he earned his MA in Anthropology in 1982, and his PhD in 1987. From 1987 to 1989 he was a lecturer in anthropology at Harvard University, and a post-doctoral fellow in the Harvard Academy. After that he fulfilled a life-long dream by moving to Christchurch, New Zealand, where he taught Hinduism in the Department of Philosophy and Religious Studies for 11 years. In 2000, he took up the Chair of Ethnology at the South Asia Institute in Heidelberg. Professor Sax has published extensively on pilgrimage, gender, theater, aesthetics, ritual healing, and medical anthropology. His major works (all published by Oxford University Press, New York) include *Mountain Goddess: Gender and Politics in a Central Himalayan Pilgrimage* (1991); *The Gods at Play: Lila in South Asia* (1995); *Dancing the Self: Personhood and Performance in the Pandav Lila of Garhwal* (2002); *God of Justice: Ritual Healing and Social Justice in the Central Himalayas* (2008); and *The Problem of Ritual Efficacy* (with Johannes Quack and Jan Weinhold, 2010).

Chapter 12

Experiencing Sanskrit dramas in Kerala

Epic performances and performers

Bruce M. Sullivan

Preamble

This chapter concerns the practice of enacting sacred dramas in Kerala, south India. The tradition, known as Kūṭiyāṭṭam, is about 1,000 years old in its currently employed style of enactment, with roots even older than that in India's theatrical practices. In 2001, UNESCO (the United Nations Educational, Scientific, and Cultural Organization, the UN's cultural preservation agency) named a group of human activities as "Masterpieces of the Oral and Intangible Heritage of Humanity." The practice of dramatic enactment known as Kūṭiyāṭṭam was one of the two Indian traditions to receive this designation. During a series of visits between 1992 and 2006, I used photography, videotaping, and interviewing of performers and supporters to document this practice. This fieldwork led to the publication of translations of two complete dramas and studies of these and other dramas of the Kūṭiyāṭṭam tradition. This chapter describes my encounter with the rare and fascinating Hindu religious art form of Kūṭiyāṭṭam, in which performers enact dramas to enable an audience to experience *Rasa*, a state of emotional consciousness that is both religious rapture and joyful appreciation of the artistry.

Narrative

The great actor Ammannūr Mādhava Cākyār was 75 years old when we met. I had arranged to interview him at his home, where he also taught the next generation of actors and musicians the techniques and traditions of Kūṭiyāṭṭam performance. It was 9 a.m. and he seemed to be exhausted as we talked over cups of tea, as if even conversing was too much effort. His low energy level rose a bit when I asked what types of roles were the most difficult to enact. He told me that dying on the stage was the most challenging part, not only because of the range of emotional expressions that entailed, but also because one needed to master breathing techniques so that the death throes would be realistic. I asked for details on the mastery of breathing, and he said that it was *prāṇāyāma*, the control of breath and energy as taught in the yoga tradition. That evening at 6 p.m., Ammannūr Mādhava Cākyār made his torch-lit entrance onto the stage as Rāvaṇa, the King of Demons, and in the course of his two-hour performance without a break he crouched, leaped onto a stool and stood atop it on one foot, and at another moment he lay prone on the stage. It was hard to believe that I was watching the same man who earlier that day had appeared to be so exhausted!

Whether his *prāṇāyāma* practices or the adrenaline rush of performing for an audience was responsible for Ammannūr Mādhava Cākyār's energetic enactment, I became accustomed to seeing actors draw on their inner resources through 15 years of experiencing Kūṭiyāṭṭam performances. These actors were traditionally all members of a few families of temple servants who had the right and religious duty (*dharma*) to perform Kūṭiyāṭṭam. Male actors are called Cākyār; while females of this social group (or *jāti*) do not perform, the associated *jāti* of the Nambiār takes part, the males as drummers, the females (Naṅṅyār) as musical accompanists and actresses. Cākyārs are quasi-Brahmin temple servants; they receive Vedic initiation, but learn drama texts and techniques rather than the *Vedas* and ritual procedures. All Cākyārs I have seen wear the sacred thread (*yajñopavīta*) at all times. Through the years I have been told by various Cākyārs, Ammannūr Mādhava Cākyār being the first, that they are descended from the epic bards (*Sūta*) who composed poems about warrior heroism and recited the poems *Mahābhārata* and *Rāmāyaṇa*. These compositions provide the stories on which most of the Kūṭiyāṭṭam dramas are based, and Sūtas appear in those works as associates of the warriors and Brahmins. For perhaps the last 600 years or so, Kūṭiyāṭṭam performers have been temple servants, and as such their ritual purity is of crucial importance. According to tradition, ritual purity must be rigorously maintained; how they do this is revealing of some of Hinduism's central values.

In the Kūṭiyāṭṭam tradition, as Ammannūr Mādhava Cākyār described to me in detail, Cākyārs experience special ritual procedures to mark their status as actors. They are initiated into the acting profession in a ritual supervised by the chief priest of a temple, an event that includes the placing of an image of the deity Rāma on the head of the actor as *mantras* are recited. The actor is sprinkled with consecrated water that has been used to bathe the temple's primary icon, an action similar to the distribution to devotees of blessed food and water from the temple as *prasāda*, or God's grace. Additional rites of devotion (*bhakti*) are performed as lamps lit from the flame that burns before the temple's icon are waved before the actor, and the Brahmin temple priest blesses the actor at the start of his or her career as a performer. Moreover, prior to every enactment of a drama, each performer traditionally would be consecrated by ritual actions of Brahmin temple priests. The performer gives gifts to the priests, and prays to his or her chosen deity (*iṣṭa-devatā*) for inspiration and protection during the performance. Actors to whom I have asked the question "which is your chosen deity?" most often have answered "Śiva." These actors have told me that they do not care whether the temple's deity is their chosen deity, and often have added that all the images of God are only forms God takes for our benefit. After the performance, the actor walks into the temple sanctuary, still in costume except for the headdress, to worship and to receive blessings from the priest. At the conclusion of this ritual, the actor returns to the

Figure 12.1 Rāvaṇa, the demon villain in the *Rāmāyaṇa* epic, makes a dramatic entrance

theater to sprinkle consecrated water on the stage, on himself or herself, and on the audience. The actor then invokes the Gods and asks their forgiveness for any errors anyone in the troupe committed during the performance. After completion of this ritual, the performer's consecrated state ceases as he or she leaves the stage.

As a performer of Kūṭiyāṭṭam, Ammannūr Mādhava Cākyār embodied the traditional values with which he had grown up. Thus, when Mārgi, an organization promoting Kūṭiyāṭṭam in the state capital of Thiruvananthapuram (Trivandrum), built a small theater structure for a troupe of performers led by Ammannūr Mādhava Cākyār, it was placed in the Valiyaśāla neighborhood beside the wall of a temple dedicated to Śiva so that he and the other performers could be consecrated by the priests and bathe in the temple tank before performances. This is the site of most of my experiences of watching Kūṭiyāṭṭam enactments.

Each performance begins with the sound of drums. Nambiārs play the drums at the back of the stage before and throughout a performance. The most important instrument in Kūṭiyāṭṭam, the *mizhavu*, is a large pot-shaped copper drum about a meter across; the small opening at the top is covered with leather, resulting in a loud, distinctive sound when struck with the hands. Each *mizhavu* drum is encased in a wooden frame on which the Nambiār may sit while playing it. Two of these drums are regarded as an absolute requirement for a Kūṭiyāṭṭam performance. I was fascinated to learn that when a new *mizhavu* is made for use in temple performances, it is treated as if it were a Brahmin: the drum is initiated in a sacred thread ceremony, consecrated for its religiously significant performances, and given a funeral when its life is ended (for example, by a crack in the drum's body). Its ritual purity is as rigorously maintained as that of the performers themselves. In addition to the two large *mizhavu* drums, two *iḍakka* drums (a cylindrical drum shaped like an hour-glass and played with a curved stick) are also played for Kūṭiyāṭṭam dramas. Small cymbals often accompany the drums, and are played by Naṅṅyārs seated to the right of the drummers and facing the center of the stage. The drums lead the musical accompaniment to Kūṭiyāṭṭam, and the speed and intensity of the drumming signals the shifting emotional moods of a dramatic enactment.

Every theatrical performance I have seen has taken place in the evening. It begins with at least one actor (and sometimes two or more) taking the stage and facing the drums, while screened from the view of the audience by a cloth. The actor turns around, the curtain is removed, and the character stands revealed to the audience for the first time. Standing like an icon on the small stage, the dazzling colors of his costume pale in comparison to his facial makeup, a swirl of vivid red, white, black, and avocado green. Communicating silently in a language of intricate gestures and postures, the rapid movements of his eyes and brows contrast sharply with his motionless lower body. He may not speak for an hour, yet he can enact his own emotional state, then the actions and qualities of another character who had been on stage earlier, and then can return to his former role again. An actor in Kūṭiyāṭṭam embodies an array of expressive techniques that convey both actions and emotional states with eloquence.

The actors insist that their performance of Kūṭiyāṭṭam is a religious duty and they compare it to doing yoga or saying a prayer. Ammannūr Mādhava Cākyār told me that when he performs, he is not cognizant of the audience, and is performing for God. Traditional Kūṭiyāṭṭam enactments are devotional offerings to God, offerings made within the temple compound by consecrated temple servants. In fact, as I discovered on my first visit to the temple at Iriñjālakuḍa, the theater building faces the main shrine building across a courtyard, and for performances the doors of each building are wide open so there is a direct line of sight from the stage to the icon in the other building. God is in the audience, in the form of the icon that faces the stage.

Traditional Kūṭiyāṭṭam temple theaters have small stages, only slightly raised above floor level. In Thrissur (Trichur), the former capital of the state of Cochin and a major cultural center in central Kerala, the ancient Vadakkuṃnāthan Śiva Temple, the site of the largest temple theater, has a stage only 6.5 meters per side. Mārgi's newly-built theater in Valiyaśāla outside of the temple compound has a smaller stage, perhaps five meters wide and four deep. The audience sits on the cement floor, which is covered only with very thin woven mats. I found that bringing a pillow for the two- to three-hour performances made for a more comfortable experience. The audience was always diverse, including men, women, and children of all ages, and often foreign visitors as well. Usually I was accompanied by my scholarly coworker, N. P. Unni, a professor of Sanskrit who was interested in Kūṭiyāṭṭam dramas; his family was of the temple servant class (but with a different role as garland-makers, not Cākyārs). Frequently one of the male elders present in the audience would provide an informal, running commentary in English on the drama being enacted for the benefit of nearby foreign or first-time audience members. Professor Unni and I often whispered about the Sanskrit verse being recited. One of the first times we attended a performance together, I asked him why the actor had recited a verse of Sanskrit, made a series of gestures and movements, and then recited the same line again. He said that the idea was to give full expression to the emotional tone of that moment. Since he is more adept in interpreting the conventional gestures that convey meanings, I often asked Professor Unni for clarifications on what particular emotional state was expressed by a series of eyebrow movements or a hand motion.

I attended a conference in 2006 that was sponsored by the government of India and UNESCO, and held at a multi-purpose theater building at Vyloppilli Samskriti Bhavan, a Kerala government cultural complex that houses the historical society, archaeological survey, languages institute, and other offices. The theater looks traditional from the outside, except for its secular setting, but has a very large stage raised above the floor over a meter, an arrangement unknown in temple theaters. The conference included performances of Kūṭiyāṭṭam on the stage, as well as talks

Figure 12.2 Professor N. P. Unni, whose office wall displays a large photograph of Max Müller

by scholars and performers delivered from the same stage with microphones and electric lighting. The audience sat in chairs, and this remains the only occasion at which I have seen Kūṭiyāṭṭam performed while I have been seated in a chair.

Actors recite their lines in the ancient language of Sanskrit, or related dialects of Prakrit (vernacular languages, in ancient times). The style of recitation, however, distorts the pronunciation in ways similar to how the singing of opera distorts European languages. As a result of being perplexed at the first performances I attended, I began taking with me the text of the drama being enacted so that I could follow the lines recited from the script. But I never needed more than a page or two of the play's script at a time, because they perform only a small portion of any drama's text in a night of acting. Only small segments of a drama's script are portrayed each evening because performers have developed a language of gesture as part of their enactment style, and added a great deal of material to the received texts of the dramas. Over the centuries they have written down this material as performance manuals that guide their dramatizations.

As I learned from conversations with actors, the received texts of the dramas they enact have been modified in all of the following ways:

1 repetition of lines, typically reciting each line three times;
2 elaboration between lines, and between repetitions of the same line, by inclusion of additional material not composed by the playwright but by the actors themselves;
3 elaboration on all spoken parts through extended silent depictions by gestures and facial expressions;
4 interruptions during the enactment, such as discourses by the Brahmin clown figure (*vidūṣaka*), or flashbacks (*nirvahaṇa*) presented as introductions of new characters, either of which may last for days;
5 performance of a single act of multi-act dramas instead of the entire text, presentation of which may still take weeks due in part to the addition of material introducing the act.

Twice I have sat for two hours watching a performance in which an actor and actress enter, and then he recites his four-line verse in Sanskrit and remains on the stage alone, acting out his emotional reactions to the sight of the woman with whom he is in love. He proceeds to represent in movement and facial expressions how he imagines her, including her own emotional reaction to him and a scene of her maids adorning her, conveying this shift of character without a change of costume or makeup, instead through the conventional gesture of tucking his lower garment into his waistband. From this, the audience knows that he has begun enacting her character. The actor returns to his own character (Arjuna, here called Dhanañjaya), and exits the stage as the actress enters performing the role of Subhadrā. After depicting her character, she imagines the heroic man she has met and proceeds to show how heroic he is, drawing and shooting his bow at the demon who accosted her earlier. Eventually she resumes enacting her own character, and is rejoined on the stage by the hero for the conclusion of the night's performance of some two hours. This segment, from the middle of Act One of "Subhadrā-Dhanañjaya," is one of the most striking examples of a single actor performing more than one character, all without change of costume or makeup.

Aside from the issue of stamina for sitting on the floor to observe these dramas, other aspects of the scholar's body enter into the process of studying Kūṭiyāṭṭam. The food of the region is delightful, colorful, and fragrant with the many spices Kerala grows (cardamom, cinnamon, coriander, and pepper). Coconut, chilies, rice, and fish also figure prominently. Kerala has a tropical climate, as it is very close to the equator and borders the ocean. Moist in all seasons, the weather ranges from warm to hot. With tropical heat and moisture, and rice growing in standing water most of the year, mosquitoes thrive in Kerala. My arrivals seem to be greeted with particular enthusiasm by that community, the news spreading quickly among the mosquitoes that a new restaurant has opened and merits a taste. Nothing appears to deter them, but on my most recent trip I thought I had found a technological solution: solar-powered mosquito repelling electronic devices from a well-known outdoor supplier. I bought two and hopefully, almost religiously, used them, but noticed that I was still being bitten. Use of them stopped one evening when I had set them up by my bed, one on either side like stereo speakers, but then I looked over at one of them and saw a mosquito calmly sitting on the black plastic "mosquito repelling" device waiting for a meal! I have concluded that study of Kūṭiyāṭṭam will include this contribution to the well-being of the mosquitoes of Kerala.

For me as a scholar observing Kūṭiyāṭṭam enactments, one of the most challenging aspects to documenting this tradition photographically is the lighting. Traditionally, lighting would be provided only by a brass lamp with three wicks that burn coconut oil at the front of the stage. Performances are typically at night, and the single lamp sheds very little light. As a consequence, actors often approach the lamp for moments in which subtle movements of the face are used to signify emotional states. The fact that light was not extensive also led to the use of a white beard-like addition to the makeup along the jaw-line, the effect of which is to reflect some of the scarce light onto the actor's face so that expressions would be more visible. Performers often, and understandably, request that no one use flash photography. In such dim conditions, cameras often produce blurry images because of the longer time of exposure required. Making a video recording is similarly problematic. Now, however, electric lighting is the norm, at least for the more dramatic moments in a performance, and often for the entire event. While the addition of light is welcome from the photographer's perspective, it can also be glaring. This innovation is only the most visible of many changes Kūṭiyāṭṭam has experienced in recent decades, a development that makes this particular historical moment all the more interesting for the study of this ancient tradition.

Discussion

Over the past 1,000 years, the Kūṭiyāṭṭam tradition became very closely tied to the Hindu temples in Kerala. Sixteen major temples in Kerala have (or had) theater buildings specially constructed within the temple compound. Some are still functional, such as the copper-tile roofed theater building at Vadakkuṃnāthan Temple in Thrissur (Trichur). Others have fallen into disrepair or have collapsed and are no longer used. With the establishment of an independent, democratic government of India in 1947, the traditional pattern of royal support for temple activities was brought to an end and new patrons have emerged. Performers and temples have both been profoundly affected by this social change in Kerala; indeed, even the audience has changed.

Land reforms have largely eliminated the income of temples by terminating ancient land grants, and have thus deprived temple servants such as Cākyārs of the income from land cultivated for them by others. As a result, performers have been compelled in many cases to find other means of making a living. Moreover, some actors and musicians stopped performing altogether when temples were opened to citizens in caste groups of lower status, beginning in 1936. Female performers have been profoundly affected by the near-disappearance of the matrilineal system that had kept a Naṅṅyār in her mother's home; now they typically live with their Nambiār husbands. These developments have thinned the ranks of performers, but have also resulted in the diversification of those who perform. In recent years, Nairs and members of Kerala's other social groups have taken up Kūṭiyāṭṭam performance, partly due to a state mandate that requires acceptance of members of all social groups in the state arts university, Kerala Kalāmaṇḍalam, at which Kūṭiyāṭṭam is taught. Social change in recent decades has led to a new situation, in which not all Cākyārs act and not all Kūṭiyāṭṭam actors are Cākyārs.

With the cessation of kingship in the mid-twentieth century, Kūṭiyāṭṭam performers began to search for new patrons to support their sacred art form. Centers of Kūṭiyāṭṭam instruction and performance have developed, and each one is quite different from the others. The previously mentioned Kerala Kalāmaṇḍalam has offered instruction in Kūṭiyāṭṭam and other art forms since 1965 without regard to caste status, and is now a state university. The Mārgi center in Kerala's capital Trivandrum began teaching the practice of Kūṭiyāṭṭam in 1981, and received a six-year grant from the Ford Foundation in 1988. Ammannūr Chachu Cākyār Smaraka Gurukulam is a family-based organization operating since 1982 with support from the Sangeet Natak Akademi in New Delhi; Ammannūr Mādhava Cākyār was the main guru until his death in 2008. Natanakairali, a research and performance center for a variety of traditional performance art forms, is closely associated with the former center and has been very active in presenting Kūṭiyāṭṭam outside Kerala, including other countries. Kerala's Śree Śaṅkarācārya University of Sanskrit (founded in 1993) has a department of theater in which Kūṭiyāṭṭam is prominently featured, and also stages regular performances. Nepatya Centre for Excellence in Koodiyattom (founded in 2004) includes traditional performances but also innovative adaptations such as *Macbeth* in Kūṭiyāṭṭam style. No performance manual exists for a drama such as *Macbeth*, of course, so actors must create their interpretation rather than relying on the extensive manuals that guide traditional enactments. Kūṭiyāṭṭam is now performed more often in such secular settings as a result of grants from the state and central governments, foundations, and new patrons, and sometimes for ticket-buying audiences, than in traditional temple theaters.

The traditional goal of enactment of a drama such as the Kūṭiyāṭṭam plays is to enable the audience to experience *Rasa*, or aesthetic enjoyment. The ancient Sanskrit text about performance, the *Nāṭyaśāstra* by Bhārata (perhaps third century CE) presents not only practical instructions on how to perform a drama, it also presents an aesthetic theory that describes how dramatic enactment can communicate to an audience and achieve artistic success. Bhārata emphasizes that an audience member's purpose in attending a Sanskrit drama performance is to experience the *Rasa* that the work of art can facilitate. To relish the *Rasa* intended by the playwright and performers is to have an aesthetic experience brought about by an effectively presented drama viewed by spectators who (because of their nature and experience) are qualified to appreciate the depiction. In the *Rasa* theory, a dramatic work is a precondition, presentation of which allows the audience member to experience not merely a personal emotional state (*bhāva*) tied to one's particular experiences in life, but a generalized state of emotional consciousness that is joyful aesthetic appreciation. That is the *Rasa* experience. Bhārata's *Rasa* theory explains how one can experience an emotional response while witnessing a drama (for example, rapid heart rate and agitation at seeing the heroine threatened on the stage), yet at the same time having the awareness that one is witnessing an enactment rather than real life, so there is no need to rush to the heroine's aid. For Bhārata, eight (and for the later tradition, nine) *Rasas* can be experienced, and the theory was later applied to poetry as well as drama. Performers of Kūṭiyāṭṭam are well aware of this aesthetic theory and have told me that it is their aim to enable audience members to experience *Rasa*, as the playwright had intended.

The various centers of Kūṭiyāṭṭam training and performance have developed different approaches to enactment. Some insist that performances should be traditional, with all the elaborations of line repetition, use of gestures, and so forth, without which the audience could not experience *Rasa*. Advocates of this approach favor presentation only of dramas for which performance manuals are available, not applying the Kūṭiyāṭṭam style to other dramas (even Indian dramas, and certainly not dramas such as William Shakespeare's *Macbeth*). Other supporters and performers of Kūṭiyāṭṭam insist with equal conviction that to remain of interest in the present time enactments must be streamlined by elimination of repetitions and interruptions, that instead the playwright's script should be performed in a straightforward manner. The result of this approach is that enactment of an entire drama is possible, even a drama with multiple acts being performed in one evening. Advocates for this accelerated pace of performance observe that audience members do not have the leisure time to attend night after night, and that their

Rasa experience is dependent on viewing the entire play, including the resolution of its plot in the final scene. Stylistic diversity has thus become a feature of present-day Kūṭiyāṭṭam enactment.

A larger issue is raised by the performance of Kūṭiyāṭṭam globally, before audiences not traditionally included in Hindu temple settings. The *Rasa* experience is said to be attained by spectators who are prepared (by prior experience and their very natures) to have that experience, but are today's audiences prepared? Audiences in Kerala itself have changed significantly in recent years. Few in an audience now know Sanskrit well enough to understand the lines recited in Sanskrit, and fewer still the lines recited in Prakrit. This is due in part to the fact that Kerala's educational system was transformed from a Sanskrit-medium tradition to English-medium education emphasizing technology and medicine. Thus, despite Kerala's population being the most literate in India, Sanskrit knowledge is not widespread. On the other hand, Kūṭiyāṭṭam audiences in Kerala now include foreign tourists and scholars, and performances take place outside Kerala for audiences entirely new to the tradition. Audiences are much more diverse than ever before. But is the *Rasa* experience available to them as spectators for these enactments? The question remains relevant whether the performance in question is traditional in style or in the modernized, streamlined style.

A very interesting new development in the history of Kūṭiyāṭṭam was initiated by G. Venu, founder of the Natanakairali center. In 1995 he led a troupe of performers of assorted caste backgrounds to the Haripad temple, where a partially ruined theater building had not been the site of a performance of Kūṭiyāṭṭam for almost a century. In staging a performance at this temple site, Venu crossed the boundary and blurred the distinction between the sacred setting of the temple (open only to temple servants) and the secular setting of stages outside the temples (open to anyone). Additional similar performances in Kottayam and Haripad in subsequent years constitute a new tradition, in which performers not entitled by birth to Kūṭiyāṭṭam enactment engage in the practice in temple theaters, sites formerly closed to them.

The activities of all these centers, their performers and their supporters, to keep the small tradition of Kūṭiyāṭṭam alive are usually described as cultural preservation efforts. Recognition by UNESCO that Kūṭiyāṭṭam was a "Masterpiece of the Oral and Intangible Heritage of Humanity" was widely hailed in Kerala, and indeed, in India more generally, as beneficial in that international endorsement of the cultural significance of the practice would attract new performers and patrons. In recent years this does seem to be happening. The tradition of Kūṭiyāṭṭam, however, is not monolithic or centrally organized; the various centers compete with each other as well as cooperating with each other. Precisely what constitutes the "tradition" of Kūṭiyāṭṭam is a contested point. Would it be the ancient practice of performing in temple theaters, now a rare, possibly dwindling tradition? Would it be the modern practice of performing in a secular setting, perhaps a theater near a temple for the convenience of performers who want a priest's blessing, or an auditorium for an audience who bought tickets? Would it be the practice of reviving performance in temple theaters, perhaps even rebuilding theaters to allow groups to perform in these reconstituted sites who could not have gained admittance to the temple compound three generations ago? At the moment, each of these varieties of Kūṭiyāṭṭam can be found, so we should regard all of them as part of the ancient tradition, now manifesting new forms, sometimes in new locations.

The late, great actor Ammannūr Mādhava Cākyār said that dying on the stage was the most difficult and demanding type of enactment to perform in Kūṭiyāṭṭam. Its supporters and those who relish the experience of aesthetic enjoyment made possible by the artistry of Kūṭiyāṭṭam practices and performers are now hopeful that they will not witness Kūṭiyāṭṭam itself dying on the stage. The ancient tradition seems to have found new life both through adherence to ancient practices and through innovative reinterpretations of tradition.

Readings

For a short overview of the Kūṭiyāṭṭam theater tradition, see Farley Richmond, "Kūṭiyāṭṭam" in *Indian Theatre: Traditions of Performance*, F. Richmond, D. Swann and P. Zarrilli (eds). Honolulu, HI: University of Hawaii Press, 1990, pp. 87–117. Translations and studies of some of the dramas in the repertoire include the following: Edwin Gerow (trans.), "*Ūrubhaṅga*: The Breaking of the Thighs," *Journal of South Asian Literature* 20 (1985): 57–70; Barbara Stoler Miller (trans.), "*Karṇabhāra*: The Trial of Karṇa." *Journal of South Asian Literature* 20 (1985): 47–56, both of which

Figure 12.3 Hanumān and Rāvaṇa, well-known characters from the *Rāmāyaṇa*

were reprinted in Arvind Sharma (ed.), *Essays on the* Mahābhārata (Leiden: Brill, 1991); Clifford R. Jones, *et al.* (eds) *The Wondrous Crest-Jewel in Performance* (Delhi: Oxford University Press, 1984); N. P. Unni & Bruce M. Sullivan (eds and trans.), *The Wedding of Arjuna and Subhadrā: The Kūṭiyāṭṭam Drama "Subhadrā-Dhanañjaya"* (Delhi: Nag Publishers, 2001), and *The Sun God's Daughter and King Saṃvaraṇa: "Tapatī-Saṃvaraṇaṃ" and the Kūṭiyāṭṭam Drama Tradition* (Delhi: Nag Publishers, 1995). A recent study with many references is Bruce M. Sullivan's, "Dying on the Stage in the *Nāṭyaśāstra* and *Kūṭiyāṭṭam*: Perspectives from the Sanskrit Theatre Tradition," *Asian Theatre Journal*, 24, no. 2 (Fall 2007): 422–39.

Author

Bruce M. Sullivan (Ph.D.) is Professor of Religious Studies and Asian Studies at Northern Arizona University. Among his four books are *The Wedding of Arjuna and Subhadrā* (2001) and *The Sun God's Daughter and King Saṃvaraṇa* (1995), each a translation and study of a Kūṭiyāṭṭam drama coauthored with N. P. Unni (see above).

Chapter 13

Learning about Hindu practice

Fighting late-colonial attitudes and discovering temples and festivals

Paul Younger

Preamble

I learned about Hindu religious practice only after hurdling a whole host of barriers that were set in place when I arrived in India in 1957. Some of these barriers were left over from the colonial era when missionaries spread the word that temples were filled with evil superstition and universities were taught that only India's philosophical systems were worthy of academic study. Fortunately, I discovered a village of leather workers or Chamārs where a great deal of religious practice was going on, and, while I could find no university department interested in what I had discovered, my interest had been piqued and I looked forward to a time when I could find out more.

After I had been teaching for some years, I stubbornly went ahead and spent a year living among the priestly families of the great Śrīraṅkam temple in south India, and that gave me an opportunity to discover their festival practices and to learn how many of their wives and relatives also visited the nearby Śaiva and Goddess temples with very different religious practices. Having gained new confidence, I then went on to the Śaiva temple of Dancing Śiva in Citamparam and spent a number of years learning about its religious practices.

Realizing that the religious practices of individual temples were unique to that location and rooted in the local festival traditions, I started to study some south Indian festivals that constituted religious traditions unto themselves with little or no temple base. What this long process of discovery has now taught me is that in an agricultural society such as India, traditions of religious practice develop locally and change very little over time, as families continue in the way of life and worship of their ancestors.

Narrative

My narrative is divided into two main parts. In the first section, I will discuss colonial encounters, focusing on missionaries, the Banaras Hindu University, and Chittapūr village. In the second section, I will describe my exploration of two temples, the Śrīraṅkam Temple and the Citamparam Temple.

Fighting through the colonial cloud

I arrived in India in 1957 to study at Banaras Hindu University. That was ten years after the end of the colonial era and I was surprised to find that I had to deal with issues left by that era everywhere I turned. I was a brash 21-year-old American at the time and was eager to identify with the new post-colonial world then emerging in every corner of the globe. I had started with two years of work in the black community of Trenton, New Jersey. There, a group of black women had been very effectively using the techniques of non-violent action taught by M. K. Gandhi by linking arms and moving into crowds to limit the drunken brawls and violence in their community. They had brought me into their organization and given me challenging tasks that ranged from facing down violent mobs to petitioning the school board to locate a school so that it did not take away the community's one piece of parkland. With this experience, I arrived in India as a student hoping to do more Gandhian style work there.

Missionaries

My father had spent a lifetime sending money to and praying for missionaries, and I naively thought they might make good allies in my new setting of Banaras. The first Sunday in Banaras I attended the Anglican church I had seen on my way to the university from the railway station. The service was primarily in Hindi and was led by an Indian priest. However, a missionary, Alan Neech, was supervising. He introduced my friend and me to the congregation and steered enough of the service around to English that we realized that our arrival had reactivated a colonial era arrangement. Standing outside later, the Indian priest pointed to his house near the church and invited me over for tea while he explained that most of the congregation belonged to a low caste and were living in the hut-like houses at the back of the compound. Rev. Neech and my friend soon arrived to announce (in English) that we were going by car to Neech's missionary compound some five miles away for lunch, and to explain to the Indian priest (in Hindi, so he would know his place) that he should get on with other work. (A few weeks later the priest would come to the university and complain about the social and economic disparity between himself and Rev. Neech, and a few weeks after that we heard that he had been sent off to a rural outpost.)

As we waited for lunch, the colonial story unraveled. The ten-acre compound of flowering trees and the huge rambling house were meant for four missionary families, but the Neeches, while the only occupants at the time, still needed a cook, a cleaner, a gardener, a clothes-washer, and a watchman. Mrs. Neech had trained as a medical doctor, but was currently not using that training. The only school the couple felt they could put their three children in was in the deep south of India. So Mrs. Neech maintained another bungalow there to be near their children for six months of the year and to accompany them on the three-day-long rail trips home for holidays. Rev. Neech explained that there were no Christians in Banaras except for the lower-caste folk who were required to attend the Anglican church in return for their housing, and the four Anglo-Indian families for whom he put on a traditional English service once a month in the ornate little Anglican church in the cantonment or military barracks area of the city where the colonial officers once lived. (Good railway jobs had been reserved for Anglo-Indians in the colonial era and these four families still worked in the railway). He acknowledged that a person named R.C. Das had a Christian *āśrama* or meditation centre right on the riverbank and held conversations with Hindu holy men, but Neech thought of him as a misguided fool. He was at the time even more irritated by the fact that the young man he had employed to sit and sell booklets in the storefront chapel in the busy city center had copied Das's style of wearing the orange clothes of a holy ascetic. Recognizing my interest in Hindu worship, he advised me that the temples were run by greedy priests trained in black magic, and reported that he knew of cases where foreigners were drugged and robbed in those settings.

It was not long before I stopped going to the Neech's house for lunch, and in Banaras the missionary presence was easy to avoid. Nevertheless, it is helpful to see how widespread the awareness of the colonial era missionaries was if I skip ahead a couple of years and describe my similar experience in a very different part of the country, at Serampore College in Bengal. Serampore College is described in several accounts of missionary work in India as the location where the model missionary, William Carey, went and translated many Indian texts before starting the first theological college in India. I wanted to go to the college primarily to read texts in Vedānta philosophy with J. G. Arapura, a leading scholar of Vedānta who was then teaching there. I had already finished two years of a three-year program in theology at Princeton Seminary, so I thought it might also be interesting to finish a third year with Indian classmates in Serampore. William Stewart, the missionary principal, objected to my presence, and especially to my need of a scholarship and my disinterest in missionary housing and food. (The housing was a sore point at the time because Dr. Arapura and the other Indian faculty were still not allowed to use the missionary housing even though some of the large missionary quarters were occupied by bachelor instructors.)

During that year, I arose to jog at the crack of dawn every day to avoid the hot humid air of the rest of the day. The road in front of the college went along the banks of the Hooghly River, which was a branch of the Ganges. I loved the sense of holiness the river gave to the town and noted with joy the many clay images devotees would build on the bank of the river for their morning worship. One day as I returned to the area near the college there was a major shouting match at the riverbank. Just as I approached, Rev. Wenger, one of the theology faculty who was wearing heavy boots, pushed an elderly man aside and with a mighty swing of his boot kicked the man's clay image into the river. A huge crowd quickly gathered and the police, who arrived with them, escorted Rev. Wenger back into the college grounds. A few days later he agreed to avoid the police investigation by taking early retirement back to England.

Banaras Hindu University

The vulgarity of the colonialism still carried on in the behavior of missionaries of the 1950s was easy to spot and it was not long before I decided to avoid them. A much more difficult challenge at the time was figuring out why Indian professors in the university were still wrestling with the Orientalist reconstruction of Indian history that Frederick Max Muller and other colonial scholars had set in place. In this case there were no representatives of colonialism physically present, and the university was reputed to be at the heart of the nationalist struggle. In fact, it had been started by Madan Mohan Malaviya, a stalwart in that struggle. The College of Indology at Banaras Hindu University (BHU) was especially central to the nationalist cause and was really a graduate center attached to the Arts College whose students focused on the Indian heritage. The five major professors, however, had been trained by colonial scholars, and in retrospect I can see that they were still struggling with the view of Indian history set out by colonial scholarship.

Frederick Max Muller was a German Protestant youth when he arrived in Britain early in the nineteenth century to continue his study of Sanskrit. He was given the job of directing the work of the Indian pundits who compiled the four volumes of Ṛg Vedic hymns and was soon a celebrity scholar even though he never was given the professorship in Sanskrit at Oxford that he so coveted. What is interesting is the way he used his strong-minded Protestant opinions to set forth a full-fledged colonial view of Indian history that ranged far beyond his scholarly work as an editor of Vedic hymns. His view rooted itself in a Protestant preference for rationally set out and romantically derived views of the natural order, and he thought all religion started in such reverence for nature. For him the ritual parts of the *Ṛg Veda* could be set aside and an early version of the glorification of nature could be found in the earliest of the hymns. To make this view historically credible he arbitrarily assigned those hymns the date of 1500 BCE and said they were composed in Central Asia and brought into India by the invading Aryans. Continuing on, so that his opinions were fully colonial, he argued, without any scholarly investigation whatsoever, that all later religious developments within India were forms of blind, Roman Catholic-like ritualism, and he thought this was particularly unfortunate because according to his theory the Aryan invasion had brought India some awareness of the noble ideas of nature worship that had influenced German Protestantism.

In 1957, a century after they had first been set forth, Max Muller's opinions were still the focus around which scholarly tasks were being taken up in the Indology College of Banaras Hindu University. The principal of the college was Dr. Raj Bali Pandey, and as a Brahmin of north India he was still an admirer of Max Muller and was fascinated by the hope that Aryan Brahmin leadership might still be able to set India on a proper intellectual course. His own scholarly work, however, led in a very different direction, and his widely read book on *Hindu Saṃskāras* provided an authoritative account of the daily rituals in which Hindu practice was rooted. Dr. A. K. Narain's book on the Indo-Greek coins had won him wide respect in

Britain. His conversion to Buddhism also fit in well with the Orientalist reading of Buddhism as the Protestant-like voice of the Indian tradition, and his focus on the Greek, Indian, and Buddhist contacts in the northwest of India provided a kind of neo-colonial echo in the historical period to match Max Muller's Aryan speculations about similar contacts in the pre-historical period. Like Dr. Narain, Dr. V. S. Pathak had been trained in epigraphy by his colonial teachers by reading the Buddhist inscriptions of the Mauryan and Sunga periods, but as a local Banaras Brahmin he knew there were inscriptions on all the later Hindu temples as well and was determined to learn to read them too some day. Dr. V. S. Agrawala had already spent a lifetime studying the vast array of Hindu art found in temples large and small in the different regions of the country, but he felt thankful to have finally been appointed to a position in a major university and just resigned himself to the fact that the exams would be based exclusively on the colonial era texts of primarily Buddhist art put together by Benjamin Rowland and Ananda Coomaraswamy. And, finally, Dr. T. R. V. Murti, who was renowned at the time for a book called *The Central Philosophy of Buddhism,* which dealt with the logic of Mādhyamika Buddhism that fascinated Western scholars, spent most of his time reading texts privately with students who knew he was a devout follower of Vedānta and a brilliant interpreter of its theological texts. Each of these professors was at the time providing students with an understanding of the Orientalist-derived questions about the role of Aryans and Buddhists in ancient Indian culture, because, as they understood it, the role of the university was limited to the set of questions established by the colonial intellectual heritage. Put another way, their personal interests in things Hindu were not yet part of the university curriculum.

Fortunately for me, it was possible at the time to step outside of the colonially defined worlds of the missionaries and the university and get a sense of the religious life of other people. My classmates thought I would be thrilled to witness the different ritual ceremonies (*saṃskāras*) that took place in their families and I attended numerous weddings, naming ceremonies, and other auspicious events in their homes. They were less sure that I would be comfortable accompanying them while they took offerings to the monkey hero/deity Hanumān at the Sankat Mochan temple just before exams, but they let me come. Down at the *ghāts* or stairs into the holy Ganges, they were less comfortable with my questions about the funeral pyres and other ritual activities we saw, because they took it as given that they would not understand rituals designed for other families and castes and I should not be asking about such matters either. In the great Kāśi Viśvanātha temple of Śiva as Lord of the Universe, located near the *ghāts*, they also found it difficult to understand any of the rituals, but, because that was not a personal or private form of worship, they did ask the priests a few questions and agreed that we might understand Hindu ritual better if students were to be taught something about it. At the time, however, it was taken as given that Hindu ritual was not to be studied in the university, even though all of the professors were working on Hindu ritual practice in their own studies.

Chittapūr village

The Hindu students at BHU had not quite bridged the gulf between their colonially defined university subjects and their family-based ritual life, but in the village of Chittapūr nearby, the colonial cloud no longer limited what I could learn about Hindu practice. I had been visiting the village for some time to practice speaking in the local Hindi dialect when the Gandhian movement at the university asked me to live in the village and assist the villagers in a work project that involved building a brick culvert to provide access to the Harijan or untouchable part of the village. Once I was living in the village, I discovered that the community life of the untouchables or *chamārs* (traditional leather workers) involved quite a bit of religious activity that no one had pointed out to me as a visitor because it was so much an integral part of their daily life. Now they explained to me that *chamārs* like themselves did not normally go to temples, but they worshipped by visiting the gravesites of revered *bīrs* or heroic figures from their community. There were many such gravesites in the Banaras area, but in their own village there was now a new one because they considered a person named Chedi Lal, who had died just months earlier, a divine being. They had buried him rather than cremating him so that his presence would remain with them, and his gravesite at the edge of the village was now a place of worship. They took me to the gravesite and I began going there regularly to witness the worship-like activity going on.

The stories about Chedi Lal that they retold for inspiration were actually a bit confusing. The oldest story seemed to be that he had once been a servant boy in the Women's Hostel of the university and had learned English from a Christian south-Indian woman in charge of the hostel. Under her tutoring he was supposed to have read the entire Bible. A second set of stories was that he had been influenced by the Gandhian movement among the students of the university and had brought a Gandhian leader to the village. The Harijan members of the village had all agreed to give their land to the village or form what at the time was called a *bhoodan* village, and as a result Chedi's wife began teaching women's classes, and weddings and other rituals always included every Harijan family in the celebration. A third set of stories described how after his wife died in childbirth, Chedi began to hold a weekly prayer group in which they sang hymns to the god Kṛṣṇa, and took vows to give up the eating of meat and consuming of toddy or the local alcohol drink. This last initiative had divided the Harijan community between those who took these vows and called themselves *bhagats* or devotees, and the majority of the Harijan villagers who were called *nonbhagats.* I was thrilled to be able to understand such a unique worship system so clearly. However, when I asked my professors about it, they were curious but were not sure it should be called "Hinduism" and were quite sure I could not make an academic study of it in any case. At this point I felt that the colonial warnings about the deep mystery and evil intentions of Hindu ritual were wrong, but the only real academic option the university offered me was to start my thesis on early Buddhist thought. I started that thesis in Banaras and finished it in Princeton University.

Temples

Quite apart from the fear-mongering of colonial views of Hindu ritual, I could see that there was an enormous amount of ritual in Indian life and that it took many diverse forms. It included elaborate life cycle rituals, huge temples with many fulltime priests, and informal ritual patterns decided on by devoted villagers such as those I met in Chittapūr. Years later I was still pondering this deep trust Indians had in ritual when I had a chance to talk with Dr. T. R. V. Murti about my plan to study some of the great Hindu temples. He laughed at the fact that I had earlier allowed myself to be influenced by the colonial opinions on these matters and suggested that I just walk into the temples and see how ordinary everything seemed.

The Śrīraṅkam Temple

In my characteristically naive way I headed for Śrīraṅkam temple on an island in the Kāvērī River of south India, reputedly one of the largest and historically most important temples in all of India. My wife at the time was Susie Oommen who was raised in the "Syrian Christian" community of Kerala and was taught as a little girl that she should not go into Hindu temples. She was also taught, however, that she was of Namboodri Brahmin stock, and decided to join in this venture into the Śrīraṅkam temple. On the plane to India we had met the son of the retired collector of Trichinopoly District, where Śrīraṅkam was located, so he offered to take us to the temple for our first visit. Surprised to see a sign saying "Hindus Only Allowed" as we approached the fourth of the seven concentric gateways into the temple, he decided to improvise. Without consulting us, he made an agreement with the priests standing nearby that they would guide us into the inner sanctum and explained that we were Brahmins from Kashmir unfamiliar with the worship routine. That ruse worked especially well when Susie overheard them using it and jumped in to explain that in Kerala she had been told that Namboodri Brahmins were originally from Kashmir and she was bringing this complicated Brahmin heritage to Śrīraṅkam to see how it fit with the local temple tradition. We entered the inner sanctum of the temple and had a full description of the ritual from the priests on duty there.

During the next year I was privileged to practically live within the walls of the temple. Mr. Narayana Iyengar was from an ancient priestly family and in addition to his priestly duties had served as a judicial magistrate before his retirement. Now that he was retired, his religious duties occupied his entire life and he was delighted when his heart specialist, who was my co-brother or the husband of my sister-in-law, asked him to give me a hand with my research. The routine was that I would arrive at his apartment built into the fourth of the concentric walls of the temple at six o'clock every morning as he finished the prayer cycle begun at 4:30 a.m. Over our large brass tumblers of decoction coffee – a special decoction made days earlier by each Brahmin priestly family to which boiled milk was added at the time of consumption – he would point out the various astrological features of the day and the times for prayer that were important to observe or the temple rituals or festivities that might happen in various parts of the temple later in the day. Sometimes I had to rush off to festivities of various kinds, but most days the busy ritual times were later in the day and I was able to go out through the north gateways of the temple to the Kollidam River (the northern branch of the river as it passes the island) just down a steep bank from the outer or seventh temple wall. During much of the year the Kollidam bank was a vast network of quiet inlets where virtually the entire population of the island bathed each day in the sacred waters. Most days I spent two to three hours at this quiet river bank, bathing, praying, and reading, arriving somewhat later than most of the bathers after my lengthy chats with Mr. Iyengar. After seeing me at the temple for a year, people began asking me if I felt like I was in Vaikuntha or heaven and whether I planned to stay permanently. I explain more about what I learned at Śrīraṅkam in the Discussion section below.

I was actually growing a bit restless in Śrīraṅkam and feared that the scholarly work people might expect me to produce about that temple was somewhat different from the observations that I was making during my time there. As I hinted above, one of the mistakes Western scholars made in approaching Indian religious practice was to look for something that seemed familiar and then to over-interpret it in all sorts of ways. The idiosyncratic link that Max Muller saw between Ṛg Vedic hymns and his own love of nature mysticism was just an extreme example of this tendency. A much more common form was for scholars to look for a version of Christian theism in the Vaiṣṇava (Viṣṇu-centered) teachings of Rāmānuja, a renowned twelfth century figure based at Śrīraṅkam. Scholarly friends had been asking me if this was the line I was going to take, and I had not found it easy to explain that living in Śrīraṅkam what I had noticed was not so much a familiar theism but a ritual practice rooted in all sorts of local traditions. What I was trying to figure out was where these local traditions had come from, why they differed from the religious practices of the Śiva temple a mile away on the eastern end of the island, and, even more so, why they differed from the traditions of the temple of the goddess Māriyamman in Samayapuram about five miles away. People went to each of the three temple settings for specific reasons, and while the government had decided to place them under one administrative office and forced them to help one another in a variety of ways, they had been very different religious traditions for centuries. Narayana Iyengar valiantly tried to help explain the differences by noting that his daughter-in-law who was childless was always sneaking off to pray to the goddess Māriyamman and explaining that "the Śaivas are all around us, they worship the whole cosmos. They are the landowners. They provided the Cōla rulers. We are on an island. We are in Vaikuntha. We just love God." I knew that I had learned a lot about Hindu ritual in Śrīraṅkam, but to get a better perspective I decided it was time for me to go and study a Śaiva temple community.

The Citamparam temple

Citamparam is on the southeast coast of India just beyond the northernmost branch of the delta that allows the Kāvērī River to flow into the Indian Ocean. The area

Figure 13.1 Devotee in Śrīraṅkam Temple (Photo Rodrigues)

was called Tillai after the poisonous scrub tree that grows along the salt-water creeks near the coast, and legend has it that the temple site was originally a place where ascetics tried to live an austere life. At some point a worshipping community called the Mūvāyiravar or the Three Thousand settled there and began the worship of Dancing Śiva in a little wooden hall. We first hear about the place from pilgrims such as Maṇikkavācakar who came there from his position as a minister in the Pāntya government of Maturai, but in the ninth century Ātitya I, the Cōla king who was building irrigation canals up and down the Kāvērī River valley, put a golden roof on the little wooden hall and tried to bring it within the Cōla cultural domain. Over the next few centuries Cōla kings continued to come there and build concentric walls around the little hall as they did in other places, but the endogamous worshipping community that was there continued to lead the worship, and the community that now calls itself the Diṭcitārs or Initiated Ones claims that it still continues its original tradition.

While working in Śrīraṅkam, I had learned to read the many inscriptions on the temple walls, the ritual manual, and the various hymns used by the priests, so when I arrived in Citamparam I began doing some of the same work and the priests were in awe. They themselves could not read the inscriptions, and, while they had community accounts about the origin of the wooden hall, the gold roof, and the legendary storybooks such as the *Koil Purana*, they were afraid to ask too many questions lest the community's monopoly on the management of the temple might be called into question. Because they had formal meetings every 20 days and a rigidly maintained rotation of leadership, it was not long before they had discussed my role and welcomed me into their midst and took me to every secret corner of the temple to show me what could be learned there. I chose not to ask permission to do dating tests on the wooden hall and gold shingled roof, but I was able to examine them at length. I handled the jewelry and watched the deity bathed by the four priests who handed over care to four new priests at the 20-day priestly rotation. I crawled into the basement under the hall where ascetics are reputed to have sometimes meditated until their bodies passed on. And I stood in the tower from which priests jumped to their death when Vijāyānakara kings tried to alter the ritual routine. I will explain more about the routine at Citamparam temple in the Discussion section below.

While I worked for years on what would be a major book on the Citamparam temple and its festivals, I struggled with the central question, which had bothered me ever since I first arrived in Banaras, as to why Hindu ritual routines were so varied and so flexible. Even the great temples of Śrīraṅkam and Citamparam had priestly traditions that were unique to their local history and festivals that tied them to the local geography. I found myself asking whether there were situations where those local traditions had not subsequently been overlaid by newer traditions and elaborate temple walls built by medieval kings. Were there local ritual traditions that had clung more tenaciously to their older form?

Discussion

My discussion centers on Hindu rituals, temples, and festival traditions. After discussing the nature of Hindu ritual, I will illustrate the theory set forth by providing examples of ritual from the Śrīraṅkam Temple, the Citamparam Temple, and the festival tradition of Ayyappan.

The nature of Hindu ritual

Dr. Murti had come to Canada to teach after his retirement from Banaras and because he had left his family in Banaras he often ate with me and my Indian wife. He was a brilliant scholar of Vedānta and understood that persons became "realized souls" when their *ātman* was freed of its karmic associations and recognized that it was one with Brahman or Reality. What I had not expected to hear from him was how the variety of ritual practices supported the quest for the realization of

Brahman. Taking his own case as an example, he pointed out that vegetarianism and daily yoga practice were essential to keeping the physical, emotional, and mental life (*rūpa, vedana,* and *manas*) disciplined. Going on up the seven levels of psychic life, he went into great detail to explain how the life cycle rituals or *saṃskāras* dealt with the *karma* marks or *saṃskāras* inherited from previous lives, and how other forms of temple devotion and meditation led to control of the ego or *ahaṃkara* and the universal vision or *buddhi,* two of the higher levels of the self. While some of his ritual life was predetermined by his role as a scholar, he was very supportive of his wife's many rituals, of his son's fondness for the Sankat Mochan temple of Hanumān, and of the ritual forms I told him I had seen in Chittapūr. In his view it was Western religions that would have to explain why ritual forms such as baptism and communion could be elevated to absolute requirements for salvation, and argued that the great variety of ritual in Hinduism was evidence of how the variety of persons gave *saguṇa* (with attributes) form to their longing for Brahman, even as they longed for a fuller (*nirguṇa,* without attributes) realization.

The Śrīraṅkam temple

The island setting provides the symbolic explanation of the holiness of Śrīraṅkam. The great Kāvērī River runs west to east and carries the water of the Western Ghāts or the Kerala mountains that catch the monsoon when it first hits India. Its wide river valley cuts through the otherwise dry plain of Tamilnātu. Śrīraṅkam Island is halfway along this river valley, and the Cōla rulers had the foresight to build their first capital of Uraiyūr beside the huge outcropping of rock on the southern bank just opposite the island. This enabled them to develop extensive irrigation canals all along this southern bank and to even divert water south of the island as the water levels dropped after the end of the monsoon.

The holiness of the island itself was recognized by the Cōlas, and the deity in the inner sanctum is an eight-foot long form of Viṣṇu sleeping on a coiled up island created by the great snake Śesa in the midst of the primeval sea. The Original or Ādi Festival was apparently a giant picnic which was even used as a metaphor by a first century poet trying to describe his lover's sad face when he wrote: "Your face has lost its luster and resembles the sandy and thickly wooded river bank in Arangam with the hearths quenched and things strewn hither and thither after the celebration of the Paṅkuni festival" (Aham 137). The festival is still celebrated in the temple during the 10 days before Paṅkuni (March-April) Uttiram and is a reenactment of the themes associated with the island setting. For the duration of the festival the power of the central deity is transferred into a small image in the form called Aḷagiya Maṇavāḷan or the "Handsome Groom" and he takes four trips in the four cardinal directions. On his first trip to the west he joins in a picnic with the agricultural laborers. The joke in this case is that he hears a mother calling to her son "Reṅka" to come and get a snack she has prepared for him, and the deity, pretending that he heard his name "Raṅka," takes the snack. Today crowds of laborers feed each other that special snack as they sing out the two names in a joyous refrain. On the second trip he crosses the northern branch of the river where he meets with some business persons. On the third trip he crosses the southern branch of the river and enters the Cōla's capital city where the princess Kamalādevi falls madly in love with him. He lingers there too long and leaves behind the broken-hearted princess who becomes the symbol of *viraha bhakti* or the love-in-separation that characterizes all humans who long for the deity who eludes them. And, finally, on the fourth trip he goes to the eastern end of the island to a Śiva temple where he greets the famous Goddess Akhilaṇḍēśvari who returns his greeting by offering him coconut juice. When he returns from his triumphant and fun-filled trip as a bridegroom prepared for his marriage, he finds the doors to the chamber of the bride, Raṅkanāyaki, closed. She had heard about the time with the princess and she was not pleased. He offers a variety of excuses and finally the saint Namālvār has to intervene and convince her to go ahead with the marriage. The informality and beauty of this ancient festival celebration was a delightful new insight into the origins of temple worship for me, and helped me see how the spontaneity of the village worship I had first seen in Chittapūr could underlay the worship patterns of even the most sophisticated temples.

In the case of Śrīraṅkam Temple, the original spontaneity and link with the local geography had, of course, long been overlaid with rich priestly tradition as well. We know that the eleven legendary hymn singers or *āḷvārs* who lived between the third and the ninth centuries all sang in the temple. There are now shrines to each of them built into the outer walls of the temple as concentric outer walls were added over the centuries. Vaiṣṇava teachers or *ācāryas,* including the most famous Rāmānuja of the twelfth century, also taught in the temple and there are monastic residences there from which they worked. After Rāmānuja's time, the priesthood split between those who interpreted his teaching as closely following Sanskrit texts and came to be called the Vaṭakalai, and the majority or Teṅkalai who thought his genius lay in combining the Sanskrit argumentation with the sense of *prapatti* or surrender to God that is emphasized in many of the *āḷvārs' hymns* in Tamil. I was surprised to see the minority or Vaṭakalai priests serving in the inner sanctum, but the vast majority of the 2,000 priests that one sees around the temple have the forehead markings of the Teṅkalai. In the Adhyayanōtsava Festival the Teṅkalai dominance becomes even more visible as the *āḷvārs' images* are brought to a seminar-like room where every one of the 4,000 Tamil hymns is sung to the accompaniment of ritual dances. Although most of the 2,000 priests now hold secular jobs and serve in their family's traditional priestly role only a few times each year, there are hundreds of priests in the temple on a daily basis and daily worship and festival preparation make the temple grounds a busy but quietly reverential place at all times.

The Citamparam temple

The figure of Dancing Śiva at Citamparam is a representation of the cosmic cycle and many hymns refer to the five stages of the cycle, with the drum symbolizing creation, the hand of reassurance preservation, the fire destruction, the foot on the demon the quiet of oblivion, and the kick of the leg the grace of renewal. This cosmic cycle is mentioned frequently in the medieval hymns, and worshippers clearly have it in mind when they approach the dynamic dancing figure in reverence. My own interest, however, began to wander, much as it had in Śrīrańkam, to the festivals and the possibility that this rich tradition had its origin in much simpler concerns about the local geography and the all-important question of fertility.

The two major festivals in the temple today are very cosmological in their emphasis in that they take place to mark the winter and summer solstices, when the sun starts its northern and southern courses respectively, but the winter festival still preserves a couple of popular fertility rituals that have to be crowded into the schedule between the morning and evening processions. Because the date of the festival corresponds with the coldest time of the year, women, and especially unmarried girls, are encouraged to bath in the chilly local streams during the early morning hours and pray for a lover to make them fertile. The prayer on their lips during this time is that of the saint Maṇikkavācakar, and during the festival his image is brought to the famous wooden hall each afternoon so that the deity can honor him as the women sing. An even more explicit focus on fertility takes place on the eighth afternoon of the festival when the most popular procession of all is inserted into the crowded schedule when Śiva appears as a naked beggar and the women in the crowd interpret his nakedness erotically and go into a frenzy. While the processions for these festivals take place just outside the fourth concentric wall of the present temple that was built by the later Cōla rulers around the twelfth century, the legend books and hymns more often refer to the Māsi (February-March) Makham Festival when the deity was taken to the wild local Goddess Piṭāri (Kāli) at the edge of the Tillai forest and then on to the fearsome sea. This festival is now rarely carried out because of the expense of clearing the forest roadway, but an ornate thirteenth-century building was put around the forest location of the Goddess and one of the Diṭcitār priests is now assigned to serve her. In order to show me the extreme heat of the crude life-sized image of the Goddess, the priest asked me to assist him as he handed me the soiled clothes of the Goddess and bathed her in oil (rather than the water, juice, honey, and milk that would be normal substances used in the bath).

Festivals

It did not take me long to realize that while the great south Indian temples had important festival traditions, some of the most famous ritual traditions of south India centered on their festival traditions. The most ubiquitous example of just such a ritual tradition during the years I was doing research was the festival of the deity Ayyappan that took place deep in the mountains of Kerala each year. For years I had been asked to join the rest of the family in a small temple in Chennai while my co-brother, the heart specialist, joined a group of male friends in taking a vow to go to the Ayyappan temple together. The group was made up of medical people, judges, and distinguished civil servants and was hardly a representation of the hunting groups that had traditionally ventured into the forest full of dangerous animals, but they revered the original ritual and followed it as best they could. Similar groups, chanting antiphonally "Ayyappan saranam," "Swamiye saranam", and addressing one another as either "Ayyappan" or "Swami", even poured through the Citamparam temple and disturbed the regular routines of worship on their way to the distant forest.

In 1986 I was teaching in a college in Kerala and we watched as our whole town was crowded with groups going up to the nearby mountain forest for worship. A student explained that he lived even closer to the forest and had often joined in a group with his father and uncles to go to the forest temple. My two sons were university age at the time, and it did not take us long to organize a group under the student's leadership and to start fasting to purify ourselves for the journey. On the mountain path we met dozens of other groups and then closer to the temple hundreds and maybe thousands of groups. (If the police reports are right there are six or seven million who visit the temple in 41 days, or about 200,000 per day.) Suddenly I realized the answer to my question about the variety and flexibility of Hindu ritual. What was important here was the group and the vow the group had made to call one another "Ayyappan" or "Swami" for the duration of the festival. There was a kind of ritual nucleus there that could be replicated thousands or even hundreds of thousands of times as groups formed and sacralized their ritual practices, whatever they were, by agreeing to follow a ritual practice together.

Some of the group leaders talked about the Pantalam king nearby that had found the baby Ayyappan while hunting in the forest, others talked about the ancient

Figure 13.2 Festival outside gateway of Citamparam Temple

Christian trade route nearby or the Muslim warrior who had assisted Ayyappan. Many had a story of how Śiva and Viṣṇu had miraculously conceived the baby Ayyappan, and many more explained the all-male crowd by recounting the story of how Ayyappan's planned marriage had to be postponed each year as he kept his vow to initiate new devotees before getting married. What was important was that people made ritual vows along with others and that the traditions established by these vows had been both strong enough and flexible enough that millions of people could continue to carry on traditions that were probably millennia old.

Conclusion

Learning about Hindu ritual practice when I first arrived in India was hard work because I had to fight off a set of mistaken colonial assumptions and pioneer every step of the way. The major mistake the colonial era made in its approach to Indian religion was to assume that all religious traditions were centered on a revelatory experience and that all religious practice was in some sense developed from that central experience. That pattern was characteristic of the nomadic population of west Asia where Western religious traditions began, but India had developed as an agricultural society and people tended to stay on the land they cultivated and develop their cultural traditions locally. As a result, what had developed in the Indian situation was a much decentralized pattern of religious practice. Regional communities gave form to their initial longings for the divine by arranging annual festivals that gave places to all the many social groups in the society and defined their links with the divinity and the cosmos as best they could. Sometimes outside myth and priestly practices were added later, but even those additions usually took into account the earlier traditions.

Given this social base of religious practice in India, it turned out to be a relatively straightforward matter to study temples and festivals in the Indian context. Dr. Murti's advice that I should go into the temples and "see how ordinary everything was" proved largely correct. In large temples such as Śrīraṅkam and Citamparam there are complex historical issues to sort through, but there is no atmosphere of secrecy and deep mystery. People view their traditions as socially defined, or what Dr. Murti called in theological terms "*saguṇa* traditions," that assist them in their final quest for *nirguṇa brahman*. They are both deeply proud of these traditions and eager to explain them to an outsider. Now that I have gone on to study the diaspora Hindu communities established by the Indians who settled in indentured societies such as Guyana and Trinidad, and, even more recently, near where I live in Canada, one can see this process of forming a "*saguṇa* tradition" at work, and the anxieties of the colonial-era scholars look all the more ridiculous.

Figure 13.3 Younger with Susie Oommen and son, and Diṭcitār priest family (on the photo left)

Readings

For an overview of Hindu philosophy, see my *Introduction to Indian Religious Thought* (Philadelphia: Westminster Press, 1972). A general introduction to the Viṣṇu-centered Śrīraṅkam temple is "Srirangam", in George Michell (ed.) *Temple Towns of Tamil Nadu* (Bombay: Marg Publications, 1993), while a comprehensive study of Citamparam is found in *The Home of Dancing Śivan: The Traditions of the Hindu Temple in Citamparam* (New York: Oxford University Press, 1995). For more detailed treatments of temple festival traditions, see my article "Ten Days of Wandering and Romance with Lord Raṅkanātaṉ: The Paṅkuṇi Festival in Śrīraṅkam temple," *Modern Asian Studies* 16.2, 1982. Another version of this study is found in "Wandering and Romance with Lord Raṅkanātaṉ: The *Ati* or "Original" Festival in Śrīraṅkam," in *Playing Host to Deity: Festival Religion in the South Indian Tradition* (New York, Oxford University Press, 2002). Also see, "Singing the Tamil Hymnbook in the tradition of Rāmānuja: The Adyayanōtsava Festival in Śrīraṅkam," *History of Religions* 21.3, 1982, and in George W. Spencer (ed.) *Temples, Kings and Peasants* (Madras: New Era). It was rewritten as "Singing the Tamil Hymnbook: The Adhyayanōtsava Festival in Śrīraṅkam," in *Playing Host to Deity: Festival Religion in the South Indian Tradition*, (New York: Oxford University Press, 2002). A study of a ritual tradition beyond the temple-centered milieu is "Return to the Mountains: The Ayyappaṉ Festival in Sabarimalai, Kerala," in *Playing Host to*

Deity: Festival Religion in the South Indian Tradition (New York, Oxford University Press, 2002).

Author

Paul Younger (Ph.D.) did postgraduate work in Banaras, Serampore, and Princeton. He taught for many years at McMaster University in Canada and is now Professor Emeritus. For many years his research focused on south India and Sri Lanka, but he now concentrates on the diaspora Hindu communities and especially the Hindu communities of Canada. On this work, see *New Homelands: Hindu Communities in Mauritius, Guyana, Trinidad, South Africa, Fiji and East Africa* (New York: Oxford University Press, 2010).

Index